Bangor
in the Eighties

Written and Compiled
by Terence Bowman

BALLYHAY BOOKS

Published by Ballyhay Books,
an imprint of Laurel Cottage Ltd.,
Donaghadee, Northern Ireland.
Copyrights reserved.
© Terence Bowman 2012.
Contributed texts are copyright of individual contributors.
Photographs are reproduced by permission.
Printed by Gutenberg Press, Malta.
ISBN 9781900935 937

Bangor in the Eighties is dedicated to Annie Stephens (née Roycroft) on behalf of the many journalists who owe her so much

Contents

Author Acknowledgments

My efforts to chronicle Bangor's history in the final decades of the 20th Century now produce a third volume, and I am once again indebted to the many people whose support has made the project possible.

As I also explained in the introduction to *Bangor in the Seventies,* the book's chronology provides information that is largely in the public domain. However, I am mindful that, despite the passage of time, wounds can still be very raw. To all those who have helped me to recount details of Troubles-related tragedies, please accept my sincere thanks.

My thanks also go to the many other contributors, from so many different walks of life, for their ready willingness to put pen to paper and share their memories.

As ever I enjoyed the support of the North Down Museum, its manager Patricia Hamilton and staff. I also consulted *Spectator* back issues at three locations: the Heritage Gallery in Downpatrick Library (my second home for nearly four months), Bangor's Carnegie Library and at Central Library in Belfast.

Troubles-related information was again verified through *Lost Lives* (Mainstream Publishing, 1999, 2007) by David McKittrick, Seamus Kelters, Brian Feeney, Chris Thornton and David McVea.

I am grateful to the *Spectator,* including Editor Paul Flowers and Deputy Editor Helen McDowell, and to its former reporters who so willingly shared their Eighties memories while holding down various positions of responsibility.

Special mention again goes to Jonathan Coates of the *Newtownards Chronicle,* who tracked down hundreds of pictures from the *Spectator* negative archive, and also to my good friend Niki Hill, who proofread the finished book.

Terence Bowman, October 2012

Introduction

by *County Down Spectator* Editor
Paul Flowers

In many ways the Eighties – more than any other decade – was the period that directly led to the Bangor we have now. And it may be that in the Eighties Bangor finally lost any claim to its time of innocence as finance rather than social largesse became the driving force in the town's development.

The physical, political and social frameworks of Bangor underwent such a sea change during those 10 years that there likely hasn't been a decade with such profound significance before or since. The Eighties witnessed the emergence of our current seafront with the impressive and structurally striking piers replacing the beaches and wooden infrastructure that had served Bangor so well for so long.

Politically, against the backdrop of seismic national change, there was an almost constant flirtation with new political entities that eroded the traditional Council make-up to such an

Paul Flowers joined the *Spectator* in 1980 and became Editor in 1987. He is still there. This picture shows him at the printing press in 2011 with one of the final broadsheet editions.

extent it has never been the same again. It wasn't just the obvious parties either. North Down's reputation for choosing its own path electorally – confirmed by the continued selection by voters of Jim Kilfedder as MP – was enhanced by the appearance of candidates for the Campaign for Equal Citizenship (which ultimately led to the emergence of local Conservatives), the continued success of the Alliance

Party and even at one stage the Natural Law Party.

Entering the Eighties as the largest party on North Down Borough Council the Ulster Unionists were already finding their power base being eroded by the DUP, leading to the current state of affairs where the DUP are the strongest party the Council has seen in over 30 years.

The juggernaut that has become the Bloomfield Shopping Centre and Retail Park was conceived in the Eighties, while the redevelopment of Queen's Parade was not only mooted but work actually began on its transformation.

Paul has written the paper's motoring column for more than three decades. This image reflects one of the more unusual stories he covered – the arrival of the Sinclair C5 in 1985.

Socially, Bangor was a town trying to absorb a rapidly growing population, swollen mostly as a result of migration patterns that diluted its 'traditional' population. And all this played out against a landscape coloured, as ever, by the continuing terrorist and sectarian violence that caused so much personal heartbreak.

To be fair, it was a time of confidence with money surprisingly easy to get hold of despite rising interest rates. The schemes and projects that were started in the Eighties were forward-thinking and promised a vibrant and progressive town designed to proudly face a new century.

The Bangor we knew was on its way out though. By the end of the decade the town's highly successful Drama Club and Operatic Society were close to losing the jewel in their crown in that the Little Theatre was becoming a liability rather than an asset, while the last surviving cinema, the Tonic, had closed its doors in 1983. It was eventually replaced by a cineplex and the ability to attract the big name entertainers who had regularly visited the town was gone for ever.

It is almost impossible now to appreciate that Pickie Pool, the Tonic and the Little Theatre (and latterly the Bangor Castle Leisure Centre) were the main venues of activity.

Many local sports teams achieved considerable success during the Eighties but the increasing importance and influence of money in the world of competitive games was to catch them unready to participate at the highest level in the future. And curiously it was the Eighties that first saw the introduction of pay and display car parking.

The decade did see the Queen's Court get a new lease of life as a roller disco but this proved only a passing phenomenon. And in a further nod to the ending of an era Caproni's went up for sale, eventually, like so many of the town's other landmarks, to become living accommodation. The iconic Barry's Amusements was ultimately destroyed by fire and it was fire again that brought the existence of the Queen's Court to an end.

Another entertainment complex, the Savoy Hotel, also succumbed to 'progress' and shut its doors.

While Bangor had been the site of Northern Ireland's first out-of-town shopping centre – the Springhill complex – it was joined by the highly successful Clandeboye enterprise. The latter's demise – yet another fire victim – was to clear the path for the creation of Bloomfield.

The closure of the Bangor gas industry – another end of an era event – allowed what is now the Flagship Centre to get the go-ahead, along with a redrawing of the town centre's roads system. But while that was slowly making progress, the current difficulties of town centre traders were somewhat foreshadowed by the departure of Robinson and Cleaver and indeed a number of other town centre stalwarts.

It all sounds a bit depressing but the march of progress, while

How the *Spectator* reported Paul Flowers' appointment as Editor in 1987, when he took over the role from Joy (Jo) Bannister

regretted at the time, was not noticed for the groundswell of change that it was. Yes we noticed and lamented the passing of various icons of Bangor's more illustrious past, but such was the confident and forward-looking atmosphere of the time that we all expected them to be replaced with something even better.

Bangor was actually a nice place to live in the Eighties. Not only was it a relatively safer environment compared to elsewhere in the Province, it also had good housing and schools, and the nightlife was second to none – as long as you liked discos.

Despite being a comparative newcomer to the town (I arrived in 1966), there was nowhere I would rather have been, judging by the regular reports on the news and the limited experience I had of life outside Bangor while attending college in Belfast. It was a good place to be a journalist on a weekly paper too. People at that time were more inclined to talk about the events around them, unlike today when that openness has been replaced by reticence and conversely a desire to live your life over social networks.

I suspect Bangor will never again see a decade of such sustained change. It wasn't so much a roller coaster of a period, more a gentle slide. It remains a pivotal time in Bangor's history and one that represented the town leaving its past behind and gearing up for what promised to be a bright new future.

Soundtrack
to the Eighties

The only chart going in which Cliff Richard sits comfortably between The Clash and The Cult. Well, comfortably is perhaps an exaggeration. In alphabetical order, the favourite songs or album tracks as selected by contributors to *Bangor in the Eighties.*

ABBA – *The Winner Takes It All*

AC/DC – *Hells Bells* and *You Shook Me All Night Long*

Bee Gees – *You Win Again* and *One*

Bill Wyman – *Je Suis Un Rock Star*

Bonnie Tyler – *Total Eclipse Of The Heart*

Bowie and Queen – *Under Pressure*

Bruce Springsteen – *Born In The USA* and *No Surrender*

Cameo – *Word Up*

Chaka Khan and Rufus – *Ain't Nobody*

The Clash – *London Calling*

Cliff Richard – *Wired For Sound*

The Cult – *She Sells Sanctuary*

The Cure – *Love Cats*

Cyndi Lauper – *Girls Just Want To Have Fun* and *Time After Time*

David Bowie – *Ashes To Ashes*

Depeche Mode – *Personal Jesus*

Dexy's Midnight Runners – *Come On Eileen*

Duran Duran – *The Chauffeur*

Electronic – *Getting Away With It*

Frankie Goes to Hollywood – *Two Tribes*

Fun Boy Three – *Our Lips Are Sealed*

Grace Jones – *Pull Up To The Bumper*

Guns N' Roses – *Sweet Child O' Mine*

Human League – *Don't You Want Me*

Irene Cara – *Flashdance…What A Feeling*

Japan – *Ghosts*

Kate Bush – *Running Up That Hill*

Kelly Marie – *Feels Like I'm In Love*

Lionel Ritchie – *All Night Long*

Madonna – *Like A Prayer*

Men Without Hats – *The Safety Dance*

Michael Jackson – *Bad*

Murray Head – *One Night In Bangkok*

Neil Young – *Rockin' In The Free World* (electric version)

Pat Benetar – *Love Is A Battlefield*

Paul Simon – *You Can Call Me Al*

Police – *Every Breath You Take*

Prefab Sprout – *King Of Rock And Roll*

Prince – *Purple Rain*

Psychedelic Furs – *Pretty In Pink*

Scritti Politti – *Wood Beez*

Simple Minds – *New Gold Dream*

The Smiths – *That Joke Isn't Funny Anymore*

Soft Cell – *Tainted Love*

Spandau Ballet – *True*

Style Council – *You're The Best Thing*

Talking Heads – *Burning Down The House*

Technotronic – *Pump Up The Jam*

Tenpole Tudor – *Swords Of A Thousand Men*

Thomas Dolby – *She Blinded Me With Science*

U2 – *Pride* and *With Or Without You*

Van Halen – *Jump*

1980
IN THE SPECTATOR

The next decade must bring a solution to Ulster's difficulties. It is inconceivable that a bunch of gun-toting hooligans with no more support than the deranged rabble of socio-political cripples and no more encouragement than the intransigence of die-hards who won't talk to one another should hold a province to ransom for 20 years.

Still closer at hand, people in Bangor are looking forward to improvements at the seafront. Replacement of the wooden end of the North Pier by something more concrete will hearten Queen's Parade, and a smartening up of Queen's Parade will cheer all Bangor.

A week is a long time in politics, 10 years is a long time by any human standard. Perhaps the best we can wish for one another is that, whatever changes we may encounter along the way, we shall emerge from the Eighties wiser, more tolerant, healthier (on average) and happier (all round) than we enter them.

Editorial in the 4 January 1980 edition of the *County Down Spectator*

Bangor native Alan Mills returned home for the first time since emigrating to Canada 27 years earlier to enjoy the Christmas and New Year holidays. His Bangor relatives included sisters Ruby McNinch and Ida Millar, along with sisters Adeline Diamond (Belfast) and Doreen Fulcher (London).

Alan Mills and his sister Ruby McNinch – together for the first time in 27 years. *43-7-9*

Former Bangor Grammar School pupil Paul McDowell (27) moved from BBC Northern Ireland to front *John Craven's Newsround* while the programme's regular host was on holidays. By the end of the decade he would be sports editor at Ulster Television.

The Bangor and District branch of the British Rheumatism and Arthritis Association – only the third in Northern Ireland – was formed at a public meeting in the Old People's Club at Castle Park on 15 January. Chairman was Jean Hazlett, secretary was Molly Marshall and treasurer was Norman Mallon.

Former Bangor Mayor Charles F. Milligan recalled, in a letter to the *Spectator*, seeing Halley's Comet over the town in 1910. The paper had indicated in an editorial that it was set to return in 1986.

North Down MP Jim Kilfedder – former Unionist, Official Unionist and Ulster Unionist – announced the formation of Northern Ireland's sixth Unionist party, the Ulster Progressive Unionist Party (UPUP). He declared the "revival of idealism" was vital for Northern Ireland and "slogans and political jargon are no substitute for policies."

Subsequently, to avoid confusion with a similarly-named group in North Belfast, the party was renamed the Ulster Popular Unionist Party.

Fears were voiced for the future of Pickie Pool, which was costing North Down Borough Council between £7,000 and £8,000 to keep open during July and August. Income in 1979 had amounted to just £479, from 5,918 juvenile admissions and 720 adult swimmers. In contrast, 250,000 had visited the new indoor pool during the same year.

After receiving a deputation from interested groups the Council reversed a previous recommendation to close Pickie, but instead to open it for three months during summer 1980 to gauge its popularity.

Cllr Hazel Bradford declared: "Pickie is a way of life. With any luck we will have a good summer and good support for the pool. It is a service we provide to the Borough and its visitors. Pickie is a part of both old and modern Bangor."

The 75th anniversary of Rotary was marked by the Bangor club with a ball in the Culloden Hotel and a service of thanksgiving in St Comgall's Parish Church in February. Guests at the ball were welcomed by Bangor president Evan Ward and his wife Heather (president of the Bangor Inner Wheel Club). Mayor George Green, Town Clerk Jack McKimm, Aldermen and Councillors attended the service in their ceremonial robes.

Bangor brothers James and Cyril Picken were airlifted to safety by an Irish Air Corps helicopter after their 40ft. yacht ran aground off the County Dublin coast. Shallow water had prevented the Howth lifeboat, which had put out in mountainous seas, from reaching them.

Bangor man Dick Cheyne, of Hazeldene Avenue, won a trip back to Japan, where he had been held captive during the Second World War. The 60-year-old civil servant was serving with the Royal Marines when he was reported missing, presumed killed. In fact, he was alive and in Nagasaki when the second atomic bomb exploded.

Former prisoner-of-war Dick Cheyne, back home in Bangor after a return visit to Japan, presents a plaque from the Mayor of Nagasaki to Alderman George Green, Mayor of North Down. 190-18-10

The 13-day trip back to Japan was his prize in a competition run by Scotland's *Sunday Post,* in which entrants identified a place they wished to visit.

It was announced in late March that work to repair and extend the North Pier – including the removal of the famed wooden section – would begin the following year and was expected to continue into 1983. It was the first element of North Down Borough Council's seafront development scheme, with subsequent phases following over the next decade as the money became available.

GO-AHEAD FOR NEW NORTH PIER

Between 250 and 300 local workers took part in a North Down Trades Council-sponsored march through the centre of Bangor on 2 April to highlight their opposition to government spending cuts. It was one of 14 demonstrations held around Northern Ireland. Marchers gathered at the McKee Clock where they were addressed by Trades Council president Andrew Barr.

Julie Milligan (8) presents a bouquet to Miss Jane M. Woods on behalf of Kilcooley Presbyterian Church Sunday School.
410-9A-9

A special evening was held at Kilcooley Presbyterian Church in early April to mark the retirement of Miss Jane M. Woods, one of Ireland's longest serving Presbyterian deaconesses. She had served in that position for 34 years, including six at Kilcooley.

Celebrating their 60th wedding anniversary on 5 April were Alex Gray and his wife, the former Gertrude Madeleine Thompson. They were married in First Bangor Presbyterian Church in 1920 and lived for 59 years at 1 Railwayview Street, a house built by Mr Gray's own grandfather.

The Rt. Rev. Dr. Robin Eames, who had served as curate in St Comgall's from 1963-66, was named as the new Church of Ireland Bishop of Down and Dromore. He succeeded the Rt. Rev. George Quin, from Bangor, who was retiring.

Environment Minister Philip Goodhart cut the first sod at Whitehill Drive for a private housing association scheme for the physically handicapped. The site would provide 14 units at an approximate cost of £250,000.

HERITAGE CENTRE FOR CASTLE COURTYARD

North Down Borough Council received proposals in early May to create a local heritage centre in the rear courtyard of Bangor Town Hall. In addition to providing the town with a means to display its proud past, it would also ensure the restoration of neglected buildings associated with the historic castle.

Following the acquisition of a four-acre site on the Clandeboye Road, close to its junction with the Rathgael Road, Bangor Free Presbyterian Church held a stone-laying ceremony on 14 June to mark the site for a new hall and Sunday School complex.

Officiating was the Rev. Harry Cairns, minister of the church, and the address was given by Moderator Dr Ian Paisley. Named the W. P. Nicholson Memorial Free Presbyterian Church, it was opened on 6 June 1981 by Dr Paisley.

The Rev. Harry Cairns, minister of Bangor Free Presbyterian Church, lays one of the foundation stones at the site of the church's Sunday School and hall complex. *304-20A-10*

Carol Mitchell and husband Raymond, from Marquis Avenue, welcomed three American visitors from Annapolis, Maryland, to their home. Carol had been exchanging letters for a decade with penpal Jayne Sisson and her visit in July, accompanied by parents William and Kathleen Sisson, was the first time they met.

Monty Python's Life of Brian was screened in the Tonic for a fortnight from the end of July after North Down Borough Council declined an invitation to attend a preview along with their Belfast City Council counterparts.

Instead, they decided to leave the verdict to the British Board of Film Censors, which had awarded the film an AA certificate (only those aged 14 and over were allowed to see it). Belfast Council opted for an X certificate (only for those over 18) but this proved unacceptable to the distributors and the film was not shown in the city.

The Abbey Street car park (opposite Bangor Railway Station) was divided in half by the Roads Service to create a free parking area and a pay car park. The first hour was free while a whole day (seven hours) cost 80p.

Placard-carrying protestors at the Tonic in late July 1980, at the opening of *Monty Python's Life of Brian*. Members of the Free Presbyterian Church, they believed the film was sacrilegious and blasphemous. *71-6-11*

Roads Service agreed to the free parking area after hearing objections from Northern Ireland Railways. The company feared business on the busy Belfast commuter line would suffer if drivers faced paying twice to travel to work.

The former Queen's Court Hotel on Queen's Parade was given a new lease of life, reopening on Friday 8 August as Rollerama and offering roller-skating sessions for as little as £1 (including skates). There was a separate disco (with quadraphonic sound) and a spectator gallery, as well as other amusements such as video games.

However, the venue faced competition with the former Milanos ballroom on Seacliff Road reopening on the same day as a roller-skating rink, teenage disco and restaurant – BJ's on Oceanside. For the opening two days of BJ's both admission and the use of skates were free. Courtesy coaches operated from Bangor Railway Station and the McKee Clock on the first Saturday.

Eighteen-year-old James McCann, from Prospect Road, was given an unconditional offer to study Geology at University College, Oxford, having passed 13 O-Levels and five A-Levels. The former Bangor Grammar School student had attended night classes at Bangor Technical College to study for his French A-Level, which he passed with a B grade. His other grades were two As (Maths and Geology), a B (Chemistry) and a C (Further Maths).

Work began on 2 September on the £531,000 first phase of the Bangor seafront development scheme, its ultimate aim being to provide a 600-boat marina. Phase one involved repairs to the Central and North Piers, demolition of the wooden portion of the North Pier and replacement stonework to extend it to provide the first 'protective mole'. The total cost of the complete marina project was estimated in 1980 at £2.14m.

It was announced that over 100 jobs would be created over the next two years at the Bangor factory of Coronary Care Systems Inc. The two-year-old company, which employed 42 people at the Balloo Road Industrial Estate, made mini-defibrillators, which literally shocked heart-attack victims back to life. The jobs boost followed a £250,000 order from Japan.

Actor Colin Blakely, a former member of both Bangor Drama Club and Bangor Amateur Operatic Society, compered the gala reopening of Belfast's Grand Opera House on Monday 15 September.

North Down Borough Councillors said Vietnamese refugees – known widely as Boat People – would be welcome in Bangor, but not in Housing Executive homes as there was already an acute housing shortage in the town with its 1,500-strong waiting list. Members had been asked to agree to the allocation of up to five Housing Executive properties to Boat People.

An alternative location, suggested by Alderman Jimmy Hamilton, was the old Coastguard Cottages in Holborn Avenue, which he described as being "ideal" for a small Vietnamese community.

Bangor's renaissance as a tourist destination was confirmed by Northern Ireland Tourist Board figures which showed the town was second only to Portrush/ Portstewart for overnight visitors.

The Queen's Parade premises of the Young Men's Christian Association (YMCA) were officially opened on 14 October by Arsenal manager and Bangor native Terry Neill. He had been in Northern Ireland to attend the centenary dinner of the Irish Football Association and took time out to perform the opening ceremony.

The Royal Hotel completed a £100,000 renovation scheme, which provided the redesigned Balfour Room restaurant, the Coffee Shoppe and Oak Bar, along with a new disco called Samantha's. The Dempsey Room was for small functions while the Sun Trap was for "lazy sun-lovers."

Former West Church (Bangor) member the Rev Ivan Warwick was ordained and installed as a minister of the Church of Scotland at the end of October. He took charge of the linked congregations of Lintrathen, Kilry and Glenisla.

Radio One DJ Paul Gambaccini (left) with Coachman's DJ Jon Antony at the Rathgael venue before taking to the stage to entertain a large crowd in October 1980. It was the American-born DJ's first visit to Bangor. 1-2-12

Mayor George Green quit the Official Unionist Party and joined Jim Kilfedder's Ulster Popular Unionist Party. Alderman Green, who retained his membership of Vanguard, claiming it was no longer a political party but a pressure group, accused the Official Unionists of being "dishonest with their electorate in their approach to devolution."

A Bangor FC training session at Clandeboye Park came to an abrupt end on 13 November after a gunman walked onto the pitch and fired a number of shots at player Matt Bradley. The Belfastman – a centre-half with the club since the beginning of the season – was uninjured. Loyalist paramilitaries were blamed for the assassination bid.

Mr Bradley, who also played Gaelic football for the St John's club in the city, told Bangor officials he would not be playing for the Seasiders again. Goalkeeper Peter McCarron also quit the club.

Tughan Court, which provided 42 sheltered dwellings on a tree-lined site at Bloomfield Road, was officially opened on 21 November by the James Butcher Housing Association. Residents were under the care of warden Gail Morrow. The opening ceremony was performed by Fred C. Tughan CBE, a pioneer of sheltered housing in Bangor.

The *Spectator* published in colour for the first time on 5 December 1980. Credit for the breakthrough went to the Clandeboye Traders' Association which added full colour to its Christmas advertising.

Amanda Doggart, from Alandale, became the first female in Ireland to hold the Diploma in Funeral Directing – at the age of just 19. The former Bangor Girls' High School pupil was the fourth generation of her family to enter the undertaking business. She worked for Messrs James Russell and Co. (Bangor) Ltd. The family business, W. L. Doggart and Son Ltd., of Newtownards, had a financial interest in Russell's.

The bells of Bangor Parish Church pealed out to welcome in 1980. Jim McBride (conductor) gives a helping hand to the youngest ringer, nine-year-old Simon Thomas. On the left is Jim's son William (12). *41-4-9*

Kilcooley children who raised £114.94 for Kampuchean refugees over the preceding holiday period. The youngsters had organised a sponsored walk and were loud in their praise for Constable Fred Dowie, neighbourhood officer, and Constable Tom Patterson, RUC Community Relations. *71-12-9*

Pupils from Kilcooley Primary School who paid a visit to the Cabra Towers activity centre near Castlewellan in February 1980. Included with the group are Mr J. A. Rutherdale, teacher in charge, along with Miss P. Gowdy and Miss O. Hanna, who accompanied the children, and principal Mr Alan Glenn. *152-7A-9*

The Kindergarten Sunday School at Ballyholme Parish helped to celebrate the 25th anniversary of the creation of the Parish in March 1980. *275-15-9*

Fifth Bangor Brownies, Bunnies and leaders with their new flag which was dedicated in March 1980 at Wesley Centenary Methodist Church. *274-10-9*

Officers and committee members of Bangor Women's Institute at their annual dinner, which was held in The George in March 1980. Back (from left): Mrs R. Richardson, Mrs R. Magee, Mrs R. Cummings, Mrs C. Mills, Mrs E. Bridgham. Front (from left): Mrs M. Hamilton, Mrs E. Hanna, vice-president, Mrs E. Major, president, Mrs K. Watkins, secretary, and Mrs J. Whyte, treasurer. *361-4-9*

The drama group at Kilmaine Primary School chose the story of *Robin Hood* for their annual production. Back (from left): Ian Rolleston (Little John), Helen McMullan (Alan A-Dale), Julie Aylward (Robin Hood), Stephen Jess (Sheriff of Nottingham). Front (from left): Donna Witherspoon (Willie de Wolf), Madeleine Goldstrom (Red Riding Hood) and Kirsty Nelson (Maid Marion). *26-8A-10*

The cast of Bangor Drama Club's production of *Sailor Beware* in July 1980. Back row (from left): Marie Gildea, Mollie Moorhead, Geoffrey Miller, John Knipe, Margaret Wylde. Front (from left): Richard Kelly, Graham Neill, Alison Gordon and Marion Logan. *479-9-10*

The Bangor Schools Action Committee invited representatives of 22 different charities to a meeting in the Seacourt Teachers' Centre to receive cheques arising from a successful fundraising walk earlier in the year. Awards were also made to two of the most successful contributors, Rhoda Davidson (front, left, who raised £201 out of Glenlola Collegiate's contribution of £1,332) and Mark Weir (front, right, of Bangor Grammar School, who raised £74). Included are SAC members, including secretary Marsden Fitzsimmons (back, extreme right), representatives of local, national and international charities, and

North Down Borough Council Deputy Mayor Terence Morrow (back, centre). *286-10-10*

Children who attended a storytelling session in August 1980 under the auspices of the summer activity scheme at Kilcooley Primary School. Included are readers Ailsa Donaghy and Rosalind Holmes, along with scheme helper Pat Smyth. *125-3-11*

Bangor rock band Motion Pictures were new on the scene in August 1980, combining cover versions with their own material. From left: Mark Crockard (18), James McCreedy (19), Mark Armstrong (19) and Marty McConnell (18). *137-13-11*

Friends and neighbours of Olive D'Agosteno (née Craig) staged a get-together to mark her return to the town in August 1980 after a 22-year absence. Olive, accompanied by husband Walter and son Donald, was joined by sisters Audrey and Eileen and brother Jim, who were also back in Bangor for the first time since the family emigrated to Massachusetts some 28 years earlier. Guests were entertained to Irish dancing by Jane Herron and Margaret Craig. *147-5-11*

Members and officers of Seventh Bangor Cub Scouts who attended the County rally in September 1980. *407-6A-9*

Guides who received their Queen's Award at the annual meeting of the North Down County Girl Guides in October 1980. Back row (from left): Lorraine McGibbon, Susan Greer, Karen Halford, Susan McKee, Rosemary Finlay, Heather Dunlop, Heather McKinney. Front: Rosemary Kirker, Rosemarie Ferguson, Annaliese McCrea, Michelle Porter, Sarah Tennant, Elaine Sterritt and Denise Lemon. *504-5A-9*

The girls of Ward House at Glenlola Collegiate raised £1,800 for the Cancer Scanner Unit at Belvoir Park Hospital in November 1980. The presentation was made by House captain Hilary Rodgers and vice-captain Jenny Dales to Sister Jean Masterson in the presence of House head Doris Hutchieson and some of the 160 girls who took part in a fundraising starve-in. *77-7-12*

Fred Yeates (left), popular crossing patrolman at St Comgall's Primary School, receives a gift to mark his retirement after six years' service from principal John O'Hanlon. He had won the Lollipop Man of the Year title in 1978. *114-3-0*

The cast of *Beastie and the Beaut*, the Christmas 1980 production at St Columbanus' High School. *252-8-12*

Cast members of *Sleeping Beauty*, the third annual pantomime to be produced by the youth club at West (Presbyterian) Church. Produced by John Morrow and William McClelland, the stars included Joanne McDonald as Princess Marigold and Gillian Weatherup as Prince Florizel. *251-4-12*

Judith Gillespie
remembers...

I moved to Bangor in 1976 when I was in my teens, and it was like moving to a different part of the world. Until then I had lived in a very troubled part of North Belfast and I couldn't believe how relatively peaceful Bangor was and how it had avoided most of the ravages of the Troubles.

That is not to say, of course, that it totally escaped. I can recall the town centre bombs and the Bangor families tragically bereaved through terrorism. But compared to where I had come from, Bangor was normal, carefree and almost exciting – note, almost.

The weather somehow seemed to be much better too. Simple things like meeting friends for coffee or a Charlie's burger on the seafront, going shopping before Christmas in Bangor town centre when the shops exceptionally opened late night, Blue Lamp discos at Pickie, walking to the beach and spending the whole day diving off the boards at Ballyholme – these were all new experiences for me.

I finished my schooling at Regent House Grammar School in 1981 and so was not a full member of the Bangor schools set. But through Church, hockey, badminton, tennis and youth organisations I made many close Bangor friends who remain close friends today. I used to get the Bangor bus home from school, together with some notable

Deputy Chief Constable Judith Gillespie OBE today

Judith Gillespie has been the Deputy Chief Constable of the Police Service of Northern Ireland since June 2009.

She joined the Royal Ulster Constabulary (RUC) in 1982 and became the first ever female Chief Officer (Assistant Chief Constable) in the history of Northern Ireland policing in May 2004.

A native of North Belfast, Judith's experience of growing up in one of the most 'Troubles' affected areas of Northern Ireland placed in her a desire to want to help people and from an early age she set her sights on becoming a police officer.

After two unsuccessful applications to the RUC, Judith went to Queen's University Belfast to study French and German, but when a third application was successful she left QUB to pursue her policing career.

She is passionate about ensuring that policing makes a real and meaningful difference in those areas that matter most, namely helping vulnerable victims and encouraging others to realise their full potential. In that regard, in 2007/08 she spent time on attachment to the Police Staff College in Bramshill, Hampshire, as a Syndicate Director on the Strategic Command Course, helping to support, develop

Judith Gillespie won the All Ireland Associate PE Solo competition in March 1989, following the All Ireland Brigader finals in Dundonald. *345-4-40*

personalities – Eddie Irvine being one, although he was a few years below me at school. Even then he was quite a character and always made his presence felt on the school bus.

I worked during school holidays in Baillie's Gents' Outfitters in High Street. This was where I learnt the old-fashioned skills of customer service, and the value of going the second mile to help customers find what they were looking for. In those days it was a rather throughother place with much of the stock held in cardboard boxes upstairs. But James Baillie (senior) knew his clientele, and through that mutual trust customers were allowed to take garments home 'on appro'. He was a Ballymena man, not prone to hyperbole, but I remember when my mother called into the shop and asked how I was getting on, and he paid me the ultimate compliment by telling her: "Judith knows the stock". Given the disorganisation of the upstairs storeroom, that was a compliment indeed.

The 1980s was a significant decade for me. I joined the Royal Ulster Constabulary in 1982, I married Ian – a Bangor man – in 1983, and I was promoted to Sergeant in 1986. I also continued my lifelong association with Girls' Brigade and, after many years of trying, managed to win the All Ireland Associate PE Solo competition in 1989. That was the year I decided to retire from GB competitions. Some would say not before time! I have made a few comebacks since, by special request, but never to solo work.

Girls' Brigade was a big influence on my young life. Our Captain, Pearl Hassard, was the most wonderful example of commitment, care, organisation, selfless service and Christian love you could imagine. When she was Captain, she was a stickler for the highest standards in everything, including preparation, neatness and bearing. Perhaps that's where my passion for good turnout in police uniform comes from. She was extremely supportive of and interested in my police career, and even to this day remains so. She was responsible for ensuring my photograph appeared in the *Spectator* after I won the Baton of Honour for the best all round recruit in my Squad in Enniskillen when I joined the RUC.

Judith the outstanding recruit

There were only four young ladies in the squad of ninety recruits who passed out from the RUC training Depot in Enniskillen last week. And one of those four, a twenty-year-old Bangor girl, gained three of the four main awards — the School Prize, the Efficiency Shield and the Baton of Honour for the outstanding recruit. Judith was only allowed to receive the Baton of Honour, with which she was presented by the Lord Mayor of Belfast, Councillor Mrs. Grace Bannister.

David Soul Tickets

Donaghadee Police report that they have in their possession two tickets for the David Soul / Brotherhood of Man concert at the Tonic Theatre in Bangor at the start of June.

The tickets were found in Donaghadee and handed in to Police — so anyone who has let tickets stray should contact Donaghadee Police.

Obviously working in the RUC in the 1980s brought particular challenges and some great sadness. Over the years I made many great friendships and because you didn't always work closely to home we tended to pool cars and travel together. I used to travel every day from Bangor to Andersonstown RUC Station with two Constable colleagues. I remember clearly how one of them tragically took his own life shortly after I had left on promotion and his funeral at Kilcooley Presbyterian Church was one of the saddest I have ever attended.

Whilst service in the RUC in the 1980s brought bereavement and injury to the door of many Bangor folk, there were also very rewarding and happy times together with colleagues who lived in the town. I guess we all felt relatively safe in Bangor in the knowledge there were many police colleagues nearby. It was a supportive community where I felt truly at home, although I often reflect with sadness that police, who wanted to serve the whole community, felt it necessary to live in a limited number of small communities like Bangor.

That said, I do recall one incident in the early 1980s at my parents' home when I was a Constable. In those days female officers were not armed and felt extremely vulnerable. I had returned home from a late shift at around 2am and as the headlights of my Mini car swung

and train future police leaders in the UK Police Service.

Academic successes include a BA Honours in Public Policy and Administration and a Masters in Applied Criminology from Cambridge University.

Judith was appointed Acting Chief Constable in August 2009 and continued in that position until the appointment of Matt Baggott in September 2009.

In her role as Deputy Chief Constable she has responsibility, amongst many other things, for the PSNI's Diversity Strategy and Gender Action Plan.

Judith received an OBE in the Queen's Birthday Honours List in June 2009 and an Honorary Doctorate for Public Service from Queen's University in July 2012.

Judith likes to keep fit

and can often be seen running the streets of her local neighbourhood. She frequently takes part in charity runs and one of her highlights was successfully completing the Great North Run in 2011.

Married with two daughters, Judith has a dog called Charlie and is a passionate Chelsea supporter.

into the driveway of my parents' home they caught what looked like a shadowy figure lurking in the garden. I was petrified – and then gasped with relief when I realised it was my older brother's wetsuit hanging out to dry on the clothesline!

I also enjoyed participating in many tournaments at Bloomfield Squash Club with police colleagues and Bangor members of the club, and even won a tournament – owing largely to the very generous handicap allocated to me.

I consider myself very privileged to have spent my teenage years and adult life in Bangor and I'm pleased my children have had such a happy childhood here too. It is a wonderful town with wonderful people who have supported me and continue to support me in my career.

1981
IN THE SPECTATOR

Town Clerk Jack McKimm and Supt. Tom Brown of Bangor RUC agreed in January to draw up recommendations for the Borough Council on possible bye-laws to prevent the abuse of local parks by drinkers. At that time there was nothing to prevent people from drinking alcohol out-of-doors so long as they were not causing any trouble.

Plans were revealed in January for a new fire station and a replacement for the Carnegie Library. The Northern Ireland Fire Authority was hoping to acquire a portion of land that extended into the grounds of Bangor Girls' High School at Castle Street, while the South Eastern Education and Library Board gained the Council's support for a new district library on land it already owned at Castle Square.

RUBIK'S CUBE A WINNER

If anyone had told me that a two-inch cube made up of 27 other cubes could hold my attention for most of an afternoon—and still leave me perplexed—I would have told them exactly where to go.

Well this one does. Known to all and sundry as Rubik's Cube it has been achieving widespread publicity lately.

Followers of Swap Shop will have seen this magnificent little toy in action. The idea sounds simple—each side of the full cube is a different colour, with all sides twistable, so that after a few elementary twists the colour scheme is lost entirely. The idea is to get each side of the cube back to its original colour.

First the good news—it has been done in 24 seconds. The bad news is that there are three thousand million variations on the cube patterns and the chances of getting it right have rather similar odds.

The Borough Council devised plans in January for a summer train service for holiday visitors between Pickie Pool and Ballyholme. There were additional proposals for Bangor Sunarama, which Councillors heard was "a kind of indoor beach with sand, sea and artificial sun, to be developed by private enterprise."

Jim Kilfedder's Ulster Popular Unionist Party struck a formal agreement with the Unionist Party of Northern Ireland – founded by Brian Faulkner and led, in 1981, by Anne Dickson. Their aim, while not merging, was to become a major political force offering a "better alternative" to the electorate.

The marina development received a major boost with news in February that the European Regional Development Fund would be injecting £715,710 into the project towards the construction of new breakwaters and improvements to the existing quays.

Sedi Rutledge, sub-postmistress of the Oakwood Avenue Post Office, was elected president of the Northern Ireland branch of the National Federation of Sub-Postmasters.

Long-time favourite The Coffee Pot at 110 High Street was replaced in March by a new business, The Pizza Parlour – the first such venture in the town. It was run by Jasmine McAdam, assisted by mum Jean Scott.

The Eastern Health Board insisted in March it had no plans to change the role of Bangor Hospital. A spokesperson dismissed rumours the main part of the hospital would be turned into a geriatric or psycho-neurosis unit, with no facilities for consultants and no out-patients department.

Alderman Bertie McConnell's long political career drew to a close with an announcement he would not seek re-election in the May local government elections. He had joined the former Bangor Borough Council in 1958 and also represented the town at Stormont – the first and last person to do so. Mr McConnell, who was blinded in the Second World War, was also elected to the Assembly and Constitutional Convention of the mid-1970s as a representative of the Alliance Party.

The town's newest church, the John Wesley Free Methodist Church at Towerview Crescent, was opened and dedicated on 11 April. The minister was the Rev. Philip Talbot and the church was declared open by the most senior member, Mrs A. Wylie, who received the key to the door from builder David Connolly.

Thieves who broke into the animal pens at Ward Park on 5 May made off with 15 guinea pigs, 12 blue baldpate pigeons, four white doves, two black fantail cocks and a white rabbit. Local pet shops were warned to be on the lookout for the stolen animals and birds.

A young policeman from Bangor was killed by a booby-trap explosion in Belfast on Monday 27 April 1981. Constable Gary Martin, who was married with two young sons, was killed in Andersonstown when a hijacked delivery van, which had been blocking the junction of the Glen Road and Shaw's Road, blew up without warning.

Constable Martin had searched the back of the vehicle and the cab but found nothing. He then volunteered to drive the lorry away, but when he placed his hand on the front seat a mercury-tilt device exploded. This "awesome bravery" was praised by the coroner at the subsequent inquest.

The Irish National Liberation Army admitted responsibility for the attack that claimed 28-year-old Constable Martin's life and also left two other policemen seriously injured.

The eldest of four children, Constable Martin had joined the RUC four years earlier and was based at Woodbourne in Belfast. He was well known in his home town as a former taxi driver. A "gentle giant" – he was 6ft 3in and powerfully built – he was well-liked for his cheerful and helpful manner.

The cortege leaves Ballyholme Presbyterian Church, with the guard of honour being made up of fellow officers from Woodbourne RUC Station. *326-18-13*

Senior RUC officers were among the mourners at the funeral for Constable Gary Martin. *326-20-13*

His widow expressed the hope there would be no retaliation for Gary's death, as that might only leave other children without a father and other wives without a husband.

The funeral service on 30 April in Ballyholme Presbyterian Church – where the couple were married – was followed by interment in Clandeboye Cemetery. The Rev. Donald Watts and former Moderator the Very Rev. Dr. William Craig officiated. The service was conducted with full RUC honours.

The May 1981 local government elections saw 46 candidates contesting the 20 seats on North Down Borough Council. Prior to voters going to the polls two long-serving members, who were not seeking re-election, were conferred with the Freedom of the Borough – Alderman Jimmy Hamilton and the aforementioned Alderman Bertie McConnell. Successful candidates were as follows:

Ballyholme and Groomsport – Eddie Mills (Unionist), Raymond Trousdale (DUP), Bruce Mulligan (Official Unionist), Bill Bailie (UPNI), Donald Hayes (Alliance).

Abbey – George Green (UPUP), Campbell McCormick (DUP), Wesley Graham (DUP), Cecil Braniff (UPUP), Albert Magee (Alliance).

Bangor West – Mary O'Fee (UPUP), Terence Morrow (Alliance), Alan Graham (DUP), Hazel Bradford (Official Unionist), Brian Wilson (Alliance).

Holywood – Ellie McKay (Official Unionist), John McConnell Auld (Official Unionist), Gordon Dunne (DUP), Susan O'Brien (Alliance) and Michael Clarke (Alliance).

Ten Councillors were first-timers and the new Mayor was outgoing Deputy Mayor Albert Magee. Of the 20, six represented the Alliance Party, five the DUP, along with four Official Unionists, three UPUP, one UPNI and one Unionist. The outgoing Council, following a succession of switches over its four years, was: six Alliance, six Official Unionists, five UPUP, two Unionist, one UPNI and no DUP.

Princess Alexandra visited Bangor's Debretta factory on 2 June, during which

she received a bouquet of flowers from wheelchair-bound employee Lily Heatley, a 50-year-old mother-of-two from Helen's Bay. Mrs Heatley described the occasion as one of the proudest moments of her life. She, in turn, was described by fellow workers as "the darling of Debretta."

Lily Heatley, a long-serving employee at the Debretta factory in Bangor, chats with Princess Alexandra after presenting her with flowers. Included is managing director Michael Houston. *495-12-13*

Actor Peter O'Toole visited Clandeboye House in June to hear the Borodin Trio play during the 12th Music Festival in Great Irish Houses.

George Green threatened to resign as a North Down Alderman in protest at the elevation of newly-elected member Gordon Dunne, who was just 22, to the five-strong body of Aldermen. Voting had been carried out by PR among all Councillors and Messrs Dunne and Green were joined by Albert Magee, Eddie Mills and Bruce Mulligan.

Cllr Green said elevation to Alderman was intended as an honour for service and stressed his protest was not aimed personally at Mr Dunne. "However, for someone as young as that to come in and be made an Alderman without the slightest idea of the practical side of Council work is ridiculous," he stated.

HMS *Cleopatra,* a 3,200-ton Leander class frigate, became the first Royal Navy ship of its size to moor in Bangor Bay for more than a decade. The centrepiece for 1981's Youth Expo, it proved a money-spinner for local boat owners.

North Down Borough Council closed all its halls to rock bands following incidents in the Market Hall during a concert on 27 June by Belfast band The Outcasts. The Council said considerable damage had been caused to the venue, coupled with numerous incidents of under-age drinking.

Terrorist violence returned to Bangor after seven years, with a car bomb on Saturday 22 August causing substantial damage to the Co-Op and superficial damage to other business premises in lower Main Street.

So destructive was the force of the blast that part of the car was found on the roof of the new Boots store in upper Main Street. Windows were broken in Queen's Parade, High Street and Crosby Street.

Victims of the blast included a local housewife hit by flying glass in High Street and two police officers

The scene of destruction in lower Main Street following the return of the car bombers on 22 August 1981. *443-19-14*

Devastated shops in lower Main Street. *450-14-14*

similarly injured while trying to clear the area when the 150lb bomb detonated.

The Co-Op reopened the following Saturday following a "Herculean effort" by members of staff.

A new trawler for the Portavogie fleet, *Willing Lad,* was launched from the Bangor Shipyard at Ballyholme on 27 August. The naming ceremony was performed by Elizabeth Robinson, niece of owner James McClements. The vessel had taken 10 months to build and cost around £350,000.

Eighteen-year-old Michael Douglas, from Grange Park, left the town on 6 September to begin a year's voluntary work in Spitalfields Crypt, East London, under the auspices of Careforce – an organisation that helped young Christians to get involved in practical Christian service in the community. He was a member of the Bangor Parish Youth Fellowship. Spitalfields Crypt was a long-term rehabilitation centre for homeless alcoholic men.

A leaked confidential Eastern Health Board document proposed the immediate closure of Crawfordsburn Hospital to save £600,000 a year, along with the transfer of its 101-bed geriatric unit to Bangor Hospital. It would then become a geriatric hospital after losing its maternity department.

This prompted calls in September for a new North Down General Hospital based around an improved and expanded Bangor Hospital. In addition, a committee was formed by the North Down Trades Council to fight the rundown of local hospital services.

RUC officer Alexander Beck (37), who lived on the Clandeboye Road, was killed on Monday 28 September after the police Land Rover he was driving was struck by a Russian-made RPG-7 missile. The Provisional IRA claimed responsibility for the attack, which left another officer without both his arms and a leg.

Constable Beck, who had joined the RUC just two years earlier, was survived by his wife and their two young children.

The funeral on 30 September took place from his parents' home in Kilkeel to the town's Mourne Presbyterian Church. The Rev. David McGaughey told those who had been responsible for the murder: "You cannot by the bomb and the bullet take away our views; we are entitled to them and will continue to express them. You cannot take away our wills, because every atrocity makes us the more resolute."

Bangor was placed first in the large town section of the annual Ulster in Bloom competition organised by the Northern Ireland Tourist Board. Cllr Mary O'Fee praised the greatly improved appearance of the ring road following the planting of floral displays in the various roundabouts.

North Down Borough Council entered negotiations with Shippers (IOM) Ltd. about introducing a regular cargo service between Bangor and the Isle of Man. It was hoped such a service – which would also spell an end to Minnie Delino's amusements on the Central Pier – would provide the harbour with an additional income of £3,000 per annum.

Thermomax, a new company in the solar heating industry, announced it would be opening a factory on the Balloo Industrial Estate offering employment to 60. Details of the project were announced on 16 November by Industry Minister Adam Butler.

SEE THE DE LOREAN CAR

at Springhill Shopping Centre next week

One thousand people gathered in Ward Park to pay tribute to murdered South Belfast MP the Rev. Robert Bradford, shot dead by gunmen who burst into his constituency clinic in the Finaghy Community Centre on 14 November.

Orange Order chaplain and retired Methodist minister the Rev. Henry Cooke led the service at the Cenotaph and a tribute to the politician was read out by DUP Councillor Wesley Graham.

Three hundred vehicles took part in a cavalcade around the town on 23 November in protest at a recent upsurge in violence and against the Government's security policies. The route was from the Belfast Road flyover to Main Street and High Street and then back along Hamilton Road. This was followed by a massive rally in Newtownards during which members of the Third Force were on parade locally for the first time. The Rev. Ian Paisley declared his intention to "exterminate the IRA."

The Northern Ireland Housing Executive and the Woolwich Building Society adopted the Church Street, Croft Street and Belfast Road area – a total of 126 homes – as the town's first Private Investment Priority Area. Its aim was to encourage home owners and the tenants of privately rented property to take advantage of improvement and repair grants.

Bangor Country and Western singer Tina James in January 1981 with a demo tape of her first release. By Easter 1986, when she was living in England, Tina was performing alongside Johnny Cash and George Jones at the Silk Cut Country Music Festival, held at London's Wembley Arena. 328-7A-12

Trinity Girls' Brigade senior A team, winners of the senior PE team event at the annual competitions held in Newtownards in January 1981. Back (from left): Lieutenant Karen Welsh, Susan Lovell, Diane Bates, Judith Welsh, Jeannette McClelland. Front: Audrey Gillespie, Janine Smith, Deborah Frame and Pauline Patterson. *350-9-12*

The Trinity Girls' Brigade team, trained by Lieutenant Margaret Wilsden (right), won the Brigader section at the annual PE competitions in Newtownards in January 1981. They are (back, from left): Sian McCully, Heather Shilliday, Pamela Welsh, Christine Boal. Front (from left): Sandra Gillespie, Judith McMorran, Elaine McClelland and Audrey Wilsden. *366-9-12*

Assistant band leader Alan Shreeve (deputising for leader Marshall McKee) is pictured with participants during the Bangor Young People's 'play-in' to raise money for new instruments. It was held in February 1981 at the town's Salvation Army Citadel. 15-6-13

Eighteen-year-old Lesley Allen, who had never achieved success at Bangor Speech Festival in the past – despite 14 years of competing – won a total of five trophies at the event in March 1981. She was a pupil of Miss Mollie Drummond. 152-8-13

The Bangor Girls' High School recorder consort prepare for their first concert in April 1981. Playing descant recorders are Rosemary and Allison Boyd, while (centre) Zara Hodgen plays treble, Carole Millar plays tenor and Jill Boyd is playing bass. 195-7-13

The percussion band from Clifton Road Special School with the Shannon Cup which they shared with two other schools in the class for Special Care percussion groups at Holywood Festival in May 1981. With the young musicians are conductor Mrs W. Moffett and music teacher Mrs J. Crowther. *403-4-13*

Colin Vannucci and Lee Gardner, both aged 11, with Parry the rook they adopted in May 1981 after finding it in the Churchill estate.*440-15A-13*

Ten-year-old Wendy Henning with the certificate and badge she received for completing the May 1981 Mourne Wall Walk – it was widely believed she was the youngest person to ever complete the gruelling mountain trek. *524-17A-13*

Retiring Connor House headmaster Gordon Thomson received three tables from the children on his final day at the school. Included are teachers Mrs P. McWilliam and Mrs D. McCracken. *124-16-14*

Billy Stewart (seated centre with colleagues), of Whitehill Avenue, brought his career at Bangor Town Hall to a close in 1981, having completed 33 years with the local authority, latterly as foreman joiner. Prior to the creation of the Northern Ireland Housing Executive he had spent much of his time building Council homes and carrying out repairs. *592-12-14*

Pupils of Ballyholme Primary School won themselves a £1,000 Commodore PET computer in a competition organised by the Northern Ireland Computer Centre in Holywood. The competition, open to schools throughout Northern Ireland, was entitled 'My friend the micro-chip'. The Ballyholme entry, which included a model robot, won the primary schools section. Back row (from left): Neville Longmore, Philip Campbell, Sean Crowther, Gareth Johnstone, Peter McCleary, Graeme McCandless, Simon Cummings, Janet Henry, Jason Ash, teacher Mrs Isobel Pow. Front: Kirsty Young, Gavin Maguire, Zane Radcliffe and Karen Monaghan. *33-19-14*

Children from Fairfield Park who attended a street party to celebrate the Royal Wedding in July 1981. 453-2-12

Children and pensioners from Belmont Drive who gathered together for a Royal Wedding street party in July 1981. 315-1-14

The mothers of Southwell Road organised a party for their children and friends to mark the wedding of Prince Charles to Lady Diana Spencer in July 1981. 294-19-14

George Best and his wife Angie (back, right) with some of the young people who welcomed them on a visit to BJ's roller disco at Seacliff Road in October 1981.
39-8-15

Bangor Operatic Society president Denby Bell hands over to Mayor Albert Magee for safe-keeping the trophy awarded to the Society following their success at the Waterford International Festival of Light Opera in November 1981. They finished second overall with their production of *Irene* and, in addition, gained various other awards. *122-13-15*

Assistant District Commissioner for Scouts Betty McKee (seated) was the honoured guest at a function in Donaghadee to mark her retirement from that position. Lorraine Shepherd (left) and Sandra Watson hand over a gift as a token of appreciation from Scouters following Miss McKee's many years of unstinting work for the organisation.
168-1-15

Mayor Albert Magee hands over the shield to the winning Scout troop after the final of the Bangor and District Quiz in December 1981. From left: Gareth Johnston, Connor Wilson, Jonathan Graham, Brian McShane (from losing finalists Third Bangor – St Columbanus Parish Church), Mayor Magee, David Fitzsimmons, Michael Ferguson, David McClelland, Karl Baxter (Seventh Bangor – West Church). *285-9-15*

Cup-winning pupils at the annual St Columbanus' High School prize distribution in December 1981. Included are principal Frank Kelly and Mrs Berga Nolan, who presented the awards. Back (from left): Clare McAlorum, Frank McVeigh, Robert Brannigan, Gerard Cousins, Shaun Donnan, Sean Napier, Stephen McKearney. Front: Angela O'Reilly, Susan O'Neill, Catherine Smyth, Petra Loyer, Anita Kane and Mairead McGlinchey. *278-11-15*

P7 pupils from the Glenlola Collegiate Preparatory Department enjoyed a visit to Castle Ward, near Strangford, under the auspices of the National Trust Theatre scheme. They are pictured in period costumes with their teacher Valerie Hunter. *315-3-15*

Karen Orr
(née Marsden) remembers...

Life began in 1966 when I was born in South Belfast but I was not destined to stay there. By 1978 a family decision saw us relocating to Bangor – a place we had often visited whilst holidaying in Ballywalter.

Memories of those days present images of 'chicken in a basket' at O'Hara's Royal Hotel and refreshing walks along the sea wall close to the famous McKee Clock. It wasn't long before we had settled into a new housing development called Deanfield, which was quite close to Glenlola Collegiate where I began my post-primary education.

Karen with husband Stephen Orr

As a family we worshipped at Ballycrochan Presbyterian Church which enabled me to join 14th Bangor Girl Guides and, at a later time, the Ranger Guides. I also have lovely memories of the Saturday afternoon badminton club which served a dual purpose, in that along with the fun we seized opportunities to 'eye up the local talent'!

Church life was central to my own life and at the Sunday night Youth Fellowship I made many friends,

Karen Marsden, a classically trained soprano, is one of Northern Ireland's best-known gospel singers.

She has appeared with leading gospel artistes including Michael Card, Lari Goss, the Palmetto State Quartet and Roger Bennett, along with, more recently, such well-known personalities as the late Max Bygraves and Eamonn Holmes.

Karen has frequently been guest artiste for the Royal Irish Regiment Band, as well as featuring on their album, and has been a regular performer at the annual Northern Ireland Festival of Remembrance at Belfast's Waterfront Hall.

For six years, following in the footsteps of her father Derek, Karen hosted Downtown Radio's Sunday morning request programme *Reflections*. Prior to this she hosted *Gospel Time* on Saturday nights and was a part-time newsreader for the station.

Karen has since moved on to concentrate on other areas of ministry, particularly within her local church, Glengormley Methodist.

At the same time as developing her roles as wife to Stephen and mum to Jonathan and Matthew, she pursues her career as a children's asthma and allergy nurse, for which she was honoured as RCN Nurse of the Year in June 2007.

although there were times when I think I proved to be more of a hindrance, especially when I 'played up' causing disturbances – antics which on reflection make me cringe.

Some of the best times were the activity weekends when we joined forces with 10th Bangor Boys' Brigade Company – the same company that allowed us to play snare drums for their pipe and bugle band. This was great fun, especially when we had our weekly drumming sessions and found ourselves parading along Silverbirch Road to and from church on Remembrance Sunday. Drumming was a difficult skill and I still shudder to think of 'paradiddles' and 'mummy-daddy', particularly when I remember the struggle I had to co-ordinate a drum roll when marching!

There were many badges to be worked for, one of which was for drama. This I obtained with the help of fellow Guides after we re-wrote a drama based on *Cinderella* and performed before the congregation. This early success aged 14 fulfilled a lifelong ambition of directing and being involved in show business!

Very soon after that I performed my first solo at a Thinking Day service where I was accompanied by my relatively new and still best friend Judith (Jude) McIlroy – daughter of 'Big Bob' of Bangor Grammar School fame.

Best friend Jude McIlroy and Karen in 1984

In those days I dressed stylishly from the Ballywalter Factory Shop – clingy silky polo neck tops, crimpoline smock-type dresses (which we nicknamed 'the blob'), all accessorised by American tan 20 Denier tights and my longed-for 'Granny Shoes'!

In post-primary school life teardrop sandals and nature treks were popular – remember those? We bought school satchels from the Trap 'n' Tackle shop on Quay Street, lightened our hair with the infamous 'Sun In' which created a 'wonderful' orangey-yellow glow. The 'Purdy' hairstyle was beginning to disappear and be replaced by 'Lady Diana' haircuts, high-necked blouses and blue eyeliner.

During my years at Glenlola, friends and I often congregated in Roulston's Coffee Shop which was usually bursting at the seams, not only with the girls from Glenlola, but many of the Grammar School boys too. I enjoyed after-school activities, especially roller-skating at BJ's or Rollerama and the occasional visit to Sam's Nightclub. There were also the times when pride over-ruled sense, i.e. walking three miles home in four-inch stiletto heels – I can still feel the pain.

Television served as a fall-back when we were at a loose end with *Dynasty, Dallas* and *Falcon Crest* being some of the most popular programmes. Then, if all else failed, there was also the faithful Betamax video recorder, a game of Pac-Man or Space Invaders – forerunners to the Xbox.

Like most young folk of the time, we were always looking for supplements to our pocket money, which I secured through working as a 12-year-old in the new Spar on the Ballycrochan Road. After that I progressed to the cash office in Stewarts, based in the Clandeboye Shopping Centre.

Memories of these years seem to be of long, hot summers when, as a silly young girl, I tried to improve my tan by using Flora margarine for sun oil to foster a deep tan, though in actual fact the hoped-for sun-kissed look turned out to be red and roasted skin.

One summer Jude and I took a trip in one of Laird's rowing boats which brought us into contact with another boat manned by a group of teenage boys on holiday. As usual I couldn't resist a joke and pretended I was German and was visiting my pen-pal. Jude translated for me and we laughed the whole way home as the boys were really taken in – unfortunately the experience did not help with my German O-Level, which I failed!

Karen as the King of Siam in *The King And I*, complete with bald wig. The role of Anna was played by Paula Lucas.

Karen in *Brigadoon* (1982), playing the role of Meg Brockie

The highlight of our school year was the annual musical. From second year I was always involved and, being an all-girl school, there were times when some of us had to play male roles. On one occasion, as the King of Siam in *The King And I,* I donned a bald wig, while for *Joseph And The Amazing Technicolor Dreamcoat* I had a drawn-on beard! I had to be quite creative in finding costumes, one example being for the part of Meg Brockie in *Brigadoon,* where I made a beautiful skirt out of a tartan picnic rug I took from Dad's car.

My dad, Derek Marsden, was a Downtown Radio presenter and he would often come along with his tape recorder to record excerpts which he then played on his popular programme *Sounds Like Marsden.* I felt very proud of him as he sat in the reserved seating at the front watching my every move. He, of course, had been working on my acting skills for months before the production, hoping my rendition might be worthy of a West End performance. Each role was special but probably the part of the demure sister Bianca (type-cast of course!) in Bangor Grammar School's *The Taming Of The Shrew* was particularly memorable.

For many years I was a box office clerk for Downtown Radio in the Little Theatre. I was then fortunate to tread the boards myself in 1986 as Julie Jordan in the New Lyric Operatic's production of *Carousel* – a role my mum had played 10 years earlier in the same theatre with the same company. But perhaps one of the very special times for me was when I had the privilege of dueting with the legendary Josef Locke – a wonderful performer and perfect gentleman.

My walk with God really began in Bangor as most of my socialising was centred within the church, but, looking back now, I feel I was 'frightened' into becoming a Christian after watching films like *Thief In The Night* which was about the second coming of Christ; I didn't want to be left behind, so very quickly asked Jesus to be my Saviour.

At that time I visualised God as a harsh judge but I have since discovered this was a false impression and totally opposite to the truth. My Lord is loving, giving and kind; He is my Father who regards me, along with all of His children, as the apple of His eye.

In time I moved from Ballycrochan Presbyterian to the 'big' Hamilton Road Presbyterian, which became my hub for many years as I was involved in nurture groups, '109' and the church choir, with the music group One Accord being born from this church. Wonderful times of praise through music.

During the 1980s my parents acquired a family bed and breakfast – 'Seacrest' – opposite the Long Hole on Bangor's seafront. I spent many days enjoying the view of Belfast Lough from my third floor bedroom window, marvelling at the sheer beauty and majesty of the sea; an ever-changing canvas and something I miss even today.

Growing up in Bangor during the Troubles was, believe it or not, a real privilege; we seemed to be cocooned, unaffected by the shootings and bombs that were so much a part of life for other parts of the Province. The only time I was

The musical Marsdens – Karen with her late father Derek in 1997

Karen with sons Matthew (left) and Jonathan

remotely aware of unrest was when I shopped in Belfast. There I had to go through security barriers and have baggage searched; living in Bangor was almost like being in a foreign land. Bangor seemed safe, here we had freedom to walk and meet with friends.

My teenage years were blissfully uncomplicated and I am so thankful my parents did not listen to my complaints when they announced we were going to live in Bangor. Without reservation, I can honestly say it will always have a special place in my heart!

1982

IN THE SPECTATOR

Somme veteran Norman Legge was awarded the British Empire Medal for his services to the Royal British Legion in the New Year Honours List. Aged 85 and Bangor-born, he was one of the last surviving members of Royal British Legion predecessor the Comrades of the Great War. He served in the Royal Irish Rifles and then the Royal Army Service Corps.

The investiture ceremony, held in early March, saw Mr Legge receiving the medal from Princess Anne. He passed away the following year.

The Elim Pentecostal Church at Southwell Road was packed for a special evening to mark the retirement of Pastor Alexander Wilson, who had ministered there for almost 15 years. Speakers included his son Samuel (Sammy) and Pastor Eric McComb, Superintendent of the Elim Church in Ireland.

Scotsman Alistair Brown, master of the *Thomas Grant,* commenced a cargo service from the Central Pier to Peel on the Isle of Man. The new service was made possible by the recent improvement work to the pier. The *Thomas Grant* was a 214-ton former Admiralty torpedo recovery vessel, fitted out with a one-and-a-half ton crane.

Captain Alistair Brown, master of the *Thomas Grant.* 513-10-15

Ballycrochan Presbyterian Church was given full congregational status at a Service of

Constitution on 17 January. The minister of the previous church extension was the Rev. Alex Beattie, who received a unanimous call from the congregation to remain in the position.

The Bangor Castle Leisure Centre was officially opened on 25 January by Mayor Albert Magee. The £1m leisure complex was completed a decade after the adjoining indoor swimming pool.

Management was in the hands of recreation officer Ken McKinnon. Annual membership, although not a requirement, was £5 per family, or £2.50 per adult and £1 per juvenile. It had to be temporarily suspended after 5,000 "signed up" in advance of the official opening.

Bangor's Citizens' Advice Bureau moved into the Carnegie Library at the end of January. It had been based at 74 Castle Street since October 1970. On both occasions the new premises were opened by Lady Dunleath.

North Down Borough Councillors joined a 24-hour vigil outside Bangor Hospital on 23 February, calling for the protection of local hospital services.

In early March the sub-postmaster of Whitehill Post Office was kidnapped from his home at gunpoint by a man dressed as a police officer. He was subsequently dumped from a car at Balloo Road after the business keys were taken from him. A four-strong gang then entered the post office and subsequently escaped with an undisclosed sum of money.

Councillors decided, by 11 votes to six, to ban the sale of alcohol at the new Bangor Castle Leisure Centre. Although the local authority did not have the power to grant (or refuse) liquor licences, as owner of the property its consent was required before a licence could be granted for any functions.

The first events affected by the ban were the final night of the North Down Choral Festival, hosted by the North Down Arts Committee, and a jazz evening starring Humphrey Littleton.

Paul Nesbitt, from Cotswold Drive, took part in the All Ireland Disco Dancing Championships in Dublin. He was sponsored by the Whispers Nightclub in the Groomsport House Hotel.

Disturbances in Bangor on Easter Monday (12 April) led to 64 young people, aged between 17 and 22, appearing before three different sittings of North Down Magistrates' Court, where they faced a variety of charges, including disorderly behaviour and assault. They were described as "Mods, Rockers and skinheads."

A wave from Mayor Albert Magee. *273-20-16*

The *Bangor Belle,* billed by the Borough Council as "Ireland's only road train", was barred by the Department of the Environment from travelling on public roads immediately after it was introduced in the middle of April. Nevertheless it proved a popular attraction in Castle Park, where those taking part in the inaugural run included Mayor Albert Magee, Mayoress Mrs Audrey Magee, Alderman Bruce Mulligan and Cllr Hazel Bradford.

The bell-ringers from St Comgall's Parish Church won the annual competition for the Cunningham Cup, organised by the Northern Branch of the Irish Association of Change Ringers.

A well-known business in Market Street, Annabelle's linen shop, closed at the end of April after operating for 35 years. It was run by Elizabeth Ellison, in partnership with Eleanor Adrain.

A Bangor family was keeping close watch on developments in the South Atlantic, hoping for news of 35-year-old Robert Walker, a member of the Falkland Islands task force. He was an electrical officer on the Royal Fleet Auxiliary fuel supply vessel *Tidespring,* refuelling Royal Navy vessels.

Back in Bangor were his mother Kathleen, of King Street, and brother Eddie and family, of Church Avenue. In his younger days Robert had been a member of Sixth Bangor Boys' Brigade. He was also a bell-ringer at St Comgall's Parish Church during home visits. (See picture on p81)

A service to mark the centenary of the consecration of St Comgall's Parish Church was held on 9 May, the eve of St Comgall's Day. The address was given by Most

Rev. Dr. Otto Simms, former Archbishop of Armagh and Primate of All Ireland.

Chief Constable Sir Jack Hermon received the Freedom of the Borough of North Down, on behalf of the Royal Ulster Constabulary, from Mayor Albert Magee at a ceremony in the Town Hall on 27 May. Councillors had voted unanimously to present the Freedom of the Borough to both the RUC and the RUC Reserve to mark the 60th anniversary of the force's existence.

William and Margaret Hagans, of Bloomfield Road South, became the owners of the 10,000th house to be sold to its tenants by the Northern Ireland Housing Executive. They received the keys on 28 May from Environment Minister David Mitchell.

CENTRAL CHANCERY OF THE ORDERS OF KNIGHTHOOD

St. James's Palace, London S.W.1
11th October, 1982

The QUEEN has been graciously pleased to approve the Posthumous award of the Queen's Gallantry Medal to the undermentioned in recognition of gallantry during the operations in the South Atlantic:

Queen's Gallantry Medal

Acting Colour Sergeant Brian JOHNSTON, Royal Marines, PO23116X.

Colour Sergeant Johnston, coxswain of LCU F4, was working in the vicinity of HMS ANTELOPE when her unexploded bomb detonated, starting an immediate fire which caused her crew, already at emergency stations, to be ordered to abandon ship. Without hesitation Colour Sergeant Johnston laid his craft alongside the ANTELOPE and began to fight the fire and take off survivors. At approximately 2200Z he was ordered to stay clear of the ship because of the severity of the fire and the presence of a second unexploded bomb. Colour Sergeant Johnston remained alongside until his load was complete. In all LCU F4 rescued over 100 survivors from the ANTELOPE.

On 8 June, LCU F4 was attacked by enemy aircraft in Choiseul Sound. During this action Colour Sergeant Johnston and five of his crew were killed.

Colour Sergeant Johnston's selfless bravery in the face of extreme danger was in the highest traditions of the Corps.

The QUEEN has been graciously pleased to approve the award of the Queen's Gallantry Medal in recognition of gallantry during the operations in the South Atlantic:

Bangor housewife Pat Cowan, of Lyndhurst Avenue, was mourning the loss of her brother in the Falklands conflict. Carrickfergus-born Brian Johnston, a Colour Sergeant in the Royal Marines, was attached to HMS *Fearless*. He was on board a landing craft which had gone to the rescue of victims after it was sunk.

The craft was hit by missiles and six were killed, the incident occurring on 8 June. News that Brian was missing, presumed dead, arrived the following day on what would have been his 34th birthday.

He was posthumously awarded the Queen's Gallantry Medal for "selfless bravery in the face of extreme danger" that was "in the highest traditions of the Corps."

The citation, issued from St James's Palace on 11 October that same year, refers in detail to an operation on 23/24 May 1982, during which Colour Sergeant Johnston, as coxswain of LCU F4, helped to fight a fire on HMS *Antelope* while at the same time taking off survivors after the order to abandon ship had been given. Despite the severity of the fire and the presence of a second unexploded bomb, over 100 survivors were rescued.

Colour Sergeant Brian Johnston

Mr and Mrs Thomas James Boal, of Shrewsbury Drive, celebrated their golden wedding anniversary on 22 June at a family function in the Copelands Hotel, Donaghadee. Those in attendance included sons Jim, Tom and Douglas and 12 of their 16 grandchildren.

The Bangor Parish Honorary Society of Bell-Ringers turned out on Tuesday evening, 22 June, to ring a joy peal in celebration of the birth of Prince William, first child of the Prince and Princess of Wales.

North Down Borough Councillors were furious at Health Minister John Patten's refusal to meet them to discuss the future of medical services in the area, including the closure-threatened Crawfordsburn Hospital. They accused him of treating the Council's concerns in a "cavalier fashion."

Renowned Bangor sportsman Jimmy Kirk sustained severe abdominal injuries when caught up in a car bomb explosion in the centre of Belfast on 26 June. He was one of 26 people injured when the 200lb bomb exploded in Brunswick Street.

Betty McIlroy, superintendent of the Bangor Ambulance/Nursing Division of the St John Ambulance Brigade, retired from the position after many years of service, including a spell as the Division's secretary.

A Bangor native was among seven members of the Band of the Royal Green Jackets who were killed when an IRA bomb exploded underneath a bandstand in Regent's Park, London, on 22 July.

Sergeant Robert Alexander Livingstone (30), who played the French horn and was described as a "non-combatant", originally came from Bangor, where his father still resided. His younger brother was in the 1st Battalion of the Royal Green Jackets and at the time was on a two-year tour of duty in Northern Ireland.

A new scheme envisaged the Castle Street/Market Square area becoming the new town centre, along with a new link road replacing a previously controversial proposal for a dual carriageway in the heart of Bangor.

The plan, prepared by the McAdam Design Partnership of Newtownards, was accepted in principle by Councillors at the beginning of August. They felt a public inquiry would be necessary as the proposals represented a major departure from the existing Area Plan.

It was announced that GEA Air Exchangers, which employed 55 people at its Balloo Industrial Estate plant, would be closing on 22 October. With insufficient

Placed on the market in mid-August 1982, Caproni's was demolished the following Spring to make way for luxury flats on Seacliff Road. *308-18-19*

orders to cover its costs it had fallen victim to the ongoing recession.

Two landmark Bangor properties, Caproni's Ballroom on the Seacliff Road and Barry's Amusements at Quay Street, went on the market in mid-August. Outline permission existed for the latter to be refurbished as an amusement arcade or for a change of use back to a hotel (it was formerly the Grand Hotel).

A week later the 'For Sale' signs also went up on the Savoy Hotel at the junction of the Donaghadee Road and Hamilton Road. It continued to operate as an entertainment centre (hosting discos, ballroom dancing and dinner dances) until May 1983.

Sixteen-year-old Paula Lucas took over the role of Joseph at short notice and performed commendably in the Glenlola Collegiate production of *Joseph And The Amazing Technicolor Dreamcoat* in 1982. *337-6-18*

Mark McMullan (15), from Ballyhalbert Gardens in Kilcooley, became Ulster's Pac-Man champion in late August, beating 200 other competitors at the Avoniel Leisure Centre in Belfast. After becoming All Ireland champion he went on to finish seventh in the World Pac-Man finals the following month in Paris.

Bangor student Brian McBurney climbed to the 21,000ft summit of Mt Kangyisay in the Himalayas. The intrepid 21-year-old, from Church Street, was a member of a 13-strong team comprising former Southern Education and Library Board outdoor pursuits centre temporary staff.

Cultra barrister Robert McCartney QC topped the poll at an Official Unionist Party meeting in Newtownards to select the party's North Down team for the forthcoming Stormont Assembly elections. The other four candidates were: Cllr Billy Bleakes (Lisburn Borough Council), Euro MP John Taylor, Cllr Hazel Bradford (North Down Borough Council) and businessman David McNarry.

Other candidates selected for North Down by their respective parties were: Cllr

Simpson Gibson (Ards Borough Council), Alderman Tom Gourley (Ards Borough Council), businessman Wesley Pentland and Alderman Charles Poots (Lisburn Borough Council), for the DUP; John Cushnahan, Lord Dunleath and Cllr Brian Wilson (North Down Borough Council), for the Alliance Party; North Down MP Jim Kilfedder and Alderman George Green (North Down Borough Council), for the Ulster Popular Unionist Party; Patrick Doherty, for the SDLP. Bert Gabbey put himself forward as a Unionist-UUUP candidate.

Bangor man Brian William Smyth was killed and a companion was injured in a shooting incident in the Shankill Road area of Belfast on Sunday 5 September. Mr Smyth (29), owner of Smyth Motors on the Gransha Road, had reportedly gone to the city with two other local men in connection with a car he had sold the previous Friday.

The murder took place at the corner of Crimea Street when the men got out of a silver Simca car. Three shots from a passing motorcyclist hit Mr Smyth in the chest and he died instantly. Another shot hit one of the other man, while the third was uninjured.

The victim, from Old Belfast Road, had previously served for 12 years in the Merchant Navy, reaching the rank of Petty Officer and also becoming the Merchant Navy's heavyweight boxing champion.

Brian's father stated: "He was a big soft man who would have given his last penny to anyone who needed it. He certainly had more friends than enemies."

The Baton of Honour, the top prize at the RUC passing out parade on 17 September, was won by Constable Wesley Wilson, from Bangor. He received the award from Belfast Lord Mayor Tom Patton at the RUC Training Centre in Enniskillen.

Health workers staged a local Day of Action on 22 September to promote their demand for a 12% wage increase. Pickets gathered at Bangor Hospital and Bangor Health Centre and at the weekly market in Castle Square.

PC Philip Wilson (24), a Bangor man serving in the London Metropolitan Police, received a Bravery Commendation, along with a colleague, for tackling a man who was trying to shoot them with a repeating shotgun during a siege at his flat in Poplar. He was the son of Elizabeth Wilson, Kilcooley, and the late Herbert Wilson.

The Tower House on Quay Street, a familiar Bangor landmark dating back to 1637, was reopened after an extensive refurbishment programme. It was looked upon as a potential focal point for the town's new marina.

A Bangor support group for the Northern Ireland Hospice was formed in October. The meeting to launch the new organisation was held in the Bryansglen Park home of Olive Byers, who subsequently served as chairman. The secretary was Pamela Hazel, of Seacliff Road.

Third Bangor Boys' Brigade Company celebrated their golden jubilee with a service of thanksgiving in Hamilton Road Presbyterian Church on 24 October. The address was given by the Very Rev. David Burke, who shared the role of Company Chaplain with the Rev. Trevor Morrow.

In the Assembly elections held on 20 October Jim Kilfedder once again topped the poll with 13,958 votes, and was the only North Down candidate to be elected on the first count. The Official Unionists won three seats – John Taylor (5,852 first preference votes), Robert McCartney (3,782) and William Bleakes (2,692); the DUP won two seats – Simpson Gibson (4,500) and Wesley Pentland (3,340); as did Alliance – John Cushnahan (4,416) and Lord Dunleath (3,841).

Former barrister Jim Kilfedder MP congratulates Robert McCartney QC, of the Official Unionist Party, on his election to the Northern Ireland Assembly in October 1982.
168-5A-18

Kilfedder was subsequently elected as Speaker of the new Northern Ireland Assembly, defeating Official Unionist John Carson by 31 votes to 25, thanks to the unlikely combined support of DUP and Alliance members. He thus became the highest paid politician in the United Kingdom, as he was also a serving Westminster MP – earning, in total, £32,705 plus £14,112 secretarial expenses.

It was announced that the Stewart Memorial School at Downshire Road – run then by the Incorporated Cripples' Institute and Holiday Homes – would close in August 1983, having fallen victim to financial difficulties.

The area's first waste refuse transfer station, built at a cost of £1.3m, was officially opened at Rathgael by Mayor John McConnell Auld on 8 December. The complex included North Down Borough Council's new works depot.

Joiner Martin Andrews at work on some of the new Bangor road signs at Rathgael. *406-8-18*

The Caproni's site was sold in mid-December with the developers indicating it would be replaced by luxury apartments.

A mini-roundabout at the junction of the Springhill Road with the Crawfordsburn and Bryansburn Roads came into operation on 14 December. The first accident was recorded within a matter of hours, prompting the *Spectator* to describe the markings as "barely adequate."

Prime Minister Margaret Thatcher landed by helicopter amidst Bangor shoppers on 22 December. The pre-Christmas visit saw Mrs Thatcher, accompanied by husband Denis, undertaking a whistle-stop tour of numerous Main Street shops and chatting with many local people along the way.

Prime Minister Margaret Thatcher with North Down Mayor John McConnell Auld during her visit to Bangor in December 1982. *489-12-18*

At Hoggs Gift Shop she purchased some Tyrone Crystal. She was also presented with a copy of Bangor Parish Choir's *Carols by Candlelight* LP by member Michael Thomson.

Prime Minister Margaret Thatcher's meets local children during her pre-Christmas visit to Bangor in 1982. *488-8-18*

The cast of the Bangor Abbey Players' January 1982 production of *Sleeping Beauty* in the final wedding scene of the pantomime. From left: John Moorehead (Wally Tonker), Ivan Maxwell (Willy Tonker), Eddie Shannon (Queen Mother Gertrude), Della Beck (Prince Valentine), Sadie McKee (Princess Abigail), Alex Best (Carabosse), Fiona McCausland (Honeydew Fairy) and Candice McAuley (Witch Boy). *455-7A-15*

The First Bangor Girls' Brigade Brigader team, winners of their section in the annual Ards District PE competitions held at Carnalea Methodist Church in January 1982. Back (from left): Karen Smith, Lynda Martin, Megan Liddell, Gillian Tipping, Lt. Brenda Stringer. Front: Julie Gowdy, Jackie Courtenay and Debra Osborne. *494-6-14*

Pupils of Grange Park Primary School collected money for the town's Stewart Memorial Special School at their annual carol service and at a school concert. Receiving the cheque from Barbara Turkington is Brian Russell, on behalf of Stewart Memorial Special School. Other pupils from Grange Park PS are (clockwise): Emma Bingham, Karen Drury, Philip Nixon, Jonathan Roberts and Richard Moore. Also included are Stewart Memorial principal Margaret Gilpin and Grange Park PS vice-principal William Henry. *549-18A-15*

Five of the principals in Kilmaine Primary School's production of *The Golden Goose*. Buttons (at the front) was played by Jonathan Brown, while Ugly Sisters Marilyn and Sophie were portrayed by Simon Henry (left) and Mark Hamilton (right). Also included are Kim Heron (Princess Diana) and Melanie Currie (Charlie). *602-4-15*

Two members of 14th Bangor (Ballycrochan) Girls' Brigade Company had reason to be proud of their achievements in February 1982. Seventeen-year-old Michelle Hayes (left), of Perry Park, gained her Young Leaders' Certificate for her work with the Brownie pack. She had also completed her Duke of Edinburgh Silver Award with the Rangers and was the first Guider at 14th Bangor to receive a leaders' certificate. Alex Henry (13), of Deanfield, was made a Queen's Guide – the youngest in the company. *742-12-15*

The choir of Bangor Central Primary School carried off the Claney Cup in the final class of the music section at Bangor Music Festival in March 1982. Holding the trophy is Foster Irwin, the only boy in the choir and its longest-serving member. Heather Armstrong was the teacher responsible for their success. *9-9A-16*

Cubs and Beaver Scouts from one of the town's newest troops, Eighth Bangor, with the new colours they received on 2 May 1982 in Kilcooley Presbyterian Church. The money for the colours was raised by the troop's very active Parents Committee. *326-14-16*

Angela Brown (17), who attended Glenlola Collegiate, became both the All Ireland and Northern Ireland Disco-Dancing Champion at the Coca Cola Championships in Belfast during May 1982. She was a member of the Body Language dancing team which operated out of the Savoy Hotel and also the Satin Sky rock band. *491-8A-16*

Members of Bangor Rotary Club at the local golf club in July 1982 after the installation of new president Ian Morrow (seated centre, second from left). Sitting with him are (from left): Michael Miller (vice-president), Albert Compton (immediate past president), Harry McDonough (second vice-president) and Hugo Simpson. Standing: Roy Rosbotham, Des Murray, Max Boyce, Tom Brown, John Pringle, Paul Twemlow, Raymond Boyd, Rockie Notley, Dick Wolsey, Ian Sinclair (visitor), Andrew Carnson, Bob Jellie, Canon George Mitchell, Wilson Ferguson, Stewart Miller, Dave Pauley, Gordon Finlay, Fred Eakin, Bill Bailie, Edwin Dunlop. Front: Jim Millar, Bill McClure, Jimmy Allen, Dacre Ball, David Magowan, Dr Des Tate, Jack Small and Hubert Nesbitt. *305-8-17*

Pupils from Kilcooley Primary School sent a project on new-born Prince William to Buckingham Palace, and in response received a letter, expressing the gratitude of the Prince and Princess of Wales, from Lady-in-Waiting Lavinia Baring. The children were also invited to a reception at the Town Hall by Mayor John McConnell Auld. Included are Mrs R. Brien (who helped the pupils with the project), Constable Tom Patterson (RUC Community Relations Branch) and principal Alan Glenn. *99-8-18*

Members of the newly-formed Bangor Group of the Northern Ireland Hospice were delighted when Maureen Cameron, captain of Bangor Ladies' Golf Club, chose the Hospice as the good cause to benefit from the annual bridge afternoon. Mrs Cameron (left) presented a cheque for £400 – a record sum from the bridge competition – to Olive Byers, who chaired the Bangor fundraising group. *237-20A-18*

Students from Bangor Girls' High School marked Ulster Tree Week in November 1982 by planting four trees in the school grounds to replace others lost from the front of the school when Castle Street was widened some years earlier. Doing the shovelling are Pauline Graham (left) and Catherine Getty while Audrey Craig holds the tree. Headmistress Marie Brownlee looks on. *338-18-18*

The young choristers of Bangor Abbey prepare for the Christmas Chorale, to be staged on Christmas Eve 1982. Included is organist Cecil Thompson. *424-20-18*

Billy and Lily Green, of Elmwood Drive, who celebrated their golden wedding anniversary on 18 December 1982. The couple were both born and bred in the town and married in Bangor Abbey in 1932. Billy served in the Royal Navy for 22 years and was one of only 12 survivors when his ship was torpedoed during World War Two. They had two children, Billy and Eveline, and two grandchildren, Jacqui and Billy. *472-4-18*

Members of the chorus from Bangor Operatic Society's pantomime *Cinderella* in December 1982. Back (from left): Claire Hughes, Desmond McIntyre, Pamela Hughes, Ian Thompson, Olwen Rowan, Alan Conroy, Catherine Chalice, Lisa Redden. Front: Rachel Shields, Joyce McCutcheon, Dawn Moffett and Deirdre Moffett. *498-6A-18*

Paul Russell
remembers...

Many memories remain with us from childhood and very often last throughout our lifetime. Thoughts flood back of days gone by when people seemed a lot happier with a lot less. For many of us who grew up in the Seventies and Eighties a trip to Bangor was always a treat and, when there, a visit to the Tonic Cinema was a priority.

Accompanied by my father Terry, I was fortunate to be able to visit the Tonic on many happy occasions between 1978 and 1983, when its doors closed for the last time. I realise some will say a cinema is just a cinema, a place you visit to see a favourite film, but mention of the Tonic always awakens memories for me of those trips to Bangor and, more than 20 years after its sad demolition, how special it was to so many of us.

Modern-day cinemas will never be able to match the design, grandeur and atmosphere of the Hamilton Road picture house, which was built and opened in 1936. It's little wonder I have an abiding interest in movies, especially those from the classic Hollywood period – so much of it can be traced back to those memorable visits to the Tonic and its direct link to the golden age of cinema.

I was born and bred in Newtownards where our last cinema in that era, the Regent, was sadly destroyed by firebombers in 1977. After that if we wanted to see the

Paul Russell was born in September 1971 in Newtownards, attending the town's Londonderry Primary School (1976-1983) and Movilla High School (1983-1988).

He has always viewed Bangor as his 'second home' and, hence, he has many happy memories of the town. Visits to the Tonic between 1978 and 1983, when it finally closed, inspired a lifelong interest in cinema and films.

Paul currently works for the Northern Ireland Civil Service. Married to Lesley, they have a baby daughter, Abi.

Just seven weeks before its closure (on 29 October 1983) Environment Minister Chris Patten visited Bangor to discuss North Down Borough Council plans to purchase the Tonic. He is pictured at the cinema with, amongst others, Mayor John McConnell Auld, Alderman Bruce Mulligan, Cllr Hazel Bradford and Cllr Mary O'Fee. *627-12A-20*

latest releases, or indeed a re-released classic, the nearest and indeed the best alternative was in Bangor.

Back in 1978 I was only seven but even then a visit to the Tonic was a highlight of my young life. Approaching along Hamilton Road I was always taken aback by the sheer size and grandeur of the building, along with those instantly recognisable signs which illuminated the area around the Moira Drive junction. One displayed the cinema's familiar Tonic name – for a brief time in the Seventies it was renamed Odeon by the cinema group of that name – while the other identified, in equally bold red letters, the current film and the times it was being shown.

As we entered through the highly polished Golden Doors, as I called them, where the plush carpet and the walls of the foyer shared the same deep shade of red, we were greeted by the stern-faced doorman/ security officer, who would search us as this was back in the dark days of the Troubles. Only then could we join the queue to purchase our tickets from the kindly lady in the ticket booth.

While waiting in line I liked to check out the 'Coming Attractions' posters, which were secured in white display boards on the foyer walls. Then when we reached the booth I was fascinated to watch the cardboard tickets shoot out from the counter slots. Simple pleasures in simpler times! After a visit to the cinema shop, which – needless to say – stocked only the largest packets of all types of sweets, we headed to the right-hand side of the foyer, with its grand staircase decorated in ruby red velvet patterned wallpaper.

Momentarily distracted by more posters showing the Tonic's forthcoming film and concert attractions, we arrived at the large first floor and its black and white patterned floor tiles, which we crossed to the auditorium doors with their 50p-shaped glazed surrounds. Once inside we were greeted by the glorious sight of those enormous yellow curtains that covered the cinema's huge screen.

Paul Russell now with baby daughter Abi

Seeking the best possible view, we always took our time to choose our seats, which were finished in a velvet material that matched the colour of the curtains. Thankfully those seats were very comfortable as most evening shows at the Tonic included a double feature and, running from around 7pm to 10.30pm, represented a complete night's entertainment.

During the wait we listened to the pop hits of the day as they boomed around the auditorium over the cinema's sound system. Then, right on time, the music faded, the main auditorium lights dimmed, the curtains were pulled back and what seemed like an eternity of adverts and trailers preceded the first film of the evening.

Most of those commercials must have been made across the water as the decidedly English 'voiceover' person had clearly never visited County Down and always pronounced our Bangor as Bangooorrrr.

With each visit to the Tonic my interest in the cinema and all it represented grew. My father had to remind me on a few occasions to actually watch the film we were there to see, as I tended to be fascinated by the glow of the cinema projector beaming its darting images onto the giant screen through the plumes of smoke caused by patrons' cigarettes (something that has thankfully changed in today's cinemas!).

When the first film ended there was always a brief intermission, during which many hurried downstairs to top up their supplies before the main attraction began. For those who didn't wish to venture too far the ever reliable usherette appeared in the middle aisles with her tray of confectionery and cigarettes, all illuminated by a tiny bulb – but supplemented,

if necessary, by her trusty torch in the event of a tardy customer needing to make a purchase after the house lights dimmed.

As the main feature came to a close, and especially if it had a long list of credits, there was a sudden rush by those who wanted out of the auditorium before the customary playing of the National Anthem. On more than a few occasions those impatient patrons found themselves denied a speedy exit if the film had a simple 'The End' fade-out and no credits!

The Tonic in the 1960s

When it was finally time to leave the Tonic it was always an important part of the ritual to study that illuminated sign, which was usually changed during our visit, to discover the following week's programme.

As I mentioned earlier, 2012 marked the 20th anniversary of the cinema's sad demolition. I am so very thankful that during my childhood my father took me to visit that grand lost treasure of a building. Even after the passage of so much time my memories remain vivid, serving as a lasting tribute to the Bangor entertainment centre known simply to so many generations as 'The Tonic'.

The Tonic Cinema
Time Line 1980-1986

1980

Top TV comedian Dick Emery appeared for two nights at the Tonic (11 and 12 March). *Spectator* reviewer Colin Bateman said while it was "far from a family show" it was "of the highest calibre."

"It is a pleasing trend for big-name acts to return to this Province, and we can only hope the Tonic management will continue to bring across stars. Not only does it do wonders for the local entertainment scene, but doubtless summer engagements would do wonders for tourism," he wrote.

Harry Secombe took to the stage on 17 September with members of the Ulster Actors' Company presenting excerpts from their show *The Rocking Fifties*. Also appearing were comedian Tom Raymond, soprano Irene Maguire and the Barry Nolan Orchestra. Compere was George Jones of Clubsound.

Other leading performers to appear at the Tonic that autumn included Lena Martell (fresh from a Number One hit with *One Day At A Time)* and Clubsound on 9 October; Lena Zavaroni with TV comedian Norman Collier on 20 and 21 October; and Billy Connolly on 10 November. Connolly returned for two more concerts in February 1982.

Billy Connolly, fresh from his appearance at the Tonic, is pictured with young Bangor man David Bateman. *58-13-12*

1981

The New Year arrived with news that a trio of top names, Elton John, Leo Sayer and Glen Campbell, were set to appear at the Tonic during 1981. There were "firm" dates for Leo Sayer and Glen Campbell, in March and May respectively, but nothing concrete for Elton John. In the end just Glen Campbell made it to Bangor, on 6 May.

The Tonic hosted the Freddie Starr Show for three consecutive nights – 29, 30 and 31 October – followed, on 24 November, by Welsh comedian Max Boyce.

1982

David Soul – of *Starsky and Hutch* fame – appeared in concert on 2 June, supported by 1976 Eurovision Song Contest winners Brotherhood of Man.

1983

More big names were preparing to grace the stage at the Tonic – Dionne Warwick would entertain two packed houses on 20 and 21 January; Elkie Brooks would appear there on 8 and 9 March; Welsh comedian Max Boyce was booked for 11 May, and TV double act Cannon and Ball would top the bill on 7 and 8 October.

Borough Councillors were informed on 14 June that a "categoric and final" decision had been taken to close the Tonic on 1 January 1984. The news was delivered by Denis Scott, director and secretary of building owners A. S. & D. Enterprises, who attended the meeting to seek Councillors' support for a previously refused application for a change of use to a retail outlet.

Since taking over the Tonic five years earlier, said Mr Scott, they had come to realise it would never be independently viable (i.e. as a cinema) because of growing pressure from television and the home video market and increased spending on leisure facilities.

"The Tonic was constructed in another age and for another world," he said, adding: "We've had to come to terms with this reality." Rather than leave the building empty and decaying, the company wanted permission for alternative use involving a "high-class retailer."

Cllr Campbell McCormick called in September for a feasibility study into converting the Tonic into a multi-purpose sports and arts complex utilising government grant aid. Following a meeting with Environment Minister Chris Patten, a matter of days later, it was revealed that plans were in hand for the local authority to buy the landmark building.

The Tonic's owners announced it would close earlier than planned, on Saturday 29 October, "owing to a lack of public support." The last live shows, starring Cannon and Ball and compered by Bangor man Adrian Walsh, were on 7 and 8 October, while the final films, screened from 27 to 29 October, were *Party Party* and *Porkies II – The Next Day*. Although the cinema no longer operated after that date, twice-weekly evening bingo sessions continued until 4 June 1985.

1984

Planning permission was granted in early August to convert the empty Tonic building into a large retail store. The Scott brothers had appealed against the decision of both North Down Borough Council and the Planning Directorate to reject their application, despite it having previously gained the support of the DoE's Planning Department.

The permission included a stipulation that the façade could not be altered in any way. At the beginning of September the Council turned down an opportunity to rent the property for £65,000 per annum, with the result that the Tonic went on the open market, complete with planning permission for retail use.

1985

Plans were submitted by a Dublin company to convert the Borough Gymnasium on Hamilton Road into a 200-seat cinema. Although there was support in principle for the proposal, Councillors were not particularly excited by the idea, with one claiming there was no demand for a cinema in the town as the previous two had closed down.

The Tonic reopened for one night only on Saturday 28 September for a big screen live broadcast of Barry McGuigan's successful first defence of his World Featherweight title against Bernard Taylor at the King's Hall in Belfast.

1986

The Planning Appeals Commission, sitting in Hamilton House during the final week of January, was told the Tonic would become a branch of Dunnes Stores if the Commission upheld an application for a retail outlet at the Hamilton Road site.

A High Court judge ordered the Planning Appeals Commission to hold a fresh inquiry after objections were lodged by North Down Borough Council. The local authority claimed natural justice had been denied in January and this was upheld by Mr Justice Robert Carswell.

Despite much talk about the future of the Tonic, the building remained empty and unused throughout the remaining years of the 1980s. Any lingering hopes that it could be restored as a cinema were dashed with the opening of the four-screen Bangor Cineplex at the former Crystals Arena on 15 December 1989. The iconic building was demolished after being ravaged by fire in June 1992. Four years later work started on the Tonic Fold – thus preserving the famous name for posterity.

Thanks to a dedicated group of supporters, the Tonic also lives on through the Facebook page http://www.facebook.com/pages/The-Tonic-Cinema/130173470339117

1983
IN THE SPECTATOR

Reserve Constable Brian Quinn, a well-known young man in Bangor and the wider North Down area, was shot dead, along with an RUC colleague, by the IRA in Rostrevor on 6 January.

The 23-year-old was the son of Thomas and Catherine Quinn, residents of Old Belfast Road since the mid-1970s. He was also survived by his sister and brother.

The young man's popularity was shown by the large attendance at his funeral, which took place to the Church of the Holy Redeemer, Ballyholme. The service was conducted by Parish Priest Fr Gerard Laverty, assisted by Fr Austin McGirr.

Fr Laverty stated: "He was callously and brutally cut down in the flower of young manhood while performing his duty with zeal and dedication. As Christians we must heartily condemn such acts of violence which are contrary to God's law and the teaching of the Church."

The murdered officer was buried with full RUC honours at Clandeboye Cemetery, where hundreds of colleagues gathered around the grave to pay their final respects.

A new chapter in the life of Bangor Baptists began on 8 January when their church at Ballycrochan was officially opened and dedicated.

The final dance prior to the building's demolition was staged at Caproni's on 14 January, hosted by Donaghadee Round Table and preserved for posterity by a BBC Northern Ireland film crew. Performers included The Dominoes, Dave Glover and George Jones.

It was announced that the Bangor branch of Robinson and Cleaver would close on 1 April with the loss of all 40 jobs. Managing director Angus Gordon said the Main Street store, which had opened in 1969, was "just not paying" and there was no alternative. The building was not owned by the company and there were hopes a new tenant could be identified.

Another piece of Bangor history came under the auctioneer's hammer on 26 January with the sale of the contents of Barry's Amusements while, separately, the building had been sold for an estimated £140,000.

The entire ghost train was purchased for £50, while *What The Butler Saw At Expo Tokyo*, comprising a turnstile and 27 peep shows, went for £70. The palmistry machine with hundreds of

Taking a last look in January 1983 at some of the amusements in Barry's before the auction begins. 659-2A-18

printed fortune cards went for £300 but the speedway track, complete with 12 cars, failed to find a buyer. All told, the auction realised £14,282 for seller Minnie Delino (who passed away in 1987).

Bangor native John Ekin took up duties in February as organist and choirmaster at Hamilton Road Presbyterian Church.

Oneida Silversmiths became the latest local firm to feel the impact of the recession, laying off 27 workers at the beginning of March and cutting back on production in the face of rising costs and a fall in demand. The company still employed 145 people in Bangor.

Twenty-year-old Anne Roycroft, from Bangor, was chosen to grace the cover of the 1983 PTQ magazine. As the *Spectator* noted of the Stranmillis College student: "Our Anne, unlike previous Miss PTQs, is not revealing all, or nearly all. Instead she is proving another not very well known fact – that even a duffle coat can be made to look glamorous."

Assembly member Robert McCartney announced he intended to seek the Official Unionist nomination to stand for the Westminster seat held by Jim Kilfedder since 1970.

Work on the new North Breakwater, the first element in the Bangor Harbour redevelopment scheme, was nearing completion and efforts were already under way to obtain funding for the second element, the Pickie Breakwater, which would ensure sheltered water regardless of weather conditions.

Ella Worthington became the first woman to chair the Bangor Chamber of Trade and Tourist Development Association. She succeeded outgoing chairman Jim Good at the annual general meeting in the Royal Hotel on 28 March.

McCartney seeks North Down Seat

Mr. Robert McCartney, QC, is seeking the Official Unionist ticket to represent North Down at Westminster.

Election. The Unionists' selection meeting will take place on April 28.

Mr. McCartney, up to now considered to be a strong supporter of devolution, is being labelled as an integrationist following his address at Fermanagh Unionist Association's annual meeting. In this he said that he now believed that the full integration of Northern Ireland into the United Kingdom could allay Unionists' fears about the union and would allow for "the desectarianisation of politics" in the Province.

It is not yet known whether Mr. Jim Kilfedder, Speaker of the Northern Ireland Assembly and founder of the Ulster Progressive Unionist Party, will stand for North Down or for the Strangford (Ards) seat at Westminster.

Mr. McCartney, who lives at Cultra and is an Official Unionist Assemblyman for North Down, is a comparative newcomer to politics. He has made application for nomination as the Ulster Unionist Party candidate for the new North Down constituency in the next Parliamentary General

Rat of the Week

... the person or persons who stole a bunch of fresh daffodils from a grave in Bangor Cemetery.

The Minor fish and chip shop, a local landmark at Church Street, was sold after being in the hands of the Gherardi family for 46 years. The business was unique in that the chip pans were coal as well as gas-fired.

Of Italian descent but born in Scotland, Matt Gherardi, second generation of the family to run the business, had retired through ill-health the previous November. The Minor was opened by his father George in 1937. Still with many of its original fittings, the business was sold to a Chinese family.

Regrettably Mr Gherardi passed away just a short time later, on 3 June, being survived by his wife Anne, sons Matthew, Derek and David, and the wider family circle.

The IRA admitted it was a case of mistaken identity after gunmen murdered father-of-two James McCormick (45) and wounded his wife at their Balligan Gardens home in the Kilcooley Estate on Easter Sunday night, 3 April. The couple had lived there for 10 years.

The IRA's statement expressed regret over the Bangor man's death and tendered "deepest sympathies" to the family. He was not the intended target and a "full enquiry is now under way."

Mrs McCormick was released from hospital for 48 hours to attend a private service in the home the following Thursday. It preceded the full service in St Columba's Church, Kilcooley, with interment taking place afterwards at Clandeboye Cemetery.

The Rt. Rev. Dr Robin Eames, Bishop of Down and Dromore, said there could never be any mistake about murder. "Those who set out on Sunday night to commit murder carried with them the tools of violent death. They committed a brutal murder.

"The fact the person they killed may have been a different man to that intended is totally irrelevant. No reason, no justification, no apology, no explanation can possibly affect the outcome."

Jim Kilfedder indicated he would stand for re-election in North Down, resisting what some described as the "soft option" of Strangford – his old seat having been cut in two by the Boundary Commission.

Seventeen-year-old schoolboy Gordon Bell, of Church Avenue, took third place in the Belfast Safe Driver of the Year competition, just six months after passing his driving test. He had entered the competition's R-driver class but his marks were sufficiently high to merit the overall placing. The winner was another local driver, Walter Gilmore.

The Bishop of Down and Connor, the Most Rev. Dr Cahal Daly, attended a rededication service in May at St Comgall's Church, Brunswick Road, following the completion of a £250,000 extension which provided seating for 700 parishioners. The Bishop stressed Bangor's unique place in European history because of St Comgall's abbey – "the matchless church of Bangor" – which was founded in 555AD.

Among the hymns sung during communion was *Sancti Venite,* from the Antiphonary of Bangor, which was written in the 6th Century by Bangor monks.

Members of the joint choir from St Comgall's and Most Holy Redeemer, Ballyholme, who sang at the ceremony to mark the rededication of St Comgall's Church, Brunswick Road. On the far right is organist Stephen McManus and behind him is choir leader Ann O'Kelly. 660-2-19

Jim Kilfedder retained what remained of his North Down seat with a 13,846 majority over nearest rival John Cushnahan (Alliance) on 9 June. Kilfedder polled 23,625 votes, compared to the 9,015 cast for the runner-up. Third-placed was Robert McCartney (Official Unionist) with 8,261, while SDLP candidate Cathal O Baoill (645) lost his deposit. The new Strangford seat was won by North Down Assembly member John Taylor.

Jim Kilfedder (left) is congratulated on his election as MP for the new North Down constituency in June 1983 by Alliance candidate John Cushnahan as Deputy Returning Officer Walter McDowell finishes announcing the result. Also included are Official Unionist candidate Robert McCartney and Cathal O Baoill (SDLP). 763-14-19

Bangor man James Arnold, of Ballyree Drive, a shift manager at Belfast Council's gasworks, retired in July after a career spanning just five months short of 50 years.

The Skandia Restaurant at Main Street became one of a growing number of businesses to introduce "non-smoking areas", a move praised by the Ulster Cancer Foundation.

The Good Templar Hall on Hamilton Road, built by total abstainers in 1872, was reopened following a £50,000 refurbishment scheme by the Borough Council. It was transformed into a bright, functional, multi-purpose hall.

Rubbish began to pile up in Bangor and district in September due to an industrial dispute involving North Down Borough Council cleansing staff. The strike lasted two weeks and was brought to an end when the Council warned the men they would all lose their jobs if they did not return to work.

Mayor John McConnell Auld unveils a plaque commemorating the start and finish of the North Pier contract in September 1983. Looking on is Alderman George Green, who as Mayor in 1981 ditched the first load of stones at the other end of the breakwater. 5-15-21

North Down Mayor John McConnell Auld officially opened the new £3m North Breakwater on 23 September. The breakwater had an immediate effect on shipping, with larger loads than ever before being landed at Bangor – a new record of 1,485.64 tons of coal for Charles Neill Fuels was established on 27 September.

Joy (now Jo) Bannister took over from Annie Roycroft as Editor of the *County Down Spectator,* a position the latter had held for some 30 years. In a farewell message prior to her departure for a new life in Cork, the soon-to-be Mrs Annie Stephens thanked the many readers, contributors and advertisers "who have given me the unique experience of presenting the news and views of the area."

Her successor, already the acclaimed author of four books, was the 1983 recipient of the Rothman's Northern Ireland Provincial Journalist award.

Bangor boat owner Brian Meharg was awarded a £12,000 grant by the Northern Ireland Tourist Board in October to help with his tourist-orientated sea angling business. His family had been involved in boating and fishing for some 40 years and Brian had served his apprenticeship with Eddie Laird of Laird's Boats. During 1983 he had acquired the *Bangor Crest* and the *Down Crest,* with both offering the prospect of holiday packages based on sea angling trips.

North Down Borough Council paid £18,000 at a Sotheby's auction in London in October for the medal collection – including the Victoria Cross – of Rear Admiral the Hon. Edward Barry Stewart Bingham, one of the seven sons of Lord and Lady Clanmorris of Bangor Castle. Born in 1881, he had served in the Royal Navy between 1898 and 1932. Rear-Admiral Bingham won the VC during the Battle of Jutland in 1916, when he was captured by the Germans. The gun in Ward Park was presented to Bangor by the Admiralty to commemorate his VC.

The medals are officially welcomed back to Bangor Town Hall, formerly the home of the Bingham family, in October 1983. From left: Ian Wilson, manager of the Bangor Visitors and Heritage Centre (due to open in 1984), Alderman Bruce Mulligan, Thomas Caves, chairman of the Bangor branch of the Royal Naval Association, Lt. Cdr. Patrick Knatchbull, executive officer of HMS *Caroline*, the last surviving ship that fought at the Battle of Jutland, Lord and Lady Glentoran, Mayor John McConnell Auld, Lt. Col. Tom Brooke, who brought the medals to Bangor, Cllr Mary O'Fee, Col. Robin Charley, who had drawn the Council's attention to the sale of the medals, and Town Clerk Jack McKimm. Lord Glentoran was Rear Admiral Bingham's nephew. *183-7-21*

Kilbroney Manufacturers Ltd. opened a new women's clothing factory at the Balloo Industrial Estate on 31 October. It had an initial staff of eight but hoped to create up to 80 new jobs for the town. The two-year-old company already had a factory in Rostrevor with a 60-strong workforce.

Terry Dickson, from Gray's Hill, received a medal for exemplary fire service from Environment Minister Chris Patten at the beginning of November. He was Station Officer in charge of Blue Watch at Belfast's Springfield Road Fire Station.

The Department of the Environment granted planning permission for the second stage of the Bangor Harbour redevelopment scheme. This involved a second breakwater reaching into Bangor Bay from the Pickie area, thereby providing shelter for the yachts and boats that were expected to make use of the 600-berth marina.

However, opposition was raised through the letters page of the *Spectator* to accompanying proposals for a 250-space car park along the seafront at Queen's

Parade. Objectors said it would totally alter the historical 'seaside town' quality of Bangor.

Glen Mouldings, which ran a factory at the Balloo Industrial Estate, announced in late November it would be recruiting up to 60 new workers (making a total of 140) to manufacture electric kettles and fan heaters for the international market.

The South Eastern Education and Library Board accepted a sub-committee recommendation to erect an 850-pupil co-educational secondary school at Ballykillaire in Bangor West. With the school expected to cost £3.5m and representing the biggest project in years, the Board was keen to see facilities included that would also be available for public use.

Bangor nurse Emily Rowntree, who was in her 50s, was released by the Angolan guerrillas who had kidnapped her and a colleague in the middle of November. She belonged to the Bath-based organisation Christian Missions in Many Lands.

Fighting a serious fire that had broken out in the derelict Barry's Amusements on 10 December required five fire engines and resulted in injuries to three local firemen who were trying to prevent the blaze from spreading to nearby occupied buildings.

North Down Borough Council met the following week, with members agreeing to recommend to the Historic Monuments Branch of the DoE that the building's façade should be de-listed. That would allow the whole building to be demolished; however the Council also felt members of the public should have they say on the future of Barry's.

A welcome visitor to the New Year bell-ringing at Bangor Parish Church in January 1983 was former ringer Robert Walker, home from sea with a Task Force medal won in the Falklands conflict. Robert presents a crest of his ship, Royal Fleet Auxiliary *Tidespring*, to senior bell-ringer Tom McBride, who promised it would have an honoured place in the refurbished bell tower. *513-7A-18*

Suzanne Alexander (front, left) former manageress at Roulston's Coffee Shop, upper Main Street, was setting off to a new job in January 1983, working for an Aer Lingus hotel in the USA. She was nominated for the scholarship trip by the Ulster Polytechnic, where she had studied to become a Licentiate Member of the Hotel Catering and International Management Association. She is seen shaking hands with her successor at Roulston's, Lorna Stevenson, as other staff look on. *510-8A-18*

Fifteen-year-old Jane Mulvenna, of Southwell Road, passed her Grade 4 Pianoforte examinations (London College of Music) with honours, gaining 87 marks. She received her tuition from Miss Maureen Griffin ALCM, of Abbey Drive. *654-12A-18*

Tributes were paid to Mrs Betty Buckley (centre), who was retiring after 11 years as head of the infants department at Kilcooley Primary School. Included with principal Alan Glenn and the Very Rev. Dr W. A. A. Park, chairman of the school's management committee, are pupils who made presentations during the farewell function in February 1983. Middle (from left): Andrew Power, Justin Meredith, Colin Stockman. Front: Lisa Burne, Trevor Hodson and Debbie Smyth. *671-12-18*

Principal players in Bangor Amateur Operatic Society's production of *Oklahoma*, which was staged at the Little Theatre in March 1983. *112-11-19*

Students from North Down College of Further Education in Bangor who took part in a sponsored bed push through the town in March 1983 to raise money for the Glebe House Reconciliation Centre in Strangford. *187-6-19*

The Fifth Bangor Beaver Colony was honoured in April 1983 with a visit by senior personnel from Bangor and District Scouts to mark the presentation of the Silver Beaver to leader Frances Keenan. Included are (front, from left): Beth Patterson, Assistant District Commissioner for Beavers; Lynda Millar, Beaver instructor at Fifth Bangor; Gerry Watson, District Commissioner; Frances Keenan; Betty McKee, Fifth Bangor Cub leader, and Mary Mulholland, assistant Cub leader. *349-13-19*

Competitors from Central Primary School who took part in the folk dancing section at Bangor Music Festival in May 1983. From left: Darren Moan, Lynda Flynn, Lisa McCaughey and Joanne McAuley. *508-10A-19*

Members of Mrs Irene McNeil's Junior Music Club, which she had founded in her Springhill Avenue home three years earlier as a way of introducing her daughter Morag to music without sending her to piano lessons, are pictured in June 1983. Back (from left): Jill Kennedy, Garry Webb, Lynne Munroe, Angela Ritchie, Kelly Barlow, Melanie Spence, Stephen Shaw. Front: Stuart Kennedy, Morag McNeil, Allison Graham, Claire McCormick and Jonathan Shaw. *781-7A-19*

The children of Trinity Nursery School, Brunswick Road, held a sponsored nursery rhyme competition for the Northern Ireland Leukaemia Fund. Thanks to a donation of £150 from Dunnes Stores in Bangor they were able to present a cheque for £800 to the Fund at the end of term in June 1983. Holding the cheque is Mrs Betty Small, secretary of the charity's Bangor branch, accompanied by school principal Rosemary Armstrong and charity treasurer Dennis McMorris.
747-12-19

Members of Bangor Abbey LOL 726 unfurled, dedicated and paraded a new banner on 25 June, just in time for the 1983 marching season. Picture shows officers and brethren outside Bangor Abbey church hall.
47-12-19

Auxiliary Bishop of Down and Connor Dr Patrick Walsh visited St Comgall's Primary School in October 1983 and was brought up to date on the latest technology available to the P6 class. Included are Parish Priest Fr Gerard Laverty and school principal John O'Hanlon.
107-3-21

The Rev. William McDermott (seated, centre), first minister of the W. P. Nicholson Memorial Free Presbyterian Church at Clandeboye Road, was ordained and installed on 1 November 1982 at a service attended by Moderator the Rev. Ian Paisley. With the new minister are (back, from left): John Graham, Cecil Magrath (Clerk of Session), Alan Graham, Wesley Graham, David Browne. Front: Rev. A Dunlop, Rev. William Whiteside, Rev. T. H. Cairns and Rev. Jim Hartin.
214-3-21

Keen disco dancers Denise Madden (15) and Caroline Collins (11), of Windmill Road and Roslyn Avenue respectively, were both pupils at the Sally and Tommy Robinson School of Modern Dancing in November 1983. Denise was awarded a Northern Ireland bronze and a London silver medal in the World Wide Championships, while Caroline gained a Northern Ireland bronze medal.
202-11-21

Attainment award recipients at the annual prize distribution in November 1983 for pupils attending St Columbanus' High School.
322-16-21

Charmaine Finnegan (21), from Bloomfield Walk, won the Pretty Polly Miss Lovely Legs title in Scarborough on 7 November 1983, having won her heat while on holiday in Blackpool the previous August. As well as a trophy she also received £300 in cash and £200 worth of prizes. *314-17-21*

Special prizewinners from Gransha Boys' High School at the annual prize distribution in December 1983. Back (from left): Paul McClements, Thomas Wylie, John Mann, Paul Fleming, Anil Tandon. Front: Clifford Larkin, Graeme Lowe, Alistair Russell and James Briggs. *355-12-21*

The young Oompa Loompas from Bangor Drama Club's Christmas 1983 production of *Charlie And The Chocolate Factory*. *391-6-21*

Alan Robson

remembers...

Although I've lived in Bangor more than half my life I was actually born in Newcastle upon Tyne. After passing the 11-Plus examination I attended a school in the western part of that city where one of the subjects I was taught was touch typing. I couldn't see any great need for it at the time but I learnt to type anyway.

Later, when I attended the Marine College in South Shields, where part of the course I was studying involved learning Morse Code and typing at the same time, I realised my knowledge of the QWERTY keyboard was at last useful. Indeed, little did I realise there would be a near universal use of the keyboard to enter data into a computer some 50 years into the future.

Back then when I became a radio and television engineer it was useful to be able to type notes from the City and Guilds course I attended in Rutherford College of Technology (now part of the University of Northumbria at Newcastle).

Furthermore, my Telecommunication qualifications

Pictured in summer 2012, and still as enthusiastic as ever about computers, Alan Robson uses a Compaq Note-Book with son Philip looking on

Alan Robson contributed a regular column to the *Spectator* during much of the 1980s about the North Down Micro Computer Users Club, which he had helped to found.

In addition to reflecting his personal and professional interest in the subject, the club (and the weekly reports in the paper) helped to point a generation of Bangor's young people towards careers in computers.

A native of Newcastle upon Tyne, Alan settled in Bangor with his wife Patricia, daughter Sharon and sons Michael and Philip in July 1972. Second daughter Deborah was born while they were living in Bangor.

Now proud Bangorians by adoption, they have four granddaughters and two grandsons, with most of the family circle still living in the town.

gained at South Shields allowed me to enter National Service in the RAF as a Junior Technician – mine was actually the last three-month group to be called up as National Service finished after that.

The future course of my life came from events that followed being in the forces. I served some time in Germany on what was a forerunner of GPS, but ground based, for testing purposes. After that I came to Northern Ireland for the first time, got married and then was sent to sunny Aden and subsequently Zambia where I first started using computerised equipment. It was also whilst there I had the opportunity to climb Killimanjaro and visit the Victoria Falls.

On returning to England I completed my studies in City and Guilds Telecommunications, Radio and Television, gaining two Full Technological Certificates, including colour television, FM, digital switching and computers. By then I could see computers would be the way forward for schools and industry.

I joined International Computers Ltd. following an interview in Putney and was offered a position in Belfast, which I knew would suit my wife. Once the Troubles started we were led to buy a house in Bangor. We weren't alone. So many people took up the Government's offer to move out of the city to places like Bangor, Lisburn, Carrickfergus and Antrim, a huge demand was placed on British Telecom to provide telephones – we had to wait 23 months before we could have one installed.

With a young school-attending family back then we made regular use of the Carnegie Library, which had served as a technical school in the past and thus had some rooms which previously had been classrooms.

After scouring the library's notice boards in the hope of

The logo that accompanied regular *Spectator* articles about club activities

finding information about a local computer club – and seeing none – I decided to post my own notice to establish if there would be any interest in the area.

Two people contacted me and we decided to place an article in the *Spectator* to see if we could arouse sufficient interest within the newspaper's readership area to form a computer club. To our amazement on the evening of the first meeting, on 28 February 1983, over 200 people turned up in answer to our appeal and it was decided to form the North Down Micro Computer Users Club.

Pictured in January 1984, Alan Robson's son Philip (left) operates a Sinclair Spectrum which used a UHF modulator to input to a TV using a cathode ray tube for the display. Programs were loaded from an audio tape recorder. Alan is seated at the ICL personal computer which stored the operating system, programs and data on 5¼" floppy disks and had a mono dedicated screen for the display. Beside the computer (on the right) is a dot-matrix printer. In the background are other members' computers in the upper room of the Carnegie Library where the Micro Users Club met. *456-6A-21*

The *Spectator* provided valuable support by publishing details of our monthly meetings, as well as items of interest, which I delivered to its Main Street office well in advance of the newspaper's deadline.

The South Eastern Education and Library Board charged us £3.50 for the use of an upstairs room at the library. We produced application forms for potential new members and although attendances never matched the level achieved at that initial meeting, there was a regular and enthusiastic interest in the club's activities from the people of North Down.

The ZX Spectrum computer, an early favourite among club members.

A *Spectator* photographer came along one evening and the pictures appeared alongside our regular article, which often included puzzles for readers to solve by using their computers.

Within a year the club had a membership of 150 and although only 50% to 75% attended each meeting, we

Barry Caruth (standing) and Duncan Redmill work on a future edition of *Micro Users*, the monthly magazine of the North Down Micro Computer Users Club in November 1986. *15-6A-31*

needed the room at the library for three nights each month. Indeed, such was the growing interest in home computing that when we arranged exhibitions in Hamilton House in 1984 and the Good Templar Hall in 1986, both were very well attended.

The aims and objectives of the club were:

1. To promote the use of microcomputers;

2. To provide a forum for members to exchange information, views, ideas and data;

3. To help members to educate themselves in microcomputing, and

4. To liaise with other groups interested in microcomputing.

A club magazine was printed and distributed to members and new innovations and products were discussed at meetings. However, teenagers started showing off their new games and less time was spent on educational matters.

After five years of the club making good progress in initiating the people of Bangor and district on the use of home computers I realised times were changing. I didn't renew the room reservation at the library, telling the young members they could just as easily invite their friends round to each other's homes to show off their wares.

Nevertheless the seeds of civilisation working and playing with computers had been sown. It is tempting to wonder how many of those young people who attended meetings of the North Down Micro Computer Users Club in the 1980s now use computers as an integral part of their work and daily lives – and are thankful for that early introduction they received at the Carnegie Library.

1984
IN THE SPECTATOR

Bangor's deserted High Street after the district was hit by a devastating storm in January 1984. 539-4-21

North Down was declared a disaster area by the Bangor office of Northern Ireland Electricity after snow and stormy conditions wreaked havoc during 13-15 January. The bad weather led to widespread power cuts, telephone service disruption, falling trees, structural damage and, after the thaw set in, flooding.

Thirty-six trees were brought down in Castle Park, with a further six in Ward Park, which led to Broadway being blocked. A tree fell at the Clandeboye Cemetery severing a telephone line but no graves were damaged. Another tree fell onto a house at Brooklyn Park. High Street was closed off for a time because of flying slates.

Work commenced in January on the new Visitors and Heritage Centre at the Town Hall, where the newly appointed manager was former school teacher Ian Wilson, a native of the town. The scheme involved renovating the former laundry and joiners' workshops.

Work got under way on the new Visitors and Heritage Centre at the Town Hall in January 1984. *560-9-21*

Rollerama, formerly the Queen's Court Hotel on Queen's Parade and by then lying empty, had been on the market for almost a year. Despite several approaches to estate agent Brian Wimpress, no buyer had been found.

Bangor postmaster Albert Compton ended 47 years of service when he retired on 21 February. Mr Compton, from Cleland Park North, began his career as a message boy in Enniskillen, earning almost 10 shillings a week, with an added allowance for keeping his bicycle clean! He took up duties in Bangor in 1968 but compulsory retirement beckoned when he was 61.

Bangor was named "Most Improved Place" in the 1983 Ulster in Bloom competition, organised by the Northern Ireland Tourist Board. It was also accorded second place in the large town section. The results for 1984 were announced before the end of the year, with Bangor going one stage further by lifting first place in the large town section.

Secretary of State James Prior talks to members of the Bangor Army Cadet Force, who shared the new TA Centre. *803-20-21*

A new £1.5m Territorial Army centre was opened by Secretary of State James Prior at the Balloo Industrial Estate on 17 March. A colourful ceremonial parade featured high-ranking officers and the Band of the Royal Corps of Engineers, as well as local Sappers and Army Cadet Force members. The centre was home to 112 Field Squadron, 591 Independent Field Squadron Royal Engineers (Volunteers) and the Bangor detachment of the ACF, which was affiliated to the Engineers.

Bangor fireman Frankie Millsopp, of Glendun Park, was presented with the British Empire Medal at a ceremony in Hillsborough Castle in March. He had joined the Fire Service as a part-time auxiliary member and went on to serve during the Second World War as a member of the National Fire Service. Although retired, he was still a full-time employee of the Fire Authority, serving as hydrant patrolman.

Bangor's Winston Hotel, on Queen's Parade, marked its 60th anniversary with the opening of a new extension in April. It had been owned for almost 20 years by Jack and Mary Good.

Around 20 jobs were created by Breton Foods, a company which made a range of fresh pies at the Balloo Industrial Estate, after it was taken over by the Carnmoney-based SHS distribution company. Many of its products were sold under the Farmlea brand name.

Twelve-year-old Karen Patterson, from Ballycrochan Road, who attended Princess Gardens School, was first in the Belfast heat of a public speaking competition organised by the City Council's Road Safety Committee in early 1984. She spoke on the subject: 'Drivers should be re-tested every year.' 726-17-21

The congregation of Hamilton Road Presbyterian Church paid tribute in April to the Very Rev. Dr David Burke, who had served as their minister for 29 years. Retirement presentations were made to Dr Burke and his wife Sheila at a service conducted by the Rev. Samuel Wilson, Convenor and Interim Moderator.

Hundreds of Mods gathered along Bangor's seafront on Easter Monday (23 April) to mark the 20th anniversary of the infamous clashes between Mods and Rockers on Brighton Pier. However, there was less trouble than in previous years with 15 youths being arrested during the day. Seven were subsequently fined between £50 and £75 each for disorderly behaviour.

Bangor joined the electronic age on Sunday 29 April with the opening of the town's new £6m TXE4 telephone exchange. It was the largest facility of its kind in Northern Ireland and also meant a new dialling tone and a change to all local telephone numbers – adding 47 to the previous four-digit numbers and a 4 to five-digit numbers.

The Three Degrees, described by the *Spectator* as one of the "hottest groups to ever hit Bangor", appeared at the Bangor Castle Leisure Centre on 27 April. They closed the show with their Number One hit *When Will I See You Again?*

Councillors rejected a proposal in a sub-committee report to convert the Borough Gymnasium on Hamilton Road into a small theatre for 300-350 people, in favour of providing a properly equipped theatre by utilising the courtyard and buildings at the rear of the Town Hall. The latter scheme was put 'on hold' two months later after members learned it could cost the Council £2m.

A full-sized replica of the *Golden Hinde,* the ship Sir Francis Drake had sailed

around the world 400 years earlier, was tied up at Bangor's North Breakwater from 21-31 May. The vessel was built in 1973 and subsequently circumnavigated the globe during the course of six years, following the original route including a stop-over at San Francisco, which Drake had claimed for Queen Elizabeth I in 1579.

The *Golden Hinde* reaches Bangor in May 1984. 374-5A-22

However, a return visit to Bangor in mid-August was cut short amid rumours of vandalism and threats against the well-being of the vessel and its crew.

PAUL'S TAKE-AWAY FOODS
QUEEN'S PARADE, BANGOR

Come to 'Paul's' with just a pound.
Get a bargain meal 'the best in town.'
Hurry up - do not delay.
You'll find us open night and day!
Paul's special price is hard to beat.
So come along and have a treat

THIS WEEK'S SPECIAL £1.00 BARGAIN

PAUL'S BURGER BAR

¼ lb. HAWAIIAN BURGER
served with
Pineapple, Cherry, Lettuce, Cucumber and Thousand Island Dressing
+
12 oz. CUP OF ICE COLD COKE
Great Value at £1.00

PAUL'S FISH AND CHIP SHOP

TWO SAUSAGES
ONE LARGE CHIP
and
TIN OF ICE COLD COKE
Excellent Value at £1.00

The North Breakwater in early June won the same accolade as had previously been achieved by the Thames Barrier and the Barbican Centre in London – best concrete structure completed in the United Kingdom. The Bangor scheme won in the civil engineering category – the first time any of the top awards by the Concrete Society had come to Northern Ireland.

The new Mayor of North Down was Cllr Hazel Bradford, who succeeded Cllr John McConnell Auld. Her Deputy Mayor was Cllr Campbell McCormick.

Placard-carrying residents of Silverstream Crescent, Silverstream Drive and Beechwood Gardens attended a meeting of the Borough Council's Deputations and Liaison Committee in June to protest over a planned extension to the nearby

Bangor Abattoir. They also urged the Council to move the abattoir from its residential location to somewhere like the Balloo Industrial Estate.

TemTech, based at the Balloo Industrial Estate, announced it would be adding another 30 to its 40-strong workforce, with the prospect of a further 100 jobs within three years.

Residents who gathered at the Town Hall in June 1984 to protest over plans to expand Bangor Abattoir. 536-18-22

The employment boost arose after a deal was struck with an American company to develop and manufacture medical hardware and software.

The town's new inshore lifeboat, named *Alan Ashford Thurlow*, and purpose-built lifeboat station came into operation on 15 June. The lifeboat base had been at Victoria Road, behind the Tower House, whereas the new facility on the North Breakwater, provided by the Borough Council, offered direct access to the sea.

Two local politicians were among the eight candidates who stood for election to the European Parliament in June. Official Unionist John Taylor, who was a North Down Assembly member as well as MP for Strangford, retained his seat (along with the Rev. Ian Paisley of the DUP and the SDLP's John Hume), while North Down MP and Assembly member Jim Kilfedder finished sixth, with 20,092 first preference votes.

North Down Borough Council resolved in late June to introduce bye-laws that would ban solvent abuse and the consumption of alcohol in designated parks and open spaces. Members hoped other local authorities would follow their lead.

COUNTY DOWN SPECTATOR
AND ULSTER STANDARD
Est. 1904   THURSDAY, 28th JUNE, 1984   Price 22p

COUNCIL AGREES ON BYE-LAWS TO PREVENT ALCOHOL AND SOLVENT ABUSE

Tributes were paid in late June to Marie Brownlee, first principal of Bangor Girls' High School, who was retiring. Her teaching career spanned 42 years, including teaching mathematics at the former Glenlola Grammar School in 1942 before moving the following year to Bangor Central Senior Primary School.

Miss Brownlee joined the High School's staff in 1948, when it was co-educational. In 1972 the boys moved to their new school at Gransha, with the girls remaining at Castle Street under Miss Brownlee's leadership.

The new principal was former Dunmurry High School vice-principal Bill Flynn.

It was announced in mid-August that 40 to 45 people, representing one-third of the total workforce, would lose their jobs at Oneida Silversmiths. Blame was placed on competition from foreign imports.

A computer-controlled variable programme car wash – the first in the area with such a high level of sophistication – was installed in August at the Bryansburn Road Maxol petrol station. It featured five different types of wash at varying costs (from 80p to £2).

The ruins of the former Queen's Cinema in August 1984. I 39-8-23

The former Queen's Cinema, by then operating as the Royal Bingo and Social Club and the 147 Snooker Club, was destroyed by fire in the early hours of 28 August. The alert was raised by the alarm system at the nearby Woolworth's store. The building was well ablaze by the time the Fire Service arrived but the men managed to get the blaze under control within 40 minutes. Only the shell remained, along with the charred remains of some snooker tables.

It was revealed that the Little Theatre in Central Avenue would close from the beginning of 1985 unless £30,000 was provided to bring the building up to fire safety standards. Bangor Drama Club representative John Knipe, while complimenting the Borough Council for all it had done for the arts over the years, argued it was time the local authority provided the town with a proper fully-equipped theatre with seating for around 350 people. A similar argument was voiced by Bangor Amateur Operatic Society representative John Neill.

At a subsequent Council meeting, held on 25 September, when the issue of the Little Theatre was given a full airing, it was agreed pay up to £30,000 for the necessary renovations to keep it open.

Bangor resident and North Down Assembly member John Cushnahan became the new leader of the Alliance Party in late September, following Oliver Napier's decision to stand down after 14 years at the helm. Aged 35, Mr Cushnahan became the youngest party leader in the United Kingdom.

The green cast-iron horse trough, which for many years sat at Warden's Corner (where Castle Street and Hamilton Road meet), was smashed in two by vandals at the beginning of October. It had been drained by the Council some years earlier and was used for floral displays.

Tommy Heyburn won North Down Borough Council's competition to design a logo for the new Visitors and Heritage Centre. The Bangor Bell formed an integral part of his design. 141-18-23

Eileen Gilbert, who at the age of 86 was still working up to 70 hours each week for the elderly and handicapped in Bangor, was named runner-up in a 'Pensioner of the Year' competition held throughout Northern Ireland by Legal and General. It attracted more than 400 entries.

Mayor Hazel Bradford and her former Stormont Minister husband Roy were caught up in the IRA bombing of the Grand Hotel in Brighton on 12 October. They were attending the Conservative Party Conference and, like many other delegates, were staying in the hotel.

MAYOR IN BOMB BLAST

Their room, no 638, was caught in the blast and sustained major damage. The couple managed to crawl into the corridor, which they realised was completely open to the elements with the sea stretching out in front of them.

The Bradfords eventually reached the street in their nightclothes, having sustained minor bumps and scratches from falling rubble. They lost clothes and personal belongings in the explosion, which claimed five lives and left 34 injured, many seriously.

The new Visitors and Heritage Centre was officially opened by Mrs Bradford on 16 October. The total cost was estimated at £150,000, with substantial grant aid being provided by the Departments of Economic Development and the Environment.

Items on display included the Bangor Bell, which dated from the 9th Century, and the Raven Maps, which were drawn up in the 17th Century and were exceptional because of their colour and detail.

It was agreed in early November to investigate twinning Bangor with the Austrian town of Bregenz. Cllr John McConnell Auld, who undertook to pursue the idea, travelled to Bregenz with Fr Gerard Laverty, PP of St Comgall's Church, and Canon Hamilton Leckey, of Bangor Abbey, for the unveiling of a stone sent from Bangor to commemorate the journey made by St Columbanus to Bregenz in the 6th Century. The town was celebrating its own 2,000th birthday at that time.

An application was submitted to the Planning Service for outline permission to change the Savoy Hotel into an apartment complex with no change to the building's outer façade.

Bangor and Ards Hospitals would be downgraded to community status, losing all casualty and maternity services to the Ulster Hospital in Dundonald, and Crawfordsburn Hospital would close, if proposals under consideration by the Eastern Health Board in early December were implemented. According to the report proposing the cuts, there was an insufficient population in North Down and Ards to support a general hospital providing acute services.

Jim Smith, of Silverstream Road, who retired as a Northern Ireland Electricity Service security officer in December, had not missed a single day during his 36 years with the company.

The chorus and some cast members from the Bangor Abbey Players' production of *Sinbad The Sailor* in January 1984. Included are (back, third from left): Ivan Maxwell, Percy Deering, Jim Kennedy and Mark Larmour. *515-7A-21*

Six of Patricia Irvine's pupils at the Gail Holland School of Music and Drama were awarded honours at the Guildhall School of Music and Drama speech examinations in January 1984. Back (from left): Jennifer Coghlin, Julie McAnlis, Shirley Anderson, Barbara McDade, all from Ballyholme Primary School. Front: Wendy and Lucy Smyth, of Glenlola Collegiate. *567-19-21*

The cast of the pantomime *Aladdin*, which was presented to parents and friends by pupils of Bangor Central Primary School in January 1984. *562-1A-21*

The retirement of Bangor's Harbour Master, Captain Edward White-Overton, in January 1984, was marked by a presentation function in the Town Hall, hosted by Mayor John McConnell Auld. Capt. White-Overton, who served in the position for five years after a lengthy career at sea, dating back to 1935, is seen receiving a Borough plaque from the Mayor as Council officials and other guests look on. From left: Deputy Town Clerk Adrian McDowell, Cllr Hazel Bradford, Liz Edgar, Cllr Donald Hayes, Ken Gillen, Mrs Jean White-Overton, Alderman Eddie Mills, Cllr Susan O'Brien and Alderman George Green. *599-10-21*

To commemorate their diamond jubilee, the Youth and Junior Unit of 404 Bangor, which was attached to the British Red Cross, planted an oak tree in Castle Park in February 1984. Holding the tree is leader Margaret Lyness, while also present at the ceremony were County Down secretary Maureen Heaney and Bangor Divisional secretary Noreen McNeill. *690-11-21*

The Bangor branch of Soroptimist International made its annual presentations in February 1984 to young people who contributed most to the local community. Among the winners were (from left): Sarah Stanley (second), Elizabeth McCloskey (joint first), Mrs Sadie Humphreys (Bangor president), Karen Marsden (runner-up), Valerie McCarroll (joint first) and Catherine Smyth (runner-up). *715-4-21*

The annual Emily J. Connor Award, presented at the Bangor campus of the North Down College of Further Education to the best commercial studies student, went to Maureen Fleming, of Sandringham Drive, in March 1984. She received the award from principal George Jardine. Looking on are Wilfred Crowe, head of business studies, and Margaret Curragh, senior lecturer in charge of secretarial studies. 798-3A-21

The victorious First Bangor Girls' Brigade team who took first place in the All Ireland Brigader Championships, held in Dun Laoghaire in March 1984. Back (from left): Amanda Stringer, Julie McGowan, Megan Liddell, Sara Henry. Front: Kerry McClenaghan, Gillian Erskine, Linda Gowdy and Debra Osborne. 746-6A-21

Some of the contestants who took part in the North Down Disco Dancing Championships, which were held in the Borough Gymnasium in April 1984. 177-12-22

Girls who were successful in the reel (under eight years) section at Bangor Folk Dancing Festival in May 1984. From left: Cathy Proctor, St Comgall's PS, who was first; Cathy McKenna, Towerview PS, who was second; Karen Moore, Erika Campbell and Lynne White, all Towerview PS, who were joint third. *312-9A-22*

Almost 100 pupils from Rathmore Primary School enjoyed a week-long trip to London during May 1984. As well as seeing many of the capital's familiar sights, they enjoyed the musical *Singing In The Rain* at the London Palladium and were taken on a guided tour of the Houses of Parliament by North Down MP Jim Kilfedder. Included in the picture are principal Hugh Boyd (left) and Gateway Building Society representative Fred Harrison. The children saved up for the break through the local branch of Gateway, which also made a donation towards the cost of the trip. *328-16-22*

Pupils from Bangor Girls' High School, who visited Crawfordsburn Hospital each week, organised a sponsored walk to Carnalea and back to raise funds for the hospital in June 1984. Sister Page, who received the cheque for £50, is pictured with Elaine Irwin, Kathleen Stevenson, Brenda Moore, Elizabeth McClure, Joanne Hopps, Beverley Kerr and Gillian McClure. *442-10-22*

Local organiser of the Health Education Council's *Look After Yourself!* campaign in September 1984 was Noreen Blair, from Ballyholme Road. The aim of the campaign was to encourage people to live fitter and less stressful lives. Each two-hour class consisted of slow exercises with a little aerobics followed by tea or coffee and a discussion on a health-related topic. *301-13-23*

Glenlola Collegiate sixth formers, pictured in the school's coffee bar area in September 1984, look forward to the new term ahead, despite the threat of A-Level examinations at the end of the year. *202-13-23*

Prizewinners during 1983/84 at Kilmaine Primary School received their prizes at the end of the summer term. Included are Dawn Miller (cycling), Linda Dunn (gymnastics), Jonathan Dick (badminton), Leanne McCabe (swimming), Rachel Law (Scripture Union), Andrew Thompson (cricket), Christopher Rolleston (rugby), Helena Johnston (French), Graeme Tolmie (canoeing), Clare Owen (needlecraft), Jeremy

Houston (craft), Janine Adair (netball), Ray Nesbitt (art), Andrea Ramage (athletics), Christopher Davis (chess), Wendy Branagh (effort), Andrea Johnston (music), Jonathan Watson (football), Karen McQuillan (handwriting), Clare Mark (courtesy), Stephen Shaw (drama), Carolyn Poots (excellence), Karen McKeown (girl of the year) and Jonathan Brown (boy of the year). *630-13A-22*

Members of the Bangor-based Theatrix musical theatre company were presenting *Dream World* in October 1984. The fantasy production was penned by songwriters David Cardwell and Ken Gillen (of *Eternity Junction* fame). Principal characters are standing at the back.
393-1-23

County Commissioner Clive Scoular (centre) joined Fifth Bangor Sea Scouts in November 1984 for celebrations to mark 50 years of Sea Scouting in Bangor. An open night afforded past members an opportunity to recall their time as Scouts and to view many photographs taken from the 1940s onwards.
709-7-23

Carol singers from Clandeboye Road Primary School entertained patrons attending the YMCA Christmas fair in December 1984 at their Queen's Parade premises.
769-8-23

Terry Aston
remembers...

I remember writing an open letter to the *Spectator* back in January 1984 to record my disgust at the loss of the fine building at Quay Street that housed Barry's Amusements. I did a drawing at the time which showed everything of architectural merit in the town being swept away, to be replaced by high-rise buildings and acres of tarmac.

Twenty-eight years later I am looking at how the environment of Bangor has changed and I am trying to evaluate if that period of time has measured up to my vision of the future. Being 28 years older myself, a certain amount of cynicism now clouds my vision and makes any Utopian dreams seem pointless.

But it's a bit like the curate's egg (not all bad). Some schemes like the marina project forged ahead and the area is now being revamped, while Queen's Parade remains in an even worse state

The final days of Barry's Amusements. *Picture by Terry Aston*

Terry Aston was born in the Manchester area and graduated from Manchester College of Art and Design in 1966. After further study at Leicester College of Art and Design he taught at Sunderland Polytechnic before moving to Belfast in 1969 to take up a post at the Ulster College of Art and Design, where he taught illustration and drawing in the context of Graphic Design.

His work has been exhibited in Northern Ireland, Europe and the USA. Now retired, Terry continues to draw, paint and occasionally exhibit.

For 40 of the 43 years he has lived in Northern Ireland Terry has lived in Bangor and has done many drawings of the town and the surrounding area. The close proximity of the sea, the variety of boats and the range of marine settings is a constant source of interest.

The protection of the town's architectural heritage is of enormous importance to him.

than it was back in 1984! We are now treated to an ever-changing display of artwork on the hoarding which fronts that site but behind this edifice is – surprise! surprise! – a car park!

How much better it would have been to preserve the original façades of the buildings and by doing so to have attempted to conserve the essentially Edwardian style of the town.

The rebuilding of several properties around the Queen's Parade/ Pickie area has been well done and old façades have been kept or rebuilt in the original style, which contributes greatly to visual continuity. However, the approach to the town via Gray's Hill leaves much to be desired.

Marina construction work under way

The marina is best from the town side and in good weather it has an almost continental appeal. However, vandalism, litter, dog dirt and outdoor drinkers don't help to engender ambiance.

Cars parked around Bridge Street are subject to serious damage by drunks, particularly at weekends. Tarmac often replaces paving and has spread steadily around the town, a sure sign of declining standards.

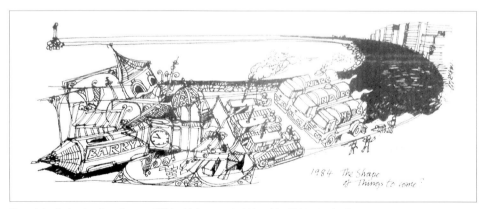

Terry Aston's drawing from January 1984, which prompted his original letter to the *Spectator*

In 1984 security was still an issue and the centre of the town was ringed by oil drums full of concrete to afford some protection against car bombs. Parking in town centre streets was restricted and people were body-searched when entering shops. Now Bangor town centre, like many throughout the country, has a lot of empty shops which look like missing teeth in almost every street.

Work was under way on the pier redevelopment scheme when Terry Aston completed this drawing

Banks and charity shops have a high occupancy profile. The businesses in the town are not as varied or as numerous as they once were due to the prevailing economic situation. It is ironic to have survived the bomb attacks only to be defeated by the economic downturn. Though the threat to charge is ever present, there are still a few free car parks in Bangor, which makes sense if the commercial centre is to survive at all.

At the moment the Flagship Centre seems about to close and that would further affect the commercial life of the town.

The redevelopment of the Carnegie Library with its new gallery is a welcome addition to Bangor's cultural life. The varied calendar of events at Bangor Castle has made an excellent contribution to the life of the town. It is, however, very tempting when one looks at the facilities elsewhere to consider what might have been. Lisburn, for instance, has the wonderful Island Arts

The Long Hole at Seacliff Road

Queen's Parade in 1988

Queen's Parade in 2012

Centre; surely a town the size of Bangor should have been moving towards such a provision?

Whilst Queen's Parade remains in its present state it is an eyesore, but it may be more desirable even now than the plans which were put forward to replace it. We should not worry too much however as things move very slowly in this town. In the unlikely event that I write again in another 28 years' time, I think the same topics may arise.

Many people care about the quality of Bangor's environment and the conservation of its heritage. For example, the Bangor West Conservation Group continually fights to preserve buildings and mature trees which are often under threat from inappropriate development.

Bangor is still a seaside town and I hope we don't completely lose sight of the sea.

1985

IN THE SPECTATOR

St Comgall's Church on the Brunswick Road was extensively damaged early in the New Year by a fire the police determined was started maliciously.

The church, which had been renovated and extended the previous year, was targeted by arsonists who set light to the Christmas crib early on Saturday 5 January, with

Parish Priest Fr Gerard Laverty behind the blackened altar of St Comgall's Church in January 1985. *875-3-23*

the blaze spreading from there. A window into an annex had been broken and spent matches were strewn along the floor. However, access to the church could not be gained from there and another window was broken, which led to the serious outbreak of fire.

Five fire appliances attended the scene – three from Bangor, one from Newtownards and a specialist hydraulic platform from Knock, on the outskirts of Belfast.

Parish Priest Fr Gerard Laverty said many messages of sympathy, as well as donations, had arrived at the church, which "have been very consoling."

North Down Borough Council, meeting three days after the blaze, agreed to send a letter of sympathy to St Comgall's, offering the Council's help in any way possible. Two DUP members publicly disassociated themselves from the letter.

The Council reconvened its Hospitals Sub-Committee for the first time since 1982 as part of its ongoing fight to maintain services at Bangor, Ards and Crawfordsburn Hospitals – all of which were under threat from new proposals being considered by the Eastern Health Board. Members subsequently agreed to donate £5,000 to a fighting fund.

Bobby Brown, of Silverstream Crescent, and William Turvey, of Henderson Drive, were recognised by the Royal Humane Society for the bravery they had shown two years earlier, in April 1983, after eight-year-old Christopher McClure fell into the Long Hole. A third man, William James Harte, also from Bangor, was honoured posthumously for his role in saving the child's life.

North Down Borough Council joined the race with Belfast City Council and Castlereagh Borough Council in late January to provide the first major ice rink/indoor bowling facility. Hopes were high that the leisure complex, to be located on the recently acquired former Forsythe's Nursery land off Castle Park Road, could be ready by the end of the year.

Councillors were told it would be possible to melt the ice and make the venue available for pop concerts, horse-jumping, fairs and many other activities. Better still, they were assured the £1.5m scheme would be privately financed and there would be no cost to ratepayers.

Concerns were immediately raised by a trio of local churches – Independent Methodist, Elim Pentecostal and Free Presbyterian – about the centre being licensed to sell alcohol. The anti-drink objections were rejected following a lengthy Council meeting devoted solely to the subject.

Government funding was scrapped in January for two schemes providing employment for 17 and 18-year-olds in community projects – namely the Basement Workshop at the Carnegie Library and Project Yacht, run by Bangor Sea Cadets. There were places for 10 trainees at each youth employment scheme.

Bangor man Colin Blakely returned to the Grand Opera House in Belfast for the first time in 20 years, when he appeared for a week in mid-February in *Other Places,* a compilation of three plays by Harold Pinter.

The End nightclub above Tania's Restaurant on Main Street was gutted by a malicious fire on 21 February. No one was hurt in the blaze which was brought under control by firemen using breathing apparatus. Owner Graham Henry said they hoped to be back in business by the summer.

Local taxi drivers, fearing their livelihoods were at risk, formed a new body in an effort to have a bye-law passed that would prohibit taxi drivers from outside the area operating in the town. The Bangor Taxi Federation was launched at a meeting in the Royal Hotel in March and involved Atlas Taxis, Anderson's Taxis, Abbey Taxis, Public Hire Stand Taxis, Four A Cabs and Bangor Taxis.

Bangor Gas manager Tim Kyle placed a full-page advertisement in the *Spectator* seeking people's views on Industry Minister Dr Rhodes Boyson's statement that the Northern Ireland gas industry would have to close. He pointed out that £97m of public money would be used to end an industry that provided work for 1,000 people, whereas £5m would provide a gas pipeline to Northern Ireland.

However, the Council voted to run down Bangor Gas during the following year, stating that to continue the undertaking without government assistance would place too heavy a burden on local ratepayers.

Another four years having passed, 31 assorted Unionists, 10 Alliance candidates and one Independent put forward their names for election to North Down Borough Council on 15 May. This time around there were 24 seats, compared to 20 in the past, with the (Official)

Ulster Unionists winning eight, and thus regaining the position as the authority's largest party, Alliance seven, the DUP six and the Ulster Popular Unionist Party two, plus one Independent.

· The highest first preference vote was achieved by Hazel Bradford (1,695 votes), who subsequently retained her position as Mayor, while one sitting Councillor, Raymond Trousdale (DUP), lost his seat. Successful candidates were as follows:

Abbey – Campbell McCormick (DUP), George Green (UUP), Brian Meharg (UPUP), Albert Magee (Alliance), Ruby Cooling (DUP), Jack Preston (UUP).

Ballyholme and Groomsport – Bruce Mulligan (UUP), Eddie Mills (Independent),

Alan Leslie (DUP), Samuel Hamilton (UUP), Donald Hayes (Alliance), Jane Copeland (Alliance).

Bangor West – Hazel Bradford (UUP), Alan Graham (DUP), Bill Bailie (Alliance), Cecil Braniff (UUP), Brian Wilson (Alliance), Ian Sinclair (UPUP), George McMurtry (DUP).

Holywood – Ellie McKay (UUP), John McConnell Auld (UUP), Gordon Dunne (DUP), Susan O'Brien (Alliance), Michael Clarke (Alliance).

The only British person to die in the Hysel football stadium disaster in Brussels on 29 May was Bangor-born Patrick Charles John Radcliffe (38). He lived with his wife in Brussels, where he worked as an archivist for the European Council of Ministers.

Thirty-nine people died and 365 were injured after rioting broke out and a wall collapsed before play began in the European Cup final between Liverpool and Juventus.

O'Corrain Heraldry, based at the Balloo Industrial Estate, signed a contract in June with an American telemarketing company to supply some 3,000 heraldic shields every week. As the contract was due to last three years the company had expectations that orders in that time could be worth £2.9m.

Bill Harvey, from Greenmount Court, celebrated his 80th birthday on 23 June – five days after completing a marathon 1,025-mile cycle run from John O'Groats to Land's End. He completed the journey in 21 days, arriving five days ahead of schedule.

Valsheda, the largest single-masted yacht in the world, made a return to Bangor Bay for the first time in 51 years, during which time she had been neglected and then practically rebuilt to her former glory. Her return, organised by the Royal Ulster Yacht Club, attracted considerable crowds.

North Down Age Concern realised a five-year dream on 25 June with the opening of an information and advice centre at 24 Hamilton Road. The premises also served as a drop-in centre and nearly new shop. The official opening ceremony was performed by Mayor Hazel Bradford.

Alex Whitla, from Christine Avenue, in his capacity as purser/ catering officer, was on board one of the first vessels to reach the scene of the Air India Flight 182 jumbo jet disaster on 23 June. The aeroplane crashed into the Atlantic Ocean after a bomb exploded on board, resulting in the loss of all 329 passengers and crew members.

He was on the *Laurentian Forest,* a cargo vessel en route from Quebec to Dublin, some 110 nautical miles west of Mizen Head. The vessel's lifeboat was used in the recovery of 15 bodies, along with various items of wreckage.

Five-year-old Michael Harte, a pupil at Rathmore Primary School, appeared as the son of leading actor John Thaw in the drama *We'll Support You Evermore,* which was set in Northern Ireland. It was broadcast on BBC1 on 14 July.

Members of the Smylie family from Bangor – George, Jean and son David – who were all injured in a holiday coach crash in Austria, returned home on 16 July. They were the only people from Northern Ireland on a Global tour trip to Rimini in Italy. The original coach broke down and they were continuing the journey in a Belgian-owned coach when it crashed near Innsbruck. The bus driver and a car passenger were killed.

Bangor staged its own Live Aid fundraiser at The Helmsman on 6 August, with £1,400 being raised before the *Spectator* went to press. The event was hosted by DJ Eddie Romero and entertainers who provided their services free of charge included George Jones of Clubsound, comedians Jackie Geddis and Sammy Mackie, The Braniffs, Teddy Palmer, Carousel, cabaret artistes Billy Donnelly, Samuel and Mary Wallace, and dance acts Klass Akt and 602 Breakdance Crew.

Pickie Pool's season ended early, on 18 August, after a disastrous summer when rain fell almost every day and attendances were decimated. However, Council tourism officer Harold Bateson dismissed suggestions the poor figures could affect the pool's chances of ever reopening.

It was claimed that Bangor's hopes of having its ice rink complex by Christmas had been dashed by "red tape". There were issues relating to the proposed site for the rink, including the disposal of Council-owned land to a private developer. In the meantime, work was proceeding apace on the construction of an ice rink at Dundonald for Castlereagh Borough Council.

Bangor Independent Christian School opened in early September at the Clandeboye Road location of the town's Free Presbyterian Church. There were 37 pupils from Primary One to Form Two, the idea being that pupils would remain at the school right up to A-Level. Headmistress was Elizabeth Rutherdale.

Bangor girl Julie Graham was crowned Miss Hawaiian Tropic (Ireland) for 1985, winning a package of prizes that included a £1,000 wardrobe, a modelling assignment and three weeks in Hawaii.

Contractors working in September on the site of a new car park for the Bangor Castle Leisure Centre uncovered a network of red-brick tunnels it was believed pre-dated the nearby Town Hall which was built in 1852.

Bone fragments, shards of pottery and the bottoms of wine bottles could be dated to the period 1650-1780, which suggested the tunnels related to one of the earlier houses on the Town Hall site, including the Bangor Castle built for the Ward family in the 1700s.

Actress Jenny Agutter *(The Railway Children)* visited Bangor in September to officially open a new residential centre. The Croft Community, based at Bloomfield Road, represented the first phase in a £600,000 development aimed at providing permanent and short-stay accommodation for mentally handicapped adults aged 18 and over.

The King's Fellowship, formerly the Bangor Christian Trust, moved into the former Milanos building on Seacliff Road, attracting 400 for their first meeting on 5 October.

DUP Deputy Mayor Campbell McCormick resigned from the Council in mid-October because he was moving to Newcastle for family and business reasons. He was replaced as a Councillor by former member Raymond Trousdale and as Deputy Mayor by Alderman Bruce Mulligan.

Environment Minister Richard Needham, having considered the legal and financial implications, gave the Council and promoters the go-ahead for the proposed ice rink complex. The new opening date was Christmas 1986.

Council meetings were adjourned for a month in late October as part of a wider protest over the presence of Sinn Fein Councillors in local authorities elsewhere in Northern Ireland. The protest was extended by a further month following the signing of the Anglo-Irish Agreement by Prime Minister Margaret Thatcher and Irish counterpart Garret FitzGerald at Hillsborough Castle on 15 November.

The Garden of Remembrance at Main Street was dedicated on 3 November by the Rev. Dermot McMorran, assisted by the Rev. L. McManaway, chaplain of the Bangor branch of the Royal British Legion. Parade marshall was Mr E. H. O'Neill and the first poppies were planted by Bangor RBL president Mr James Ashcroft and women's section president Mrs Sadie Cresswell. 11-19-26

Hamilton Road Baptist Church was filled to overflowing for the funeral of Constable David Hanson, who was murdered by the Provisional IRA on 15 November, just hours before the signing of the Anglo-Irish Agreement.

A single man aged 24, Constable Hanson was killed when a 300lb landmine was detonated under a joint Army/ RUC patrol near Crossmaglen. Another officer was seriously injured.

The funeral cortege for Constable David Hanson moves through the centre of Bangor in November 1985. 95-13-26

Pastor Kenneth Humphries, telling mourners he had known David as a young boy and their two families had been very close, stated: "David was a quiet and inoffensive young man who, having decided to serve this people and this country, some three years ago joined the RUC."

He condemned those responsible for his murder, saying: "You have committed some of the most dastardly crimes and brought death and suffering and heartache to many. Your punishment will be eternal damnation."

Interment followed at Clandeboye Cemetery. Born in Australia, David Hanson arrived in Bangor after a short time in Dublin. He attended Ballyholme Primary School and Bangor Grammar School.

Services at Bangor and Ards Hospitals faced the axe after the Eastern Health Board approved savings totalling £270,000 a year. Bangor was set to lose its 25-bed maternity unit, along with ENT in-patient services, while surgical beds would be cut to 23.

North Down MP Jim Kilfedder, in common with his 14 Unionist colleagues, indicated he would resign his seat from 1 January 1986 after voting against the Anglo-Irish Agreement.

Bangor girl Anne McAneney became Britain's first woman principal trumpeter in December 1985, appointed by Sadler's Wells Royal Ballet Orchestra. Speaking

in 2012, Anne recalled: "In 1979 I left Bangor for London to continue the music studies I had begun at Bangor Girls' Secondary School. Having completed my B.Mus course, I embarked on a postgraduate year at the Guildhall School of Music and Drama where I was awarded The Principal's Prize. I also undertook a Master's degree in Music at Reading University.

"The 1980s were very exciting for me, a time that affirmed my desire to be a professional musician. During this period I enjoyed playing with such diverse ensembles as The Ivy Benson Orchestra, West End theatre, brass ensembles and symphony orchestras.

"In 1985 I was appointed to the Principal Trumpet position in the Sadlers Wells Royal Ballet orchestra and following Philip Jones' retirement I became his replacement as flugelhorn specialist in the successor group, London Brass, a position I held for 23 years.

"I am currently Sub-Principal Trumpet in the London Philharmonic Orchestra and Professor of Trumpet at the Guildhall School of Music and Drama."

Anne McAneney today. *Picture by Richard Cannon*

Mrs Isabella McIntyre Wilson celebrated her 105th birthday at Ravara House, Bangor, in January 1985. With her is officer-in-charge Mrs Edith Stevenson. A native of Scotland and a former school teacher, Mrs Wilson had lived in Bangor with her family for many years. She died two years later, in 1987, aged 107.
877-12-23

Cast members from Kilmaine Primary School's pantomime *Cinderella* in January 1985. Back (from left): Taralisa Allen, Lynn McMurray, Andrew McCullough, Clare White, Allen Skelton. Front: Garry Stewart and Christopher Wade.
41-17-24

The cast of Glenlola Collegiate's production of *Annie Get Your Gun* in January 1985, with (at front): Diane Webb, Avril Patterson, Sharon Ritchie and Karen Marsden.
29-12-24

The Hamilton Road Presbyterian Church Girls' Brigade PE B team won the Explorers Teamwork section at the annual Ards District GB competitions in January 1985. The winning squad, with officer Anne Anderson, comprised (back, from left): Karen Craig, Katie Pringle, Rosemary Stephens, Nicola Davidson, Claire Pringle. Front: Denise Scott, Elaine Henning, Julie Pinkerton and Sarah Jane King. *33-11-24*

Seven-year-old Paul Kennedy, from Sinclair Road, with the *Snowman* video he won in a *Good Evening Ulster* competition in January 1985. It took the Bangor boy two nights to paint his winning entry. *78-15-24*

The single-seater Sinclair C5 reached Bangor in February 1985 and proved an eye-catcher at Hamilton's of Church Street, where the £425 price meant it was cheaper than buying the vehicle direct from Sinclair. Behind the wheel is Tom Scott of Hamilton's. *185-19A-24*

St Comgall's Primary School pupils were given a BMX cycling demonstration in March 1985 by Gary Harkness from Sampsons cycle shop in High Street. Also included are Constable Tom Patterson and Sgt. William Robb from the RUC's Community Relations Branch who gave a talk on cycle safety. *191-9-24*

Mayor Hazel Bradford (standing at the door) launched a new fleet of mobile libraries for the South Eastern Education and Library Board in March 1985 with the help of Bloomfield Road Primary School pupils dressed in pirate costumes. Included are (from left): Edna Gilmore, library assistant, Bangor; Rosemary Wood, mobile librarian; Richard Roy, mobile driver; Iris Blunt, mobile librarian, and John McGrattan, mobile driver. *274-8-24*

The principals and some chorus members from Bangor Amateur Operatic Society's production of the musical comedy *The Boyfriend* at the Little Theatre in March 1985. *339-12-24*

Principal actors and actresses in the cast of *Smike*, a musical version of Charles Dickens' *Nicholas Nickleby*, which was presented in March 1985 at St Columbanus' High School. *422-15A-24*

Pupils from the Rathmore Primary School partially hearing units took part in a production of *The Wizard Of Oz* at the school in April 1985. Back (from left): Karl Reid, Neil Miskimmon, Yanna Eleftheriadas, Glenda Thompson, Heather Ferguson. Front: Barry Campbell, Michael Johnston, Claire Gibney, Kerrie McIlmurry and Angela Gray. *564-7-24*

Members of the maintenance staff at Bangor Dairies who took part in a picket line in May 1985 as part of a strike over private maintenance contracts and possible redundancies. The dispute was resolved after agreement was reached with the Milk Marketing Board. *675-13-24*

Daniel Martin (11) and Yvonne McGoldrick (9), both from Bangor, won their respective competitions at the Confined Irish Dancing Festival, which was held at Hamilton House in May 1985. Daniel won the nine to 11 years championship, while Yvonne came top in the seven to nine years championship. *721-3-24*

The cast of Glenlola Collegiate Preparatory Department's production of *Aladdin*, which was produced by Ms Valerie McKinney and staged in May 1985. Principals were Marian McKee, Barbara Corry, Justine Boles, Sarah McMillan, Victoria Latifa, Kerri-Ann Elwood, Sarah Stewart, Julie Douglas, Zoe Tate, Susan Dorrity and Rachael Strahan. *732-6-24*

Plans for a factory in Bangor to manufacture guitars, and employing 15 skilled craftsmen, were announced in September 1985 by local guitar maker George Lowden. Located at the Balloo Industrial Estate, it would be the first factory of its kind in Ireland and the largest acoustic guitar factory in the British Isles. George, who had begun making guitars at High Street in Bangor when he was 22, wanted to move production back from Japan to the North Down area. *165-12-24*

Barry McGuigan officially opened a new public bar and function room at the Bryansburn Inn at the end of October 1985. He is pictured with (from left): Roy Beattie, chairman of Bryansburn FC, Tom Corran, John Crossan, chairman of Glentoran FC, Bill Heron, president of Bryansburn FC, and Sean McCabe. Messrs Corran and McCabe were proprietors of the Bryansburn Inn. *119-15-26*

Children from the St Andrew's and Oakwood Avenue playgroups enjoy stories read by South Eastern Education and Library Board staff at the Clandeboye Road Primary School book fair in November 1985. *170-6-26*

Pupils of St Malachy's Primary School dressed up for their Christmas play in December 1985. *278-2-26*

Stephen Hanson
remembers...

The 1980s changed entirely for our family on the 15th November 1985 with the detonation of a landmine outside the village of Crossmaglen in South Armagh. Media reports at the time, dominated by the signing of the Anglo-Irish Agreement that same day, simply stated that Constable David Hanson, 24 and single, died at the scene.

The first half of the decade had also seen changes for our family – as 1980 dawned my brother David was a first year student at the Ulster Polytechnic, later part of the University of Ulster, studying for a degree in combined science. Though living at home in Ward Avenue, he enjoyed student life, improving his snooker skills in the Union Bar.

At this time David bought his first car, a 1975 Datsun 120 Coupe, for £60. Held together by pop-rivets, string and blind confidence, it lasted the few months until its first MOT. He got £10 for it from Bobby in the scrapyard at Rathgael. It was replaced by a less rusty Renault 5, in which I learned to drive two years later.

David was fascinated by technology and was what we would now call an 'early adopter'. He bought the first

Stephen (left) and David Hanson when pupils at Ballyholme Primary School

Stephen Hanson writes poetry and fiction, he has an MA in Creative Writing from Lancaster University and has won the Sir James Kilfedder Memorial Bursary from North Down Borough Council twice.

He has taught creative writing for the Community Arts Forum and has been involved with the Bangor-based Aspects Writing Festival for several years. Stephen has worked for Libraries NI,

Brothers and friends – David (left) and Stephen Hanson on holiday in the early 1980s

David Hanson enjoyed a number of outdoor hobbies, including climbing in the Mournes, kayaking, swimming, boating and cycling

A proud moment in 1983 as David Hanson meets Secretary of State James Prior at his passing out parade in Enniskillen

Sony Walkman and then when they improved it, making it smaller, he bought that too. He accumulated computers, synthesizers and digital watches, passing on what he considered the obsolete ones to me.

He was, though, too much of an outdoors person to be a techno geek. He loved swimming, kayaking, boating and, above all, fell walking. It was a passion I shared with him in the 1980s, climbing together in the Mournes as well as travelling to Scotland and the Lake District.

When David finished studying at Jordanstown in 1982, he applied and was accepted into the RUC. His 12 weeks' training at Enniskillen began in early 1983. Being over six foot four he had to crouch down in the passing out parade photograph so that he didn't obscure the person behind him.

By the summer of that year he was stationed at Tennent Street in Belfast and had been allocated accommodation in the Antrim Road complex. He usually travelled home to Bangor, staying in his room at Antrim Road only occasionally, preferring to use it to make homebrew beer and wine. I'm not sure how senior officers would have viewed this cottage industry, but as he gave most of his produce to friends and colleagues no one ever complained.

Together we frequently socialised in the Bangor area, favourite haunts being The George at Clandeboye and the Groomsport House Hotel, while on Monday nights it was The Helmsman (£5 in and three free drinks). David loved music and in the 1980s was into electronic pop, including bands like Kraftwerk, Eurythmics and Japan. He loved anything you could dance to and was always on the dance floor when the DJ played the last song (*Let's Stick Together* by Brian Ferry) at The George. I think it was there he met his girlfriend at the time, Dympna.

In the late Spring of 1985, after two years in Belfast, David was transferred to Crossmaglen. The police station was one of the most heavily fortified in Northern Ireland. The village is at the heart of what was then known as 'Bandit Country' and about a mile from the border with the Republic of Ireland. In the 1980s, because of the threat of landmine attacks, roads in the area were considered too dangerous for police vehicles. All police work was carried out using Army helicopters or on foot with the support of soldiers for protection. This, combined with the IRA threat to any local people accessing RUC services, made providing policing in South Armagh challenging and dangerous.

Stephen Hanson today

In an effort to make it more difficult for the IRA to operate, the police mounted roving vehicle checkpoints on the roads in the surrounding area. David loved the rugged rural nature of South Armagh and the helicopter flights from their pick-up station in Bessbrook to Crossmaglen and into the surrounding countryside were a highlight of his time there. The station was residential, with David usually staying for four days before flying back to Bessbrook and then heading home.

formerly the SEELB Library Service, since 1985.

Though born in Belfast, Stephen moved to Bangor in the late Sixties. He still lives in the town with his wife, the artist Marie-Therese Davis, and their son Ben.

In the late summer of that year our parents moved to Lisburn for my father's work. However, David and I stayed on in Bangor renting an apartment between us. He continued to travel to Bessbrook by car, often making a detour to our parents' house on the way.

On the morning of 14th November he headed out for the last time, dropping me off in Belfast at the back of the City Hall. I jumped out of the car with a "See you next week".

The next day in work I watched the police car stop in the car park outside with no idea; even when they asked for me I never thought, but the world in that instant became strange. My belief in humanity, science and progress dimmed. How could we move on from such an emphatic full stop?

The landmine had been planted only a few hundred metres from Crossmaglen. Its detonation blew a six-metre deep crater, instantly killing David and critically injuring his colleague Mark. The bomb was triggered by remote control from a hillside close to the border, allowing for a quick escape. The only person later convicted was the engineer who designed and built the circuitry for the bomb's detonator.

David's funeral was all the things that it was supposed to be: dignified, respectful and sombre. Hundreds of mourners walked or lined the streets in Bangor and the sun shone as we buried him in Clandeboye Cemetery. His was just one of many funerals across Northern Ireland. The conflict worsened as Ulster said 'No' to the Anglo-Irish Agreement, and positions hardened for a time.

Our family received many hundreds of messages from across the UK, Ireland and beyond that gave comfort to my parents. I would like to say "Thank you" to the many people who I know and those I never met, for their help and support.

By the end of the 1980s the Troubles had ebbed and flowed for over 20 years and looked unlikely to end any time soon. In 1989 I spent a month in Australia and visited the house where my parents lived when David was born. I walked on a lot of beaches, city streets and in the desert of the Outback. I came back with some opals and a determination to write.

In the years that followed I was drawn into working with community arts groups. I was privileged to meet many extraordinarily brave people and, in a little way, I perhaps helped some gain a voice and, through their cross-community work, hear other voices. Many of the people involved in these projects had lost loved ones to the Troubles and when we shared our stories it helped bring us understanding of each other's need for healing.

Now, as I write this in 2012, the time since David died is longer than the 24 years he lived. Northern Ireland has changed so much in the intervening years and I am sure he would have been amazed and delighted by the incredible advances in science and technology. But most of all David would be proud that the people can live in peace.

1986
IN THE SPECTATOR

An 'Ulster Says No' banner was erected at the Bangor Castle Leisure Centre after a resolution was passed at a meeting of North Down Borough Council on 7 January. The same resolution called for a further one-month adjournment of Council business in protest at the Anglo-Irish Agreement and voiced support for Northern Ireland's security forces. It was passed by 15 votes to three following a two-hour debate.

John Howell (22), from Prospect Road, became the first man from Northern Ireland to complete the training course necessary to become a guide dog instructor. He was a former pupil of Gransha Boys' High School.

Vandals targeted the Bangor Cenotaph in Ward Park, as well as the First World War gun, in an early morning attack on 12 January. The cannon was painted pink and the peace figure on the war memorial was daubed with red gloss paint. The area was cleaned up thanks to the hard efforts of Council foreman painter Alf Thomas and colleague William Batten.

Bangor Chamber of Trade and Tourist Development Association voiced strong opposition to a proposed one-way traffic system

The peace figure at the Ward Park war memorial was daubed with red gloss paint by vandals in January 1986. Foreman painter Alf Thomas (left) and William Batten had the task of cleaning the figure and the adjacent First World War gun. *360-13A-26*

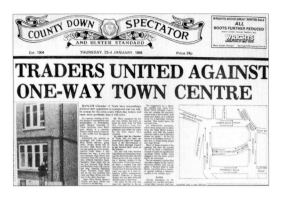

for the town centre, claiming it would cause more problems than it resolved. The scheme envisaged making lower Main Street one-way, going down, while Bridge Street would be two-way, High Street would be one-way, going up (as far as Springfield Road), and a new link road between High Street and Hamilton Road would also be one-way. Hamilton Road itself would be one-way between this road and Main Street and two-way in the other direction. Upper Main Street, Queen's Parade and Quay Street would continue to be two-way.

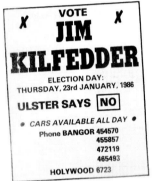

Voters went to the polls on 23 January in what was widely seen as a mini-referendum on the Anglo-Irish Agreement. In North Down voters had a choice between just two candidates – sitting MP Jim Kilfedder (Ulster Popular Unionist Party – Ulster Says No) and Alliance Party leader John Cushnahan. There was a 60% turnout, with Kilfedder easily retaining his seat – he secured 30,793 votes to the 8,066 cast for Cushnahan.

Plans were announced for a new-look Springhill Shopping Centre at a cost of £1.5m. Early in the New Year Northern Ireland's first-ever shopping centre had fallen on difficult times, with just 7,000 customers passing through the doors each week. However, with a new local owner, Cusp Ltd., hopes were high the figure would rise to 35,000 a week.

North Down Sports Council unanimously passed a resolution on 12 February regretting the Bangor Castle Leisure Centre being used to display a political 'Ulster Says No' banner. The chairman, Alderman Bruce Mulligan, abstained.

St Malachy's Primary School brought honour to the town by winning the Primary Schools section of the All Ireland Schools Peace Awards, jointly organised by the Irish Commission for Justice and Peace (which comprised the Catholic bishops of Ireland) and the Irish Council of Churches (the representative body of the main

Protestant churches). It was the hard work of the P6 class under the guidance of teacher Carmel Starr that achieved the first award for a Northern Ireland school in the 13-year history of the competition.

Teacher Carmel Starr with the P6 class along with principal Gerry O'Loan. *178-13A-27*

Local Alliance leader Donald Hayes served notice on North Down Council that he intended to take legal action if it did not resume its "legal duties" by 3 March. He pointed out in a letter to Town Clerk Jack McKimm that it was already in default of its statutory duty to strike a rate by 15 February.

Three thousand people, along with some 200 vehicles, took part in a rally in the town centre on 3 March, organised as part of the Unionist Day of Action against the Anglo-Irish Agreement. In association with a Province-wide series of rallies there was also a 24-hour strike.

The 'Ulster Says No' parade makes its way down Main Street on 3 March. *112-23-27*

Bangor's new ice rink complex had a name – Crystals Arena – and a confirmed location at the former nursery between the Bloomfield Road and the Valentine Playing Fields. Construction, according to Peter Plimley, managing director of Plimley Estates Ltd., would start at the end of March with a likely opening date in mid-October.

Fifteen-year-old Robert McKittrick, of Belfast Road, was awarded a Royal Humane Society testimonial for bravery following an incident the previous November when he saved from drowning a girl who had jumped over the sea wall at Queen's Parade.

North Down Borough Council signed the formal agreement on 25 March that signalled an end to the gas industry in Bangor. Customers were given three months' notice, prompting a gradual rundown of services to the various sectors supplied by Bangor Gas.

Petrol bomb attacks in early April on the homes of two police officers living in Bangor were among more than 160 acts of intimidation against RUC officers in the aftermath of the Anglo-Irish Agreement.

Ulster Popular Unionist Party secretary Valerie Kinghan was co-opted onto North Down Borough Council on 22 April to fill a vacancy in the Abbey area following the resignation of Cllr Brian Meharg.

A £700,000 order from the USA for racing cars boosted the fortunes of the three-year-old Mondiale company in early May. It allowed the firm to increase its workforce and almost double the size of their premises at the Balloo Industrial Estate.

The DUP's Bangor branch urged Prime Minister Margaret Thatcher to bomb Dundalk, West Belfast, the Bogside, Dublin and "all strategic headquarters of Irish Republican terrorism." The resolution was passed unanimously at the annual meeting in Hamilton House in early May.

It accused Mrs Thatcher of "double standards" in tackling terrorism, claiming she had used military force against Colonel Gaddafi but ruled out similar action against the IRA.

The Bangor United Welfare Committee, which had been launched as the Bangor Emergency Relief Committee in 1971 to help Belfast people affected by the Troubles, was officially wound up in June.

Former Councillor Mary O'Fee, who had been involved with the organisation since its earliest days, presented a cheque for £204, representing their remaining funds, to the RUC Benevolent Fund.

The British Legion Housing Association purchased the Savoy Hotel for an undisclosed sum and indicated the premises would be converted into flats for disabled people and pensioners.

The Northern Ireland Assembly was dissolved on 23 June, just four months short of the completion of its four-year term. The Dissolution Order was read out by Speaker Jim Kilfedder amid cries from Unionists of "Ulster Says No."

Mario 'Siki' Togneri, Bangor's best known barber, closed the doors of his Abbey Street business for the final time on 27 June, just short of his 66th birthday. Born and reared in the town by his Italian parents, he had entered the hairdressing business at the age of 13, serving a four-year apprenticeship in Belfast before joining James Major in the centre of Bangor. With his mother's help he opened his own business at Abbey Street in 1952.

The 70th anniversary of the Battle of the Somme, on 1 July 1986, was marked by the Royal British Legion's Bangor branch with a parade to Ward Park where the Legion wreath was laid by two Bangor veterans of the Somme, David Martin (10th Btn., Royal Inniskilling Fusiliers) and John Nicholson (36th Royal Ulster Rifles Cycling Corps). Betty Anderson laid the wreath on behalf of the Women's Section. (See picture on p153)

The North Down Visitors and Heritage Centre was awarded a certificate of merit in the British Tourist Authority's *Come to Britain* competition. It was regarded as the Oscar of the tourism industry.

North Down Borough Council resumed normal business on 26 August, nine months after introducing its adjournment policy in opposition to the Anglo-Irish Agreement. The decision was taken on a 13-6 vote and prompted a walk-out by the six DUP members as well as Ulster Popular Unionist Valerie Kinghan.

Christopher Callendar (10) and Allison Poots (10), both pupils of Rathmore Primary School, appeared as the 'royal couple' at a street party in Henderson Drive to mark the marriage, in July 1986, of Prince Andrew and Sarah Ferguson. *290-8-29*

The Roads Service began installing 'Pay and Display' machines in a number of Bangor car parks, including Bingham Street, Bingham Lane, The Vennel and Holborn Avenue, with the new system commencing on Monday 15 September.

North Down Councillors subsequently urged the DoE to replace the pay and display system with manned car parks where parking would be free for the first hour. While recognising the new scheme was preventing all-day parking for free, members feared it was sending casual shoppers away from Bangor.

The campaign against the Anglo-Irish Agreement changed tack with the first meeting of the North Down branch of the Ulster Clubs taking place in Hamilton House on 15 September.

Chairman Alan Wright, stating that political activity against the Agreement was "completely exhausted", warned the 40-strong audience: "When the time comes, North Down is going to have to be taken and held, not by people from Portadown, but by people from North Down."

A campaign of civil disobedience, organised by Ulster Clubs, was, he said, one more effort to convince Mrs Thatcher and Dr FitzGerald they could not rule without the consent of the majority. Those wishing to join the new branch were told to leave their names and addresses, with Mr Wright – warning the group would become the top target for infiltration by the RUC – stating: "You won't be joining tonight, not until those who know you have vouched for you."

An appeal was launched in early October by rector Canon George Mitchell to raise the £120,000 needed to repair serious damage and decay to St Comgall's Parish Church.

The Council was preparing in October for the introduction of the new dustless refuse disposal system – better known as 'wheelie bins'. Members agreed to seek a loan sanction for capital expenditure totalling £850,000 to cover the cost of all aspects of implementing the service, including bins and vehicles.

Bangor Chamber of Trade and Tourist Development Association voiced opposition to a business village proposed for the Bloomfield area by Crystals Arena developer Peter Plimley. The proposal, which had received planning permission, was viewed by Chamber chairman Evan Ward as a third shopping centre for Bangor, which could only further harm businesses in the heart of the town.

Five Ulster Unionist members of North Down Borough Council were expelled from the party following their return to Council business despite the continuing UUP/ DUP policy of adjournment in protest at the Anglo-Irish Agreement.

The five – Mayor Bruce Mulligan, Alderman George Green, Cllr John McConnell Auld, Cllr Samuel Hamilton and Cllr Jack Preston – while reiterating their opposition to the Agreement, said they would continue to sit on the local authority as 'Unionists'.

Bangor-born Canon Gerry Murphy was named as the next rector of Christ Church Cathedral on the Falkland Islands. Aged 60, a former rugby and cricket player for the town, and a World War Two veteran, he had previously served as Rector of Sandringham and a Domestic Chaplain to the Queen.

Crystals Arena opened its doors to the public in October, offering an ice rink and six-rink indoor bowling green, snooker hall with four tables, ice cream parlour and restaurant/snack bar. Membership of the new North Down Indoor Bowls Club, based at Crystals, topped 500 by the end of the year.

The launch of the Dunlop Commercial Park in October at the Balloo Industrial Estate, following on from the success of the local building company's industrial units, promised the prospect of employment for as many as 1,000 people. Having opened in 1982, the units, which provided purpose-built accommodation for small manufacturing and service industries, were already providing work for 350.

Sixty production jobs were lost in mid-December at the Oneida factory on the Bloomfield Road but 30 jobs were retained in distribution and warehousing, with management insisting there were no plans to shut down the Bangor operation. The job losses were the result of rationalisation, a spokesman insisted.

Councillors voted by 14 to seven on 29 December to spend up to £17,500 on a publicity campaign against the Anglo-Irish Agreement. A four-member committee had full Council powers to organise the campaign – Alderman Bruce Mulligan (Mayor), Cllr George McMurtry (Deputy Mayor), Alderman George Green and Cllr Ellie McKay.

The cast of *A Crown Of Stars*, a play for Epiphany performed by pupils of Bangor Central Primary School in January 1986. Production was by teachers Mrs M. Hamilton and Mrs H. Armstrong. *341-14A-26*

The Junior Choristers of Bangor Abbey presented a cheque for £275 to the Malcolm Sargent Fund in January 1986, having raised the money at their *Celebration Of The Nativity* the previous month. Charity representative Mr R. N. Bowman accepts the cheque from treasurer Donald Kerr and chairman Stella Robinson. Included is organist Peter Hunter. *94-9A-27*

Teachers and pupils of the Bangor School of Dance, which was run at the Good Templar Hall by professional ballroom dancers Colm and Julie Magee, in March 1986. From left: Colm and Julie Magee, Cathie Moore, Amanda Caskey and Paddy McDaid, Tracey and David Hodgins, and Steven Flannigan. Not included in picture: Barbara Nelson. *101-15-27*

The third form at Glenlola Collegiate was awarded first place (12-18 years) in the South Eastern Education and Library Board's International Year of Youth *Playback* competition, held in March 1986. Pictured with UTV's Eamonn Holmes, who presented the prizes, are (from left): Lisa Flavelle, Nicole Cairns, Vanya McWilliams and Cheryl Laird, along with teacher Judy Neville (seated). *204-7-27*

The winners of the Easter Egg Hunt which attracted hundreds of children to Castle Park on Easter Monday in 1986. From left: Rachel Fawcett (Holywood), Caroline Magrath, Jenny Milliken, Jonathan Foster, Jennifer Gray, Emma Stewart and Andrew Morrow (all Bangor). *316-12-27*

Brice Park on the Donaghadee Road was given a facelift in April 1986 by conservationists who planted a number of trees and picked up two bin-loads of litter. Pictured are (from left): Mark Boyd, Stuart Griffin, Gareth Lorimer, Nessie James, Timothy Moore and Andrew Lorimer. *399-2-27*

Bangor in the Eighties

Pupils and staff from St Columbanus' High School who travelled to Austria in May 1986 for a 10-day educational holiday, including visits to Vienna and Salzburg. 94-7-28

The playgroup at Rodney Park participated in a sponsored 'Run the World' fundraiser in May 1986 as part of the Sport Aid initiative. Some 2,000 people took part in a number of similar events around the town. 226-3-28

Former world snooker champion Dennis Taylor made it a day to remember for two young autograph hunters when he visited the revamped Clandeboye Shopping Centre in July 1986. 316-10-29

Counter staff at Bangor Post Office joined celebrations held in August 1986 to mark the 50th anniversary of the day it opened to the public. From left: William Herron, Roy Jackson, Norma Burns, William Boyd, Catherine McAlorum, Sam Walsh, May L'Estrange (acting supervisor) and Bob Alexander. *328-10-29*

Children and parents from the Mother and Toddler group, which was run each Wednesday during term time at Hamilton Road Baptist Church Hall, are pictured in September 1986. The leader was Sandra Waddell. *80-16-30*

P2 pupils from Rathmore Primary School who presented *Joey's Magic Carpet* during the traditional Christmas concert in December 1986. *155-7-31*

All 19 classes at Clandeboye Road Primary School planted a tree in December 1986 to mark National Tree Week. P2 pupils look on as Mrs H. Finlay and Shelley Riley plant a young oak tree. Included are principal Mr J. Upritchard, student Doris Cousins and organiser Mrs A. Lightbody. *117-24A-31*

Pupils from St Columbanus' High School who formed the chorus for their Christmas production of *Joseph And The Amazing Technicolor Dreamcoat* in December 1986. *161-15-31*

A surprise party marked the golden wedding anniversary of Bangor couple Robert and Elizabeth Irvine, from Silverstream Road, who were married in Bangor Abbey on 17 December 1936. Guests included their three daughters, 11 grandchildren and five great grandchildren. *202-14-31*

Donna Wilson
(née Harmer) remembers...

The Eighties proved a memorable decade for me as a teenager growing up in Bangor. I completed my secondary, further and higher education – and met my future husband!

At the start of the decade I transferred from Rathmore to 'the big school', travelling by bus to Glenlola Collegiate. Such an adventure for someone from Bangor West! I have great memories of Glenlola, where I forged many special friendships – Lesley Finn, Julie Foote, Andrea Forbes, Alison Grant, Lesley Moore, Gail Jamieson, Fiona Craig and Claire Collins, to name but a few.

In First Form Andrea and I joined the choir for the musical *Show Boat*. It proved a roaring success under the direction of the charismatic Lorna Watton, who encouraged our love of music. I took piano lessons, achieving Grade 5, and still play today.

We endured hockey all year round, wearing short skirts on our all-weather pitches which were more often flooded and enjoyed by the Ward Park ducks. Julie, Andrea and I completed our Duke of Edinburgh Award, hiking along the Causeway Coast in blistering heat – goodness knows how we managed it!

We were thrilled to be involved in the BBC's *We Are The Champions* television programme. Glenlola joined up with Gransha Boys' High and we travelled to Liverpool

Donna keeps cool in France in 1984

Donna Wilson, eldest of three children (the others being sister Nicola and brother Graham) of Wilfred and Lila Harmer, was born in 1967 and has lived in Bangor most of her life. She attended Rathmore Primary School and Glenlola Collegiate.

After graduation she joined Friendly Hotels as a trainee manager, travelling throughout England and Scotland to work in all their hotels. She met future husband Martin when they both worked at the Station Hotel in Perth. They returned to live in Bangor in 1989 and got married in 1990.

Donna joined Hastings Hotels on her return, spending 10 years at the Stormont Hotel as Assistant Manager and then Deputy General Manager, and five years at the Culloden as Events Manager.

Enjoying a first family holiday in Majorca with mum Lila, younger sister Nicola and brother Graham

Donna (left) with friends Lesley Finn (centre) and Julie Foote in 1984

on the overnight boat, sleeping in berths for the first time. Filming took place in Preston, but alas we got knocked out in the semi-finals. While we met Ron Pickering and Kenny Dalglish the icing on the cake was when we were given money for lunch expenses but instead bought chips and spent the rest at Blackpool's Pleasure Beach!

In Fifth Form Julie, the two Lesleys and I went on the infamous – for reasons I won't elaborate on – school trip to the south of France. We travelled by boat and coach and stayed in a hostel which resembled a fairytale castle!

The Eighties saw a big first for the Harmer family when we went to Palma Nova in Majorca – just like Ballyholme but with constant sunshine. Before then we'd been limited to caravan holidays at Newcastle, Tollymore and Cranfield, or a chalet at Butlins in Ayr.

On most Saturday nights Julie, Lesley and I attended the youth club in the Carnalea Methodist Centre, playing table tennis, darts, dancing and watching videos (we didn't have our own video player at the time so it really was a big treat). We participated in activity weekends in Castlewellan and Ardglass and thoroughly enjoyed the RUC's Mourne Ramble and the Blue Lamp discos. Lesley and I played badminton in the local church league, never winning 'big' – our enjoyment was in the participation.

Monday was Girl Guide night at St Gall's (12th Bangor) under the leadership of Captain Florence Hartley. Julie and I slept out under canvas at regular camps in Lorne and I remember going to Windermere in the Lake District, learning to light fires with sticks and cook meals in our billycans – all very important skills as we achieved the Queen's Guide badge in 1984.

St Gall's Grand Fete was in its heyday then and quite simply was a fabulous family day out. We all joined in the organisation and people came from all parts for the fun of the fair, with stalls ranging from hoopla, white elephant, books and cakes to wet sponge throwing. My parents' tombola stall was legendary. The Fete has recently been revived and is going strong today.

I spent my hard-earned babysitting cash in Bangor or the Clandeboye or Springhill Shopping Centres, only rarely venturing to Belfast because of the security situation. Lunch was from The Wimpy, Isobel's or Furey's, or maybe just a bag of chips from Paul's, followed by a browse around the Co-Op Superstore or Robinson and Cleaver. Smyths record store was a cool spot, while the Boulevard and the Locarno, both on the seafront, were popular places to hang out and listen to the jukeboxes.

When the weather was good we swam at Brompton, Crawfordsburn or Ballymaconnell, rowed Lairds Boats and of course every Eighties teenager will remember when Gary Davies and the Radio One roadshow visited Bangor! Likewise there was great excitement when BJ's and Rollerama opened. We all saved up for roller boots from McManus's.

A massive treat was getting a new outfit from Top Shop or Chelsea Girl in Belfast to wear to BJ's. Imagine, I skated all the way from home into Bangor, right along the Seacliff Road just to get there. BJ's was a teenager's paradise on Saturday afternoons and under-age drinking was rife – but that, of course, will be denied!

We thought Bangor was Northern Ireland's answer to Brighton, a seaside town where rival groups would congregate on bank holiday weekends. In the early 1980s, at the height of the Mod revival, hundreds of smartly dressed teenagers would jump on their Vespas or catch the train from Belfast to Bangor to meet friends and pose by the seafront. I wore ski pants, mini-skirts, twin sets and pearls, lots of eyeliner and listened to The Jam, Secret Affair, The Who and adored everything about the 1960s. The girls all wanted to be Steph from *Quadrophenia*.

As I got older it was all about the music, fashion and dancing. Our favourite haunts included The Helmsman, The George, The Coachman's, Groomsport House and Sam's, or if we were flush we travelled (half fare) by bus to The Knightsbridge in Ards or The Coach in Banbridge.

Fashion was largely led by the New Romantic music scene – Spandau Ballet, Adam and the Ants, Duran Duran, Prince. We imitated them by wearing knickerbockers, leg warmers and frilly blouses based on the romantic looks of earlier eras in fashion history. The blouses had intricate

followed by seven years as Events Manager at the Clandeboye Lodge Hotel.

In 2009 she decided on a change in career for a better work-life balance. She is now employed by North Down Borough Council, previously as a Tourism Information Advisor and Events Assistant and now working as Liaison Officer in North Down Museum.

Donna loves welcoming tourists and visitors, managing the gift shop and all room/ group bookings for the museum. She says no two days are ever the same – it's just like working in a hotel but without the bedrooms!

She and husband Martin have a son, Ross.

On a footnote – Donna is still very close to the various school friends she mentions in her contribution and together they travelled to Las Vegas in 2007 to celebrate their joint 40th birthdays, along with Karen McKee, Sharon Campbell, Heather and Deborah Emberson (11 in total).

Sadly their very dear friend Andrea Forbes was unable to join them as she had lost her battle with cancer in 2005.

Donna and husband Martin with son Ross and pet dog Rudi

stock or cravat-effect neck wrappings, deep pleated shoulder tucks or swathed crossover fabrics. All were made up in silk or polyester satin or crêpe de chine substitutes which softened the harshness of severe man-tailored jackets.

The biggest musical event of the 1980s (apart from The Jam splitting!) was Live Aid in July 1985. Unfortunately I had to work that Saturday but my parents were under strict instructions to tape it for me on the VHS. It needed more than three tapes and I camped in our living room with a sleeping bag to watch every last minute. I will never forget the heart-rending video for The Cars' *Drive*.

My first concerts were in the 1980s – Julie, Andrea and I went to see Nik Kershaw at the Maysfield Leisure Centre and Howard Jones at Avoniel.

I landed my first Saturday job at the Skandia in upper Main Street. One night we were evacuated to the Ava Bar because of a bomb scare. I was wearing my school blazer but no one cared! I loved the restaurant work and was usually there while my friends, who all had day jobs in Woolies, Wellworths, Crazy Prices or Stewarts, were out dancing. Unsociable hours? Nonsense!

Much to my teachers' surprise I left Glenlola after my O-Levels and was guided into hospitality as a career by Florence Bickerstaff (a colleague's mum and an enthusiastic mentor). I attended the College of Business Studies in Belfast, going on to Birmingham College of Food, Tourism and Creative Studies (now University College Birmingham) for my HND. To supplement my student grant, I worked many part-time jobs, including the Winston Hotel, Windsor Bars, Red Pepper Restaurant and Bangor Golf Club.

1987
IN THE SPECTATOR

North Down Borough Council commenced its campaign against the Anglo-Irish Agreement in January by launching a petition to the Queen, calling for a referendum. The petition could be signed at a total of 18 different locations throughout the Borough, including the Town Hall and Bangor Castle Leisure Centre.

A European Community funding package totalling £2.1m towards the multi-million pound Bangor seafront development was announced by the Council on 27 January.

The local authority predicted the face of Bangor Bay would be transformed during the next two years, with the construction of the Pickie Breakwater, along with a new promenade and protective Queen's Parade sea wall, being essential elements of the new marina, along with dredging and land reclamation.

The Council also predicted a completion date of summer 1989, when it believed the Pickie Breakwater would be finished and the marina would be operating.

In a separate EC funding announcement, there was a £320,000 cash injection for the Visitors and Heritage Centre, thus guaranteeing completion of its third and final phase comprising a resource centre, exhibition area, catering facilities for up to 180 people, a lecture theatre, stores and workshops. The work cost a total of

PETITION TO HER MAJESTY THE QUEEN FOR A REFERENDUM ON THE ANGLO-IRISH AGREEMENT

North Down Borough Council would wish to remind you that on Saturday, 17th January, the following locations will be available from 8.00 a.m. till 4.30 p.m. for the signing of the Petition.

1. Town Hall, The Castle, Bangor
2. Bangor Castle Leisure Centre
3. Caravan adjacent to Northern Bank, Main Street, Bangor
4. Tower House, Quay Street, Bangor
5. Hamilton House, Hamilton Road, Bangor
6. Good Templar Hall, Hamilton Road, Bangor
7. Co-op Hall, Castle Square, Bangor
8. Caravan, Seahill Road, Craigavad
9. Queen's Hall, Holywood
10. Redburn Community Centre, Jacksons Road, Holywood
11. Breezemount Community Centre, Breezemount, Conlig
12. Conlig Community Centre
13. Groomsport Boat House
14. Kilcooley Community Centre
15. Skipperstone Community Centre
16. Ballyrobert Orange Hall
17. Craigantlet Orange Hall
18. Caravan at Station Square, Helen's Bay

IF YOU BELIEVE IN DEMOCRACY YOU WILL WANT TO SIGN THE PETITION

£640,000 with the Council providing the other half.

Environment Minister Richard Needham announced in February that a new fire station would be built in Bangor – most likely on a site bordering the ring road – as part of an £18m package for the Northern Ireland Fire Authority.

The Council agreed in early March to formalise a twinning agreement between Bangor and Bregenz. A month later the chess clubs of the two towns engaged in a match by telephone – the first such encounter between an Ulster club and one from Continental Europe. The result was a 3-3 draw.

Bangor Chamber of Trade and Tourist Development Association raised the possibility of backing a candidate standing as an independent or on behalf of traders at the 1989 Council elections. It would not be easy finding a suitable person, stated chairman Evan Ward at the annual meeting in March. "Anyone who is sensible doesn't want to sit in that town hall the way things are going on," he declared.

Thermomax won a coveted Queen's Award for Export Achievement in mid-April. The company by then employed 60 people at the Balloo Industrial Estate.

'Unwanted' Education Minister Nicholas Scott is stuffed into a Campaign for Equal Citizenship collection bucket by (from left): CEC president Robert McCartney, Dr Laurence Kennedy, Conservative Councillor Paul Mangnall and North Down CEC group organiser Bill Methven. *390-7-32*

During a meeting of the recently formed Campaign for Equal Citizenship prospective Ulster Unionist candidate for North Down in the next general election, Robert McCartney, spelled out his vision of a Northern Ireland completely integrated into the United Kingdom. Mr McCartney, who at the time (28 April) was facing an internal disciplinary committee because of critical comments he had made about the Ulster Unionist Party, described those proceedings as a "heresy trial".

Three weeks later, on 19 May, Mr McCartney was expelled from the party. He indicated he still intended to contest North Down as the 'Real Unionist' candidate, having been selected by the local constituency association four days earlier. The North Down Constituency Unionist Association subsequently found itself 'disaffiliated' for putting forward a candidate for the general election.

The Ulster Unionist Party threw its weight behind sitting MP Jim Kilfedder, with leader James Molyneaux joining Mr Kilfedder for the handing in of his nomination papers and other MPs canvassing on his behalf. This was in accordance with an inter-party policy, whereby all sitting Unionist MPs were supported for re-election as part of the campaign against the Anglo-Irish Agreement. The same policy saw Jim Allister quitting the DUP because he was not allowed to contest the safe seat of East Antrim.

Seacliff Road residents voiced concern over proposals to fill in the Long Hole for use as a car park by the owners of vehicles using the new marina, as well as visitors to the area. Council development officer John Thompson admitted the authority had considered the idea but he stressed they were also looking at other proposals, the preferred option being a multi-storey car park on the gasworks site. "We are trying to avoid filling up the seafront with cars," he added.

Bye-laws targeting the owners of dogs that fouled footpaths and public places came into force on 13 May. Notices were posted around the town reminding owners of their responsibilities, including the need to carry 'poop scoops' and plastic bags to clean up after their pets.

News of the death in a London hospital on 7 May of Bangor-born actor Colin Blakely from leukaemia greatly saddened members of the town's operatic and dramatic societies, both of which he had joined in his younger days. Aged just 56, he had become a star of stage, screen and television in the years after his major career breakthrough – when he joined the National Theatre in 1963.

Blakely was a member of Bangor Amateur Operatic Society for four years, beginning with a minor role in *Annie Get Your Gun* back in 1952, while one of his earliest roles with Bangor Drama Club was in a production of *Rope,* which won the Northern Ireland Drama Festival.

Work began on the next phase of the seafront development with Mayor Bruce Mulligan releasing a truck-load of stones into the water from the South Pier on 28 May. It was estimated that 100,000 tonnes of stones would be required to complete the scheme.

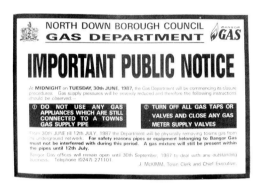

The Bangor Gas Department announced the supply in the North Down area would cease on 30 June. Customers were warned not to use any appliances still connected to the town gas supply pipe after that date.

Portrush nightclub owner Roy Crawford bought the former Queen's Court Hotel on Queen's Parade, saying he planned to turn it into a wine bar, nightclub and hotel with 30 bedrooms. He said the marina was one of the key factors bringing him to the town, along with the fact that Bangor had a larger population than Portrush, where he operated the successful Traks nightspot. The proposals were rejected by the Planning Service at the end of November.

Jim Kilfedder won the North Down seat at the general election on 11 June, but his majority was slashed from 13,846 to just 3,953, representing a 13% swing

away from the Ulster Popular Unionist Party leader. Kilfedder polled 18,420 votes compared to the 14,467 cast for Real Unionist Robert McCartney, with Alliance Party leader John Cushnahan third (7,932 votes). The turnout was 62.6%.

On 21 June Katherine Poulson became the first woman deacon in the Church of Ireland to be ordained. She was attached to St Comgall's Parish Church in Bangor. A week later her husband Ian was ordained as a priest, attached to St Mark's Parish Church in Newtownards.

The 11-year-old Clandeboye Shopping Centre was almost completely destroyed by a devastating fire which broke out on 3 July. The police indicated early on they were not treating the blaze as suspicious; rather it seemed more likely it had started in an area where workmen were using welding equipment.

Firemen dampen down the smouldering ruins of the Clandeboye Shopping Centre in July 1987. 347-22-33

Although many people lost their jobs as a result of the shopping centre's destruction, the owners, Lindore Investments, insisted that rebuilding work, costing as much as £9m, would start almost immediately and they hoped to have the centre operating again by Christmas 1988.

Former bricklayer Sam Heyburn was appointed national president and director of Youth for Christ in Australia. He had left Bangor for Australia back in 1960.

Business people and traders in lower High Street, Bridge Street and Mill Row were angered by new proposals being considered by the Council that would involve razing the whole area. Officers had proposed that the Department of the Environment should acquire the sites fronting the streets to provide a more attractive package to potential developers.

Speaking on behalf of a newly-formed Lower High Street and Bridge Street Traders Sub-Committee, which feared job losses of up to 100 if the scheme went ahead, spokesman Bill Wolsey said: "We are not opposed to the development of that area, although we doubt the need for it. We certainly don't think it needs the amount of shops they are talking about."

Bangor Drama Club paid its own tribute to the late Colin Blakely at the beginning of September with a staging of *Philadelphia, Here I Come!,* with all proceeds going to Leukaemia Research. Among those in attendance were his widow Margaret and their sons Drummond, Cameron and Hamish. A programme chronicling the actor's life was prepared by club chairman Kenneth Irvine.

INTRODUCING THE
BANGOR LITTLE BUSES

From Monday, 31st August, a new service of small buses running at greater frequency will be introduced on Bangor Town Service Routes serving **ALBANY/ CLOVERHILL** Estates via Gransha Road and **BALLOO** Estate via Gransha Road, which will also serve **BEXLEY** Estate.

There are also timetable changes and improved frequencies on other Town Bus Services.

TIMETABLE LEAFLETS available on request from Ulsterbus Office at BANGOR BUS STATION.

Ulsterbus

Following a visit to the area by Ulster Unionist Party leader James Molyneaux on 14 September, a new North Down Constituency Association was formed and affiliated to the Ulster Unionist Council.

The Eastern Health and Social Services Board voted on 24 September to close not only Crawfordsburn Hospital but also Cultra House, which provided accommodation for the mentally handicapped. Patients at the latter would be split between Muckamore Hospital, residential homes and sheltered accommodation, while the elderly residents of Crawfordsburn Hospital would move to either Bangor or Newtownards Hospitals.

Bill Wolsey (second from left), proprietor of Jenny Watts at High Street, presents a cheque for £1,000 to Neill Grainger from Combat Cancer. The money was raised in autumn 1987 by customers and staff, including a team participating in Bangor Bay raft races. Included are Gillian McMullan (North Down Borough Council) and Jane Rodgers (communications manager for Sealink, which provided raffle prizes). 397-5-34

And finally … the official twinning of Bangor and Bregenz was marked by a five-hour programme of speeches, entertainment and the exchange of gifts at the Town Hall on 21 October. The Austrian town was represented by, amongst others, Burgermeister (Mayor) Fritz Mayer. They were welcomed by Mayor Bruce Mulligan, with both dignitaries being called on to sign the formal twinning documents.

Hundreds of people gathered at the war memorial in Ward Park on 11 November in a service of remembrance for the 11 people killed in the Enniskillen Cenotaph bombing the previous Sunday. Clergy from all denominations took part in the service. Mayor Bruce Mulligan and Town Clerk Jack McKimm laid a wreath on behalf of North Down Borough Council.

The Council was warned it would face court action by the DoE if it did not remove the 'Ulster Says No' banner from the Bangor Castle Leisure Centre by 23 December. The banner was termed an 'unauthorised advertisement' by the Department and its continuing presence was a breach of the planning laws.

Brett Cunningham, of Beverley Gardens, was appointed Coastguard District Controller for Northern Ireland – the first Ulsterman to hold the position since the mid-1970s.

The former Queen's Court Hotel was destroyed by a fire early on Monday 30 November. During the height of the blaze, thought to have been caused by drinkers who had broken into the disused premises, part-time fireman Sam McCullough, deputy manager of the Bangor Castle Leisure Centre, fell more than 40ft from the roof of an adjoining building. He suffered multiple injuries and was detained in hospital for some weeks.

A former member of the Royal Ulster Rifles from Southwell Road, who murdered a totally innocent man believing he was a member of the IRA, was sentenced to life imprisonment in December. The soldier's wife was found guilty of aiding and abetting attempted murder and jailed for three years.

The victim, Clifford Clemo, a Protestant from County Mayo, was stabbed to death in the Dufferin Avenue car park on 21 January 1987.

Continuing attacks by vandals forced the town's St John Ambulance group out of the Central Avenue hall that had been their home for 40 years. Members moved in December to the nearby Red Cross Hall while they searched for suitable new premises.

First Bangor Girls' Brigade achieved considerable success in January 1987 at the annual PE competitions in Newtownards. They won first place in team work (Brigaders), along with solo firsts in scarf work and senior skipping. Back (from left): Joanne Mellon (scarf solo and team), Julie McGowan, Cathy Eddis, Jan Henry, Tara Lynch, Katrina Henry (skipping solo). Front: Gillian Erskine, Loren Gowdy and Karen Rea. *361-9A-31*

The boys of 11th Bangor Scouts celebrated 10 years of Scouting for the mentally handicapped with three days of fun and dedication in late April 1987. This picture was taken in St Columbanus Church Hall, Groomsport Road. *456-14-31*

Staff from the Co-Op in Bangor joined in the celebrations in March 1987 that marked the 10th anniversary of their sister store in York Street, Belfast. *477-14A-31*

Pupils of Kilmaine Primary School pictured during rehearsals for their pantomime *Ali Baba And The 39½ Thieves* in March 1987. Included is Barbara Law, who made the costumes. *458-3-31*

Ballyholme Primary School pupils visited Bangor Fire Station in April 1987. They were shown around the station and one of the fire engines by Station Officer Paul Vaughn. Included are teacher Honor McCracken and classroom assistant Kathleen Endersby. *204-6A-32*

The Bangor Abbey Players presented the Sam Cree comedy *The Mating Game* in the Abbey Hall in April 1987. Back (from left): Percy Deering, Lilla McGlennon, Richard Sweeney, Eddie Shannon, John Peacock, Ellie Henderson. Front: Carole Evans, Claire Jardine, Maud Thompson, Lisa Lindsay and Jean Barton. *254-10-32*

Hundreds of children took part in the annual Easter Egg Hunt on Easter Monday 1987 at Bangor Castle. It was organised by Bangor Youth Council and sponsored by award-winning butcher David Burns. Competition winners are pictured with Mayor Bruce Mulligan (back, from left): Andrew Rainey (with Julie Todd), Suzanne Foster, Alan Sloan, John Cinnamond. Front: Nicky Thompson, Cathy Millar, Mark Keenan and Peter Hopkins. *352-23A-32*

Centenarian Mrs Annie Gore, of Chippendale Avenue, is pictured outside her local polling station at Ballyholme Primary School on election day in June 1987. Mrs Gore, who was 102, was already 43 when women were given the vote in 1928. *176-17-33*

Henry and Elizabeth Mulholland, of Holborn Avenue, celebrated their golden wedding anniversary on 18 June 1987. They were married in First Bangor Presbyterian Church in 1937 by the Rev. W. J. Currie. The couple had three children, 10 grandchildren and two great grandchildren. *236-5-33*

Two 90-year-old veterans of the Battle of the Somme took part in Bangor's remembrance service at the beginning of July 1987, namely John Nicholson (36th Royal Ulster Rifles Cycle Corps) and David Martin (10th Btn., Royal Inniskilling Fusiliers). *296-17-33*

Pupils from Bangor Girls' High School who received prizes at the annual awards ceremony in June 1987. *301-6A-33*

Members of St Comgall's Temperance LOL 235, Bangor, who attended the demonstration in Holywood on 12 July 1987. *491-5A-33*

Clare Hardy, Angela Gray and Alison Hardy, along with Joanne Honeyford (not in picture), from Ballyholme, raised £110 for the Tear Fund through a bric-a-brac sale in August 1987. *180-13-34*

Ballyholme Primary School welcomed two sets of twins to P1 in September 1987: Andrew and Simon Jackson pictured with David and Adam Henderson. *227-21A-34*

Connor House welcomed these new P1 pupils in September 1987. Included is teacher Sandra Williams. *225-11-34*

Mr and Mrs James Gillespie, from Church Street, celebrated their 50th wedding anniversary on 17 September 1987. They were married in St Comgall's Parish Church in 1937 and had two children and six grandchildren.
295-12-34

Pupils from Kilcooley Primary School who took part in a harvest service at the school in November 1987.
474-16-34

Employees from the Bairdwear factory on the Clandeboye Road who took part in a sponsored walk in November 1987 to raise money for the Enniskillen Poppy Day Bomb Appeal Fund.
109-7-35

Testing their baking skills at the St Comgall's Playgroup in December 1987 are triplets Rosemary, Deirdre and Hannah Marshall, from Brunswick Road. *172-8-35*

Glenlola Collegiate's Christmas pageant for December 1987 had the theme *The Colours Of The Christ Child*. Among those taking part were these Santas (back, from left): Joanne McCready, Diane Webb, Heather Walsh, Julie Ogilvie, Linda Ruddock. Front: Claire Nicholl, Debbie Jordan and Aileen Tyney. *189-4-35*

Principal cast members of *The Christmas Dove And The Woodcutter*, a nativity play presented by P4 and P5 pupils of St Malachy's Primary School in December 1987. *219-3-35*

Zane Radcliffe
remembers...

The Eighties was my truly formative decade.

In 1980 'Catchy Kissies' was officially banned by Ballyholme Primary School headmaster Derek Cummings. It was one less distraction from my 11-Plus exam and a hopeful admission to Bangor Grammar School, which – I was reliably informed by a friend's older brother – involved a medical where they injected your testicles to make your voice break.

Thankfully, we could still chase girls at BJ's roller disco on Seacliff Road – though it is hard to catch a 12-year-old girl when you're teetering gingerly across a dance floor, on wheels, while trying valiantly not to spill her Slush Puppy.

Zane at Bangor Grammar School in1986

My initiation to the Grammar came at the pre-school camp at Castlerock. I had just returned from the legendary Ballyholme Primary trip to Holland, so Castlerock was

Some participants on the Ballyholme Primary School trip to Holland in 1981

Zane Radcliffe was born in Bangor Hospital in 1969. In 1992 he graduated from Queen's University and moved to London to pursue a career in advertising at Leo Burnett and HHCL, winning numerous gongs, including a British Television Advertising Award.

He relocated to Edinburgh in 2002 and founded his own ad agency, Newhaven, which quickly became Scotland's Agency of the Year. He has now returned to Bangor to write.

Zane is the author of three successful novels published by Transworld/Black Swan. His debut – *London Irish* – won a WH Smith 'People's Choice' Award, and was followed by *Big Jessie* and *Killer's Guide To Iceland* (a No.1 best seller in that country).

a bit of a letdown.

The Grammar School jaunts were repeated in later years at a haunted schoolhouse in Moffat. I still don't know how some of my classmates managed to get back into the Province, during the Troubles, with bags stuffed full of airguns, fireworks and crossbows. There was enough weaponry on our returning coach to arm another Falklands War.

I lived out my teens in Baylands, an equidistant stroll from the Grammar School, Ballyholme Beach and Bangor Golf Club. My summers were spent on the golf course, sometimes squeezing in 54 holes a day.

Of course, this was back in the Eighties, so I was a junior golfer by day and a New Romantic by night. This double-life often had unhappy consequences. Like the time I dyed burgundy stripes down the sides of my hair and turned up to play in an adult-juvenile tournament with my mother, versus the Lady Captain and her son. Mum was mortified as I arrived at the first tee, looking like a cross between Greg Norman and Limahl from Kajagoogoo. We still whipped them 3&2 but, nearly three decades later, Mum struggles to live with the shame.

She immediately dragged me down to The Vennel to get my hair butchered for £1. In the Eighties I wasn't the only Bangor schoolboy dragged to The Vennel to be sheared. The barber's was regularly populated by sullen-looking teens, heads bowed in resigned readiness, looking like we'd just been conscripted.

Zane on O-Level results day in 1985 at Bangor's Wing-Wah. He passed his exams but was forced to resit his hairstyle.

This was the decade that saw the closure of Bangor's Tonic Cinema. Newfangled video recorders had sounded the death knell for this amazing Thirties building, in which generation after generation of Bangor's dedicated cinema-lovers experienced the unfolding drama of chucking fruit pastilles from the circle at those watching from the stalls.

Bangor's Richard Morrow embraced the move to VHS (or was it Betamax?) by opening the town's first video rental shop, famed for its 'Spiders Web' selection of adult films in their unbranded sleeves. Happily, my older sister got a job there, so I had free access to Eighties classics like *Gregory's Girl, The Breakfast Club* and *An American Werewolf In London*.

The Eighties also saw Bangor's seafront undergo an irreversible 'facelift'. It was very considerate of the local Council to commission the building of a marina designed to accommodate hundreds of teenage drinkers… and at the very time I discovered alcohol.

It was also philanthropic of Abbey Wines to cross-promote by selling out-of-date Lamot Pils to Bangor's under-age drinkers for 20p a tin. Most of us owned fake ID crudely fashioned from Letraset (Photoshop hadn't been invented then), but any kid could get served at Abbey Wines if they concealed their head in a crash helmet or stroked their chin for imagined 'stubble'.

A Saturday night in 1985. From left: Steven Emerson, Valerie Duncan, Zane Radcliffe, Stuart Dodds and Garry Sanderson. Stuart has since made a full recovery.

BGS schoolboys didn't even attempt to conceal their age when buying 'single' fags from a sweetie jar in The Hilltop on High Street.

As schoolboys our social lives revolved around the house parties we gatecrashed, or nights out at The Coachman's (Rathgael Road), Whispers (Groomsport… '2 for 1 on Bezique') and the Co-Op Hall (now Asda's petrol station). The Girls' High also did its bit to up the teenage pregnancy rate by inviting us to the occasional disco.

Those nights were funded by my Saturday job working for Drew Davidson and family at the Carlton coffee shop.

The Carlton comprised a bakery and café on the corner of High Street and Albert Street. Like Cinderella, I was confined to the kitchen, washing dishes.

I did once have the privilege of being allowed into the shop, with mop and bucket in hand, when an inebriated female 'customer' decided to wee-wee on the floor.

I loved playing my C90 compilation tapes in the Carlton's kitchen all day. Music became very important to me in the Eighties, my thirst being quenched by local radio DJ Gerry Lang who had opened his first record shop – Musique – in King Street.

Gerry would stay late at Musique one night a week to do a stocktake of his vinyl. He would allow a few of us in to watch him open up large boxes of the week's newly-released 12 inches, letting us hear tracks before they officially went on sale.

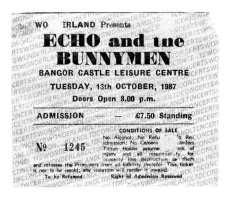

Liverpool band Echo and the Bunnymen were scheduled to appear at the Bangor Castle Leisure Centre on Tuesday 13 October 1987 – as indicated on this ticket, supplied by *Bangor in the Eighties* contributor Zane Radcliffe. There was great disappointment among local fans when the entire UK and Irish tour was cancelled at the last minute because one of the band members was sick. The local leg was rescheduled, but with a change of venue to the King's Hall in Belfast on 18 January 1988. Tickets for the Bangor concert remained valid so perhaps Zane's has some rarity value.

We felt like we were the first kids in the UK to hear the latest LPs by Talk Talk, Scritti Politti, Japan, Cocteau Twins, The Jesus & Mary Chain, Bauhaus and countless others. He introduced us to so many new bands and fresh sounds, and I still find today that it is these albums and the associated memories I return to most frequently on my iPod.

With the invention of CDs, Gerry expanded and relocated his shop to Main Street, renaming it Harrison-Musique, replete with new peppermint and pink livery. It was never quite the same. And if anyone out there has one of the original black and red Musique carrier bags, I will pay good money for it.

When The Rock Shop opened in Bangor, selling cheap guitars and tiny but affordable amps, half of Bangor's teens were inspired to form bands. Some were pretty good. I still fondly remember the last day of term double-header gig at BGS featuring The Pelican Daughters (Darryl Flanagan, Phil McDonough, Gordy Reid, Roger Brown and CJ McDaid) and Watergate (Rob Copeland, Andrew Armstrong, Tom McIlwaine, Andrew Williamson, Keith Roberts and Steven Emerson).

Steven also helped me launch a fanzine for Bangor FC, entitled *Now with Wings*. We had been inspired to create it by our experience a few years earlier selling Colin Bateman's *County Down Magazine* door-to-door. Colin gave us 10p for every copy we sold, but after months of having doors slammed in our faces, from Beverley Gardens to Dorothy Avenue (yes, they still sound like porn stars), we decided we wanted a bigger slice of the publishing pie, and *Now with Wings* was born.

The first issue caused a bit of a stir with its heady mix of potty-mouthed *Viz*-style humour and unapologetic Ards-baiting. The club was forced to issue a statement in the *Spectator* distancing itself from any involvement with the fanzine. This didn't stop the directors from slyly slipping us £1 on match days and scuttling away with their sheepskin collars up, caps down and a fanzine hidden from view inside a less offensive publication, like *Razzle*.

By then the Eighties was over and I had graduated from adolescence in Bangor to student life in Belfast. I had also graduated from New Romantic to Goth. I would still return home most weekends, largely so

Zane pictured with sons Arlo and Ferris on Father's Day, 2011

my mum could do my washing. Her machine was good with blacks.

On Friday nights Bangor's exiles would arrive home on the last train from Botanic and spill into the Matinee Club at Bangor Station, partying until the sun came up. But when the club closed its doors for the last time there was little to lure me back to the seaside, other than Bangor FC's victorious Irish Cup run and the occasional European glamour tie (I still have my Apoel Nicosia ticket).

It's taken 23 years for me to finally settle back home. When my sons – Arlo and Ferris – came along, I reflected on my own youth in Eighties Bangor and could imagine no better place for the boys to grow up. Sure, all the best sweetie shops have disappeared – Brucie's, Dalglish's, Pollocks, Wright's, See-Sea House – but Bangor still has plenty to offer them.

Who knows, maybe one day my boys will form their own band, as I once did in a garage in Sheridan Drive. Maybe they'll start a fanzine, meet their first love or nick burgundy hair dye from Boots. Whatever they do, I hope they'll have as happy a time as I did in Bangor in the Eighties.

1988

IN THE SPECTATOR

Plans were announced at the end of January for the £8.5m two-storey Flagship Centre with 35 stores and associated car parking on the gasworks site off High Street.

The Council conceded defeat over the 'Ulster Says No' banner and removed it from the roof of the Bangor Castle Leisure Centre at the end of January. It was relocated inside Hamilton House where it could be seen in the windows.

Pictured at a press conference held in Bangor Town Hall in March 1988 to announce the awarding of the contract for the new Flagship Centre on the gasworks site are (from left): John Thompson, North Down Borough Council's development officer; Kevin Milhench of Milhench Crothers (commercial property letting specialists), Mayor Bruce Mulligan and Joe McIntyre, developer. 230-9-36

Ulster Unionist Leslie Cree had a convincing win in an early February by-election in the Ballyholme and Groomsport ward. It arose following the death of Cllr Sam Hamilton, one of the elected representatives expelled from the party for supporting a return to business following the campaign against the Anglo-Irish Agreement.

Mr Cree, the official party candidate, secured 1,151 first preference votes, well ahead of second-placed candidate Sylvia Anderson (Alliance) with 711, while Robert Lyle (Real Unionist/ Campaign for Equal Citizenship) and Muriel Stringer (Unionist) received 637 and 491 votes respectively.

A Book of Condolences from the people of North Down was sent in March to the Royal Signals Regiment following the murder of two corporals in Andersonstown the previous month. Members of the public were able to sign the book at a Borough Council caravan in Main Street.

Northern Ireland's Coastguard applied to North Down Borough Council in April for permission to move from Orlock to a hi-tech complex based in the new administration buildings at the nearly completed Bangor Marina.

The new wheelie bin service came into operation on Monday 9 May, with 10,600 of the new bins being delivered to local homes in advance of the launch date.

Crystals Arena staff were paid off, the ice was melted and the doors to the sports complex were locked on 13 May, with management indicating that repairs were necessary in preparation for a major relaunch in two months' time. A statement from Plimley Leisure said it was traditionally quiet during the summer and former workers would be considered for re-employment when the premises reopened.

Glen Dimplex announced a major expansion for its Glen Mouldings operation at the Balloo Industrial Estate. Poised for a major breakthrough in the coffee filter machine market, the company hoped to create 68 new jobs in Bangor while doubling the size of the factory.

Environment Minister Richard Needham, responding to the Council's four-year-old quest for bye-laws to curb alcohol consumption in public places, said a full drinking ban relating to all Council-owned properties was unlikely for the time being.

As an interim measure the local authority introduced its own ban on all beverages, alcoholic or otherwise, at the North Breakwater. This was enforced by private security staff.

Sharp Holdings Ltd., a Northern Ireland development company, indicated in early June it was negotiating for several properties along Queen's Parade and that "hotels" would be part of its building programme.

History was made at St Comgall's Church, Brunswick Road, on Sunday 19 June when Colum Conway (26), from Princetown Road, became the first Catholic priest to be ordained in Bangor in modern times.

The grounds were bedecked in yellow and white papal flags for the ordination service, which was celebrated by Most Rev. Patrick Walsh, Auxiliary Bishop of Down and Connor.

Following discussions between the South Eastern Education and Library Board and the boards of governors of local schools regarding the future of secondary education for girls in the Bangor area, the go-ahead was given in late June for Glenlola Collegiate to move to a site behind Crystals Arena.

The future of Crystals Arena was becoming clearer, Councillors heard in August. The plan was to reopen the complex early in the New Year following a £163,000 face lift, including the provision of 400 seats for ice rink spectators. It would be run as before, as an ice rink and indoor bowling centre, but by a management company with the cost of the £1.5m complex going on the rates.

Deborah Ferguson (22), of Silverstream Drive, was the first deaf person from Bangor to volunteer her services as a full-time missionary for the Church of Jesus Christ of Latter-Day Saints. She took up a post in Coventry in early August following a training period in London.

The Troubles impacted on Bangor once again with the murder, in Belfast on 22 August, of Royal Navy Lieutenant Alan Shields, from the Ballycrochan area of the town. He was returning home from the Royal Naval Recruiting Office in Howard Street when his car blew up just after he had passed over the Queen's Bridge.

Scottish-born, Lt Shields (44) had returned to Northern Ireland to take up

his new post as head of the recruiting office at the beginning of the year after living in England for several years.

It was the first murder of a Royal Navy officer during the Troubles in Northern Ireland. The funeral service took place in Scotland nine days after Lt Shields' murder.

NORTH DOWN BOROUGH COUNCIL

SATURDAY NIGHT

DISCO

FOR 14—18 YEAR OLDS
at
BANGOR CASTLE LEISURE CENTRE
(Capacity 200)
commencing
SATURDAY, 17th SEPTEMBER, 8 p.m.
ENTRANCE FEE £1.50
*COME ALONG AND ENJOY A
NON-ALCOHOL DISCO UNTIL 11 p.m.*
Run by Recreation & Community Development Department

A new Youth Provision Sub-Committee was formed by the Borough Council, tasked with combating the growing trend of under-age drinking in Bangor. Chaired by Cllr Jane Copeland, one of the first actions was to organise weekly Saturday night discos for 14-18 year-olds in the Bangor Castle Leisure Centre, beginning on 17 September.

Councillors approved expenditure of £250,000 in early November to infill an area in front of Queen's Parade for temporary (later permanent) car parking in time for the opening of the marina's first 300 berths in April 1989.

The new civic amenity site at Rathgael Road, purpose-built at a cost of £150,000, was officially opened in November by Alderman Gordon Dunne, chairman of the Council's Technical Services Committee. It replaced the former town dump at Valentine Road.

Charles Brand Ltd. was awarded the £3m contract to complete the final stage of the Bangor seafront development. The work included infills between the North and Central Piers for boat repair and storage purposes and between the Central and South Piers for harbour car parking and the administration area. Over £800,000 was included for the building of pontoons by a sub-contractor.

At a meeting in December of Glenlola Collegiate Debating Society members voted by nine to six with three abstentions to support the motion: 'This House believes Margaret Thatcher's student loans are great!'

Proposers Alison Crozier and Barbara Anderson argued that the loans scheme, as proposed by the Prime Minister, would decrease dependency on parents and "make the student regard money management and higher education more seriously". Opponents viewed the loans as a purely economic matter which would not improve the standard of education.

A murder bid on an RUC Superintendent at his Kensington Park home on 27 December left neighbours deeply shocked although thankfully no one was injured.

The attack was the first terrorist activity over the holidays anywhere in Northern Ireland. The culprits planted a bomb underneath the senior officer's parked car. The vehicle caught fire after the resulting explosion and the force of the blast also smashed windows in nearby homes.

Margaret Reid, of Bexley Road, shows the letter she received from America's First Lady, Nancy Reagan, at the beginning of 1988 after sending her a 'get well' card when she (Mrs Reagan) went into hospital for a mastectomy. It was a short letter expressing the First Lady's thanks for the concern Mrs Reid had shown. *284-10-35*

Bangor couple Joe and Margaret Lonsdale cut the cake to celebrate their golden wedding anniversary. Married in Belfast at the end of December 1937, they had two daughters and four grandchildren. *268-5-35*

Some of the boys and girls who attended the College Playgroup, which met at the Castle Park Hall on the Valentine Road, in January 1988. Back (from left): James Clark, Conall Wolsey. Front: Aimee McAlister, Jonathan Hope and Helen Young. *329-18-35*

P1, P2 and P3 children from the Glenlola Preparatory Department who performed their play *The Magic Wishing Well* in January 1988. *359-18-35*

Seven-year-old Clare McCaughey, from Victoria Road, became the youngest contributor yet to George Jones' programme on Radio Ulster when she took to the airwaves on 31 January 1988. The Bangor Central Primary School pupil told listeners what would be happening throughout North Down during the following week. *385-4-35*

Julia Williamson from Fifth Bangor Brownies presents a cheque for £50 to Kelly and Helen Brown towards a portable ultrasonic scanner for the Royal Victoria Hospital for Sick Children. The children collected the donation by saving their pocket money for three months. Included is Brownie leader Marjorie Irvine. *351-15-35*

Red Nose fever gripped North Down in early 1988 as the UK-wide Comic Relief fundraising initiative, launched three years earlier, began to seize the public's imagination in a big way. Children from the Salvation Army Playgroup in Bangor wore fancy dress to raise money for Comic Relief that February. *425-5A-35*

Brigaders from Trinity Girls' Brigade who won their section in the Northern Ireland PE finals at Hamilton House in February 1988. Back (from left): Shirley Lovell, Debbie Jones, Louise Watson, Amanda Stringer. Middle: Tina Campbell, Susan Smith. Front: Paula Burrowes and Audrey Gillespie. *19-11-36*

Caroline Reynolds from Bangor with terrier Buttons, winner of overall and best dog prizes at a fun dog show organised by the Groomsport Village Youth Club in May 1988. *412-10-36*

Fourth Bangor Beaver Colony, winners of the John R. Patterson Memorial Trophy as runners-up in the Bangor and District Beaver Scout sports in May 1988. *384-19-36*

Children from Towerview Primary School pictured in May 1988 prior to their annual display for parents and friends. *68-5-37*

Members of 10th and 11th Bangor Boys' Brigade who took part in the Mayor's Parade, held as part of Bangor's Expo '88, in June 1988. The boys were awarded first prize in the under-16 section of the float competition. *364-4-37*

Vicky Hayes, Guide captain at Eighth Bangor (St Columbanus) for the previous eight years, was presented with a glass bowl by the Guides to mark her departure for England in June 1988. Her successor was Delores Noble. *355-4-37*

The Trustee Savings Bank branch on the Groomsport Road was targeted by thieves using a JCB earth-mover in August 1988. They used the vehicle to smash down the front of the building and the cash machine was then placed on the back of a pick-up truck which headed in the Donaghadee direction. It was believed the culprits made off with approx. £2,000. *103-9-38*

Radio Ulster's Gerry Anderson paid a visit to the Bangor Shipyard on the Seacliff Road as part of his *Detour Show* in early August 1988. There he met Elias Scott who was celebrating his 70th birthday and who was the delighted recipient of a card and cake from Rosemary McClenaghan on behalf of the employees. *134-18A-38*

Representatives of the locally-based Love Uganda charity project met North Down Mayor Donald Hayes and his wife Mary on 4 August 1988, prior to their departure for three weeks' work in an orphan village in the Luwero Triangle area north of Kampala. Among the party travelling to Uganda was *Spectator* reporter Colin Bateman (second from right). *125-6-38*

New P1 pupils in Betty Cumper's class at Ballyholme Primary School in September 1988. *389-18-38*

New P1 pupils at St Malachy's Primary School in September 1988. *379-19A-38*

Joanne Kennedy, Kelly Williams, Leann Hart, Pamela Hart, Karen Littlewood and Ross Williams, all pupils at Clandeboye Road Primary School, held a street sale at Silverstream Avenue in September 1988 to raise money for Cancer Research. They are pictured handing over a cheque for £52 to Bangor branch chairman Joy Rothwell. *348-6-38*

Pupils from Central Primary School held a sponsored one-day silence in September 1988 to raise money for the local Love Uganda charity and other good causes relating to the plight of people in Bangladesh. *472-23-38*

Members of Bangor Harmonic Society, who met each week in the minor hall of Wesley Centenary Methodist Church, are pictured in October 1988. They presented Haydn's *Creation* to local audiences that December. *486-24-38*

Olympic bronze and gold medal winner Stephen Martin gave a talk to P7 children at Central Primary School in October 1988. *46-12-39*

Members of the First Bangor Scout Group celebrated their 80th anniversary by holding one of their weekly meetings at the town's Heritage Centre in October 1988. There was a display featuring Scouting memorabilia dating back to 1908. *87-10-39*

Children from the Bangor Tumbletots group at their Hallowe'en party at the end of October 1988. *163-11A-39*

Brownies from the Bangor Division of the Girl Guides are pictured with Santa at their annual fundraising sale in November 1988. *185-15-39*

Members of the Bangor Oxfam *Hungry for Change* group fasted for 50 hours in November 1988 to highlight the plight of people living in Kampuchea (formerly Cambodia). Although it was one of the poorest countries in the world, it received no overseas aid from any countries in the West. *175-2A-39*

Centenarian Florence Lemon is pictured with family members on 17 November 1988. Born in Crawfordsburn, Mrs Lemon spent part of her married life residing in the *Spectator* buildings at Main Street where her daughter Betty (Warden) was born. *251-10A-39*

Bangor man Thomas Martin had not had his hair cut for seven years – that was until the BBC staged its annual Children in Need appeal in November 1988. Thomas agreed it was a good cause and, hoping to raise £150 in the process, left himself in the capable hands of (from left): Laura Inglis, owner of Hairways, with assistants Jacqui Bothwell and Julie Simpson. 255-5A-39

Cup winners at the annual St Columbanus' High School prize day in November 1988. Included are: Aileen McClean, Eileen Geddis, M. J. McWilliams, Fiona McVeigh, Claire McKenna, Roisin Gavin, Michael Rollo, Damian Mullan, Amanda Kearney, Derek McLaughlin, Ciara McGlinchey, Colleen McGrogan and Carena Lennon. 325-9A-39

Fifth Bangor Guides with Christmas hampers they collected in December 1988 to distribute among elderly members of Wesley Centenary Methodist Church. 411-13A-39

Pete Snodden
remembers...

Bangor is my home town; it is where I live today and where I grew up. Born in June 1980, I was raised by my parents Irene and Jackie at Dellmount Drive, just off the Gransha Road. Our house then was the last in the street, followed by wasteland and beyond that the 13th hole at Bangor Golf Club.

By the time I was six my dad had put a club in my hand, but unlike Rory McIlroy I was not to make golf my career. Looking back I do regret not spending more time on the course as a child – my swing would certainly be a lot different now if I had!

I have so many fond memories of those times: warm summer days spent walking round to Pickie Pool, having an ice cream on the seafront, or going into the Co-Op on Main Street where the Flagship Centre is now.

Dad has worked all his life whereas Mum stopped when I was born and only returned to work once I was 14. As she never drove a car, I remember either being pushed in a pram or walking everywhere when I was very young. My mum couldn't walk more than a few yards without bumping into someone she knew.

In the Eighties there was no one-way system and traffic

Pete Snodden (centre) with Mark Feehily and Shane Filan from Westlife

Starting as a DJ during his university years, Bangor-born Pete Snodden joined Cool FM after graduating and it wasn't long before he was given his own breakfast show, combining his two passions of music and presenting.

This role has seen him at the helm of the most listened to commercial radio show in Northern Ireland for eight successful years, during which he has won two prestigious awards – Media Personality of the Year at the 2008 FATE Awards and Media Personality of the Year at the GO Awards for 2009.

In addition, Pete was also shortlisted as a finalist at the 2008 *Ulster Tatler* People of the Year Awards in the category of Celebrity of the Year, but was pipped to the post by actor Jimmy Nesbitt.

Pete's belief is that the listener should feel part of the show and, with that in mind, he gives listeners the stage to share their funny stories and take part in the varying topics of conversation every morning; but Pete's fun and charming personality leads the show and his listener banter, as well as interviews with many famous faces – from Noel Gallagher to Louis Walsh and Leona Lewis to Cheryl Cole – contribute to his excellent audience figures.

Pete's first day at Bangor's Central Primary School

flowed in both directions up and down Main Street and High Street and along Bridge Street. The shops were always packed and in order to be able to see anything I always insisted on being carried on Dad's shoulders. Away from the town centre, my parents and I frequented the Clandeboye Shopping Centre. Stewarts was the main supermarket and I always remember the packing area, which was located outside the store. I would ride inside the trolley as my mum pushed it around the aisles and then, having paid for the goods, you would pack them in the mixture of boxes and plastic bags left for that purpose by the staff.

Whilst Mum was shopping I happily checked out the toys – and in particular the Star Wars figures – in Stewart Millers, on the opposite side of the shopping centre from Stewarts. On the top floor I was introduced at a young age to the '50p Shop'. It was there I discovered gel for my hair and a chain for my bike – although I quickly learned that not everything cost 50p!

As we lived just off the Gransha Road I had easy access to Ward Park where Mum and Dad would take me for walks. It was also where I got to kick a football around and discovered my love for the game. In the Eighties Liverpool were 'the' team and as my friends' brothers supported them, they soon became my team too. As I was an only child, friends were very important in my world, including the large number who lived close by and who attended my primary school, Bangor Central.

Towards the end of the Eighties we were allowed to cycle to the park on our own; once there we would climb on the cannon or play squash using a tennis racket and ball off the back wall of the tennis pavilion. This was a great game until the point you hit the ball onto the pavilion roof. I well remember one of my friends squeezing himself through the security gate at the side of the building and then heading up the stairs onto the roof from where he would throw down a horde of tennis balls that had been hit up there by other kids.

Jumping over the river was another regular pastime. We would work our way along to the largest gap, which was down towards the children's play area. I still remember my first attempt – it was at the point of the river that is now covered over on the Gransha Road side of the park, up from the tennis courts towards the car park. Let's just say there was quite a drop, jumping from one side to the other, and although I made the jump I slipped back into the water. Tears ensued as I feared what my parents would say.

From the age of about seven BMX bikes were our preferred mode of transport. *BMX Bandits* had been released and what fun and excitement there was when the Council built a BMX track at the Valentine Playing Fields. I remember going there with Dad the day it opened and not being able to build up enough speed to get over the humps!

Another local hub of social activity was the Gransha Stores. A proper 'old school' shop where you could get just about anything, I would be sent there on errands to pick up everything from batteries to tights for my mum, and from Oxo cubes to a 10p mix. Once there was a power cut in the area and we all – children and parents alike –packed into the Gransha Stores in the pitch black, splitting what candles they had in stock between us.

During the day we would kick a football off the shop wall or play on our bikes as my friends' older brothers would turn up at the shop for a can of Top Deck or Shandy Bass and a single cigarette which they sold for 10p. Tudor Spring Onion, KP Prawn Cocktail and Tayto Cheese and Onion were my crisps of choice back then, costing between 10 and 18p a packet… bargain!

Thinking back to the Eighties I have such fond memories of Christmas – going to see Santa in the Co-Op and at Stewarts, but especially the street market on the Friday night before Christmas. Main Street would be closed to cars and market stalls would line the street, from the Northern Bank right down to Bridge Street. It was a hive of activity and to me symbolised the closeness of a visit from Santa.

With the Tonic closed and all but derelict, we had nowhere to watch a film until late into the decade. Then

Outside the breakfast show, Pete also hosts Cool FM's Saturday night dance music show *The Source*, which won the Most Informative Media award at the 2006 NI Dance Music Awards. He has also made a number of TV appearances, presenting the entertainment slot on *UTV Life* and appearing as a panellist on UTV's *Late And Live* programme, as well as *The Seven Thirty Show*.

In addition, he has taken part in the BBC's *Panic Attack Celebrity Christmas Special*, *Children in Need* and warmed up for *The Friday Show* on BBC1.

He does occasionally get away from the station to go to the pub, play football or a round of golf and host high profile events such as The Magners Light Style Awards, Pepsi Sexiest Man, Red Bull Soap Box Race, Sports Relief and the St Patrick's Day celebrations in Belfast.

Pete juggles all these commitments and events to stand proud as an ambassador for the Unite Against Hate Campaign and The Prince's Trust.

He met his future wife Julia, from Carrickfergus, whilst studying at the University of Ulster in Coleraine and they were married in 2007. Daughter Ivana Shannon Snodden was born in February 2011.

Music was in his blood from an early age – Pete is pictured with his first ghetto blaster!

on a Saturday afternoon a small cinema was introduced in Hamilton House, where my friends and I would watch such children's classics as *Bedknobs And Broomsticks* and *Herbie*. The Leisure Centre was another centre of our world – it was where I learnt to swim and eventually could go with my friends on our own. Straight after the swim it would be upstairs to the café for sausages and chips. How wrong was that!

At the tail end of the Eighties the Bangor Cineplex Icebowl opened its doors. The former Crystals Arena had been transformed and suddenly the landscape of growing up in Bangor changed forever. We had an ice rink with ice that didn't melt, 10-pin bowling and a proper cinema. The kids of Bangor had arrived, and in style – in their trainers and high top boots with the tongues out.

I can't close without returning to the place where I spent most of my life in the Eighties, namely Bangor Central Primary School. During seven years of learning that I thoroughly enjoyed I played on every team going and even sang in the school choir. It was football at lunchtime from P5 onwards, plus tig and conkers. I was actually the school conkers champion back in 1989. As the new marina in the town was unveiled three of us had the great honour of being chosen to have our picture taken for the DoE road safety calendar featuring 'Ginger'. There we were pointing at Ginger, who didn't actually exist but was placed into the photograph afterwards.

It was at Bangor Central that I first developed my love for DJ-ing after my P6 teacher, Richard Hazley, introduced me

The family home at Dellmount Drive

to his Cloud turntables. A few friends and I played the music at the back of the assembly hall during school fetes and we even got to broadcast from the classroom store to the rest of our class on a Friday afternoon. It was then I knew I wanted to be a radio presenter.

Bangor, as it still is today, was a great town to grow up in during the Eighties. I can honestly look back fondly at my childhood and it brings a huge smile to my face.

1989
IN THE SPECTATOR

There were hopes that up to 250 jobs could be created in the town centre with the news that, nearly 10 months after winning the right to develop the gasworks site, the Bangor Flagship Development Company had submitted an outline planning application. It envisaged a two-level shopping centre with restaurant, multi-storey car park and multi-screen cinema complex.

Several Bangor people were among the injured in the British Midland air crash at Kegworth on Sunday 8 January, in which 47 people on a flight from Heathrow to Belfast International were killed and many others were hurt.

Gilmore (Gillie) and Vivienne Stevenson, from Gransha Road, had travelled separately to London as Mr Stevenson was doing the final part of an Open College examination on the previous Friday. His wife had gone over the next day because they wanted to attend the London Boat Show. Mr Stevenson was one of the first victims to meet Prime Minister Margaret Thatcher when she visited Derby Royal Infirmary where many of the injured were being treated.

Another survivor was Chris Thompson, of Towerview, who was also returning from the London Boat Show. Both his legs were badly broken in the crash. Bangor couple David and Sonya Seaton also survived the crash but were among the injured.

Three of the expelled Ulster Unionist members of North Down Borough Council, Alderman Bruce Mulligan, Alderman George Green and Cllr Jack Preston, joined the North Down Conservative Association. They argued that membership did not mean they had to support Conservative Party policy, which included the Anglo-Irish Agreement.

It was revealed in mid-January that the harbour rowing boats, part of Bangor's maritime heritage, would disappear when the new marina opened. Council official Ken Gillen told a meeting of the Cockle Island Boat Club in Groomsport: "The rowing boats are incompatible with the operation of harbour security and there is also a danger to the rowing boat users themselves through getting in the way of commercial traffic and bigger pleasure boats."

Plans for a second major shopping development and cinema complex, covering a 27-acre site off the ring road at Bloomfield, were lodged in late February by Scottish company SIBEC. A separate 17-acre 'roof rack' (DIY) shopping development was proposed by the same company for the vacant 17-acre site formerly occupied by the Clandeboye Shopping Centre.

Plans for an arts centre, including a 300-400 seat theatre, at Home Farm in Castle Park, were being considered by the Council. The projected cost was between £700,000 and £800,000. It was not seen as an immediate priority as the scheme would not attract European funding.

The Better Bangor Campaign, a new group formed by concerned ratepayers, said it intended to sponsor candidates at the forthcoming Council elections. It wanted to challenge established political parties with a view to "introducing a more open form of local government" through the election of "non-party political" public representatives.

The first two candidates, named in late February, were local businesswoman and former *Spectator* Deputy Editor Ann-Marie Hillen and High Street trader Colin Simpson.

Crystals Arena was placed on the market for sale or rent in early March – with early offers falling well short of the £1.5m it had cost to build. Rental offers did not exceed £60,000 a year (one-third of the amount it was still costing the Council).

The 32-bed Gransha Private Clinic,

the district's first private nursing home, was officially opened in April. Built for £1.5m, it had its own X-Ray machine, a doctor on site 24 hours a day, laundry and catering facilities, as well as an operating theatre with £350,000 ventilation system which, the owners stated, could undertake open heart surgery.

Award-winning butcher David Burns was appointed president of the Northern Ireland Master Butchers Association in April – the first time the honour had come to a business in the town.

The final two phases (of four) of the Visitors and Heritage Centre were completed at a cost of £410,000, heralding the end of the five-year building programme. The official opening was performed on 17 April by Mayor Donald Hayes. The new section of the £1m project focused on the Coastal Path and boasted various

displays, an audio-visual facility, a lecture theatre for schools, an auditorium and extensive kitchens to enable a restaurant franchise to be operated during the summer months. A highlight was the mural of the shoreline from Groomsport to Ballyholme painted by local artist Gary Devon.

Mayor Donald Hayes officially opened Bangor Marina on 28 April, saying he hoped it marked a turning point in the town's economic development. He poured fresh water from Lake Constance, presented by representatives from twin town Bregenz, into the salty waters of the new marina. It was announced that the administration building would be known as Bregenz House.

North Down Mayor Donald Hayes speaks at the opening of the Bangor Marina on 28 April 1989. 157-9A-41

Crystals Arena was sold to Regal Theatres, operators of the Strand Cinema in Belfast, in one of the last acts of the outgoing Council, with Regal agreeing to pay the authority £1.2m over the next decade. Regal said they planned to carry out a £1m programme to convert the complex into a four-screen cinema, 16-lane 10-pin bowling alley, café/restaurant, teenage disco and snooker hall. It was also their intention to retain the ice rink.

The opening of Home-Start House at Castle Street in early May marked a new phase for the charity which acted as a befriending agency for young families under stress.

The Borough Council faced major changes following the May local government elections in which 50 candidates stood for its 24 seats – 12 Ulster Unionists, 11 North Down Conservatives, 10 Alliance, nine DUP, two Popular Unionists, two Better Bangor Campaigners, two Progressive Unionists, one Independent Unionist and one Independent.

Few would have predicted the Conservatives would emerge as the largest single party with six seats. The Ulster Unionists lost three seats, leaving the party with five representatives, while Alliance lost three, leaving it with four, and the DUP lost two seats, leaving it with four.

Mayor Donald Hayes (Alliance) lost his seat, while former East Belfast Assembly member Denny Vitty was among the winners. The Popular Unionists still had two Councillors, while Ann-Marie Hillen won a seat for the Better Bangor Campaign. In addition there was one Independent Unionist and one Independent. Successful candidates were as follows:

Ballyholme and Groomsport – Leslie Cree (UUP), Bruce Mulligan (Conservative), Jane Copeland (Alliance), Ivan Thompson (Conservative), Alan Leslie (DUP), Eddie Mills (Independent Unionist).

IT'S TIME
ULSTER SAID
YES!

To: ECUAL rights with the other citizens of the United Kingdom, so that we too can have a say in how our country is governed.

To: BETTER value for money from a more efficient council, with increased powers in line with those in England, Scotland and Wales.

To: NON-SECTARIAN politics, with people being judged on their ability and not their religion

ON MAY 17th & 31st

VOTE CONSERVATIVE
FOR A REAL FUTURE

Abbey – Valerie Kinghan (UPUP), Cecil Braniff (UPUP), George Green (Conservative), Albert Magee (Alliance), Denny Vitty (DUP), Irene Cree (UUP).

Bangor West – Hazel Bradford (Ulster Unionist), Brian Wilson (Alliance), Bill Baxter (DUP), Ann-Marie Hillen (Better Bangor Campaign), Tom Miskelly (Conservative), James O'Fee (Conservative), Roy Bradford (Ulster Unionist).

Holywood – Laurence Kennedy (Conservative), Ellie McKay (UUP), Dennis Ogborn (Independent), Gordon Dunne (DUP), Susan O'Brien (Alliance).

The Mayoral election resulted in a 7-7 tie between Hazel Bradford and Ivan Thompson, with Donald Hayes (who retained the position until his successor was appointed) declining to use his casting vote as he was "not an elected member". As a result the position was held, uniquely, by Cllrs Bradford and Thompson for six months each. George Green was the new Deputy Mayor.

The 'bring-a-bottle' Matinee Club at the forecourt of Bangor Railway Station was badly damaged by an accidental fire on 12 June. Six firemen wearing breathing apparatus used five hose reel jets to bring the blaze under control.

The week-long Bangor and North Down Festival replaced the annual Youth Expo and got under way on 16 June with the selection of Glenlola A-Level student Carol Stringer, from Ward Avenue, as Miss Bangor. Other highlights included a Superstars event at the Bangor Castle Leisure Centre, where the stars included Stephen Martin, Mike Bull and Norman Whiteside, water sports and a fireworks display.

A £2.5m investment by Denroy Plastics in late June promised 70 new jobs at their Balloo Industrial Estate factory over the following three years. The expansion was largely due to a contract with South Korean firm Daewoo which made video recorders in Antrim. Denroy already employed 200 people at two locations in Bangor.

Four-year-old Gemma Marshall as Bo-Peep at Trinity Nursery School's end of term fancy dress party in June 1989. 581-7-41

Philip McCartan, of Dufferin Villas, risked his life on 19 July to save an elderly woman who had fallen into the sea near Seacourt Lane.

Ballyholme residents enlisted MP Jim Kilfedder's support in their fight against a three-storey apartment development for the Fold Housing Trust at Lyle Road. They did not oppose the scheme but felt it should be limited to two storeys. The residents' campaign proved successful.

Up to 150 new jobs were promised within a year through the expansion of the North Down Development Organisation at Balloo Avenue. Combined with the existing site at Enterprise House, it was hoped as many as 100 small businesses would be employing over 300 people.

Secretary of State Peter Brooke visited Bangor on 18 September to mark the beginning of work on the conversion, at a cost of £1.75m, of the former Savoy Hotel into 55 self-contained flats for the Royal British Legion Housing Association.

Two-year-old Karate Kid Robert Emerson joined in the fun at a fundraising raft race held in late August at Ballyholme. He was cheering on a raft entered by the Bangor Shotokan Karate Club. 106-18A-42

Traders in Bangor, Newtownards and Holywood joined forces to oppose a shopping centre at Bloomfield. Their respective Chambers of Trade decided to combine their legal representation at the forthcoming public enquiry (17 October) in an effort to see off what they described as a "devastating threat to the commercial lives of the three towns".

Bangor Amateur Operatic Society urged the Council to help save the Little Theatre, which was being put up for sale for around £150,000. The Council, in turning down an offer of first refusal, preferred the Home Farm option from earlier in the year.

Bangor Drama Club viewed any purchase of the Little Theatre as a short-term measure that would threaten the provision of a theatre/ arts centre for the town. The club indicated its willingness, as far as possible, to share its facilities with the Operatic Society during any interim period.

The South Eastern Education and Library Board gave the go-ahead for the sale of the Seacourt Teacher Training Centre off the Princetown Road. The move was opposed by the Better Bangor Campaign. It suggested trading the former Forsythe's Nursery site, which the SEELB wanted for a new school, for Seacourt which could then be used as a maritime museum or arts centre.

Councillors were advised on 18 October that the impending closure of Crawfordsburn Hospital, which they wanted to discuss with the Eastern Health Board, was no longer a proposal but a matter of fact. However, the closure would not occur until the 77 patients were satisfactorily placed elsewhere.

The introduction of the long-awaited bye-law banning the consumption of alcohol in designated parts of Bangor was delayed until February 1990 for legal reasons.

Councillors voted unanimously against any compulsory vesting of properties along lower High Street and Bridge Street to make way for the new Flagship Centre. Traders had voiced concern they would lose their businesses and it would be impossible to find alternative sites.

The town's new four-screen cinema, offering 700 seats and representing the first phase of the Bangor Cineplex Icebowl development at the Crystals Arena site, opened on 15 December. The first films shown were *Ghostbusters 2, Shirley Valentine, Back To The Future 2* and *Roadhouse.* The 16-lane bowling alley and ice rink opened in January 1990.

A £3.5m tourism grant in mid-December from the European Regional Development Fund, the second largest of its kind ever given in Northern Ireland, meant the Council could complete the marina scheme with various tourist attractions and amenities, including the 'family fun park' that would ultimately replace Pickie Pool.

Marks and Spencer announced plans to open a food store in Bangor as part of a Province-wide expansion programme that would create 400 jobs. The company indicated it would occupy a 16,000 sq. ft. site in the new Bloomfield Shopping Centre – even though the outcome of the planning inquiry would not be known until the New Year.

When it's finished, Bangor is going to be rather nice. Two or three shopping centres, a four-screen cinema, ice rink, landscaped marina, 10-pin bowling, new fire station – the list of facilities is getting to be endless. Or perhaps that should read, if Bangor gets finished, for there seem to be as many complaints about future plans for the Borough as there are people.

Everyone has an opinion on everything and at the moment it is our local traders' organisations that are getting shirty about the prospect of a new shopping centre on the edge of town, at Bloomfield. North Down Borough Council, with its finger in the pie of the new downtown Flagship Centre, would presumably be against the development.

It is difficult, however, to see why both the Flagship and Bloomfield projects cannot come into existence. Indeed, why should either back down just because they can't agree whose is the best idea?

One tends to forget Bangor had two shopping centres on the edge of town only a couple of years ago. Before the Clandeboye Shopping Centre burned down it provided a first-class service without noticeably detracting from the town centre trading community; by their very nature small shops do tend to come and go; laying all the blame on out-of-towners is not quite fair. The influx of shoppers such a centre (the Flagship) will inevitably bring can do nothing but good for the smaller traders in the town centre.

Bangor is getting very big, very fast, and with developers pouring millions of pounds into a whole range of projects we should be looking optimistically forward to a period of prosperity rather than nit-picking over who might do what, best.

Editorial in the 21 September 1989 edition of the *County Down Spectator*

Children enjoy themselves in January 1989 at the After School Club that was held each Tuesday in the Kilcooley Community Centre. 508-9A-39

Pictured at the opening of Julie Hamilton's Ballet School at Prospect Road in January 1989 are (back, from left): Julie Hamilton, North Down Mayor Donald Hayes, Mary Hayes, North Down MP Jim Kilfedder. Front: Rachel Truesdale, Imogen Clark, Suzanne Maguire and Clare Ablett. 503-8A-39

Girls from the Explorer Section of Trinity GB swept the boards at the annual Ards and District PE Championships in January 1989. Back (from left): Rhonda Mitchell, Jan Craig, Lt. Karen McCready, Lisa Kinney, Victoria Spratt. Front: Andrea Faull, Emma Heaney, Rebecca Kirkpatrick and Kim Gallagher. 84-15A-40

Pupils from Jeanne Cree's Ballet School who appeared in *Cinderella*, along with comedian Jimmy Cricket, at the Grand Opera House in February 1989. *135-13A-40*

Idle Jack (Ricky Armstrong) jumps for cover from Tommy Cat (Emma Sturdy) during the Kilmaine Primary School production of *Dick Whittington* in March 1989. Included are Alice (Catherine Menary), Sara (Ryan Stuart) and Dick Whittington (Melanie Megan). *197-4-40*

March 1989 saw a growing movement in Bangor for the provision of integrated education. This group of parents (and children), meeting under the banner of the Campaign for Children Together, organised regular meetings and launched a petition calling for the provision of a co-educational, all-ability integrated secondary school rather than a new Glenlola Collegiate. Members included Judith Thurley, Ann and Ken Sterrett, Patricia Wallace, Marie Maidment, Mary Lowry and Roberta and Harry Law. *250-8A-40*

After some 43 years of trading at Main Street the doors closed for the final time at the family jewellery business run by Fred and Amy Eakin in March 1989. It had been launched by Fred's late father John in 1946 and a familiar figure in the shop all down the years was his mother Doris (centre), then aged 91. *250-11A-40*

Children from Towerview Primary School who took part in a Peace Day rally hosted in late February 1989 by North Down Mayor Donald Hayes. *246-12A-40*

Children from Central Primary School admire the red-nosed Teddy Bears displayed for Comic Relief Day in the window of Robert Neill and Sons at Main Street. They include Nadine Ramsey, Susan Scott, Kerry Hicks, Kelly Dalzell, Rhonda King, Caroline Adams and Claire Sterling. *298-8A-40*

Pupils from Rathmore Primary School, winners of the Kenmuir Cup in the Acting Poem class at Bangor Music Festival, held at Hamilton House in March 1989. Included is drama teacher Dawn Murphy. 397-21-40

Girls from Glenlola Collegiate's Upper Sixth enjoyed themselves on their last day in May 1989. Dressed in Denis the Menace outfits they targeted unsuspecting members of staff with "water cannons and shampoo baths". 245-11A-41

Members of Second Bangor Venture Scout Troop who received the Queen's Scout Award, the highest award in Scouting, in May 1989. From left: David Henderson, William Pritchard, William Barclay, Chris Erskine and Simon McWhirter. 284-9-41

Members, leaders and supporters of the Bangor PHAB (Physically Handicapped and Able Bodied) Club celebrated 10 years in Bangor and in Northern Ireland at the end of May 1989. Local leader was Jean Leckey and their base was the Project Bangor headquarters in Dufferin Avenue. *346-0A-41*

Norman Larmour, lollipop man at Glenlola Collegiate for almost a decade, was presented with a school crest to mark his retirement in June 1989. Making the presentation were principal James Hagen, head girl Judith Larmour, Emma Hughes and Carrie Lemon. *547-1A-41*

Members of Sons of Ulster LOL 2027, Bangor, at Worshipful Master John Gordon's home prior to the Twelfth demonstration which was held in Groomsport in July 1989. *664-11A-41*

Bangor milkmen, pictured with family and friends, took part in a cavalcade around the town in August 1989 to protest over a supermarket price war which had reduced the price of a pint to as little as 18p, which impacted heavily on doorstep deliveries. The supermarkets responded to their concerns by raising prices, but to a limited extent. *108-4A-42*

Achievement prizewinners from Glenlola Collegiate at the annual prizegiving in 1989. Included are Emily Meanley, Cathy Quinn, Jennifer Blackwood, Nicola Duncan, Diane Hamilton, Melanie Spence, Pamela Dobbin and Rosamond Girgis. *502-21-42*

New pupils in September 1989 at Bloomfield Road Primary School with teachers Louise Hudson and Jill Robinson, along with classroom assistant May Patton. *165-8A-42*

The Friends of Bangor Abbey held a seminar in September 1989 on the early history of the Abbey. Those in attendance included Dean Hamilton Leckey, Ellie Leckey, Mary O'Fee, Eddie Beckett, Stella Robinson, Dr Anne Hamlin, Ian Wilson and David Comiskey. *295-4-42*

Children from the Stepping Stones Playgroup, who met in Bangor Orange Hall, enjoyed their Hallowe'en fancy dress party in October 1989. *414-22A-42*

Staff from the Carlton Patisserie with some of the trophies gained in October 1989 at the Northern Ireland Bakery Championships. From left: Alison Weir, Claire Murphy, Janet Beattie and Sharon Martin. *424-7A-42*

Chris Thompson

remembers...

I was born in the small streets of Belfast in 1956. My parents, working all hours, sent me to Methody. However, instead of going on to music college, as planned, I worked in a local sports shop as a year out. My summer job then became full-time before, in 1984, with my dad Ronnie and late mum Paddie's help and encouragement, I was involved in opening a retail business in Belfast catering for my twin hobbies of water sports and mountain sports. This was followed a few years later by a second shop in Bangor.

Life was fun and retail was very good, apart from dealing with the aftermath of the car bombs which had become a way of life for traders.

I was already living in Bangor by then, having camped, along with my parents, on people's floors for many months after our home in Belfast was burnt to the ground by a petrol bomb thrown in error by one of the many brainless entities of that time. It had destroyed everything we'd worked for; the upside was I met my wife.

Liz was from Groomsport and after getting married in 1983 our first home was in the village and then in Towerview, where we were living when our daughter Ashley was born in 1987. With both businesses expanding we had every reason to look forward to the future.

The changing point in my life occurred on 8 January

Chris Thompson in the late 1980s with daughter Ashley

Married to Liz and father to Ashley, Ryan and Aimee, Chris Thompson survived the Kegworth air crash on 8 January 1989.

1989. I left Bangor extremely early to fly to the London Boat Show, where I was buying new stock. It was a trip I always loved making. The plane that morning was brand new and despite other flights being delayed by dense fog, it was able to take off and land with ease thanks to its modern technology.

With my business completed quickly I had the choice of either catching an earlier flight home or joining the hordes for a tour around a real super yacht destined for one of the world's super rich. No contest!! I joined the queue and dreamed the same dream as everyone around me.

Having eventually made it back to Heathrow, my British Midland flight, BD092, took off on time. It was the same new plane I'd been on that morning. My seat, 1E, was at the very front and I looked forward to getting an early meal as I'd not had any lunch. The food was just being served when there was a violent bang followed by what appeared to be blue smoke coming into the plane and the most terrible shuddering and shaking.

I knew it had to be one of the two engines; it was screaming then dying over and over again, causing the plane to be jerked all over the sky. I could not even focus on the escape door such was the extreme vibration. A close friend was a commercial pilot so I was aware a plane could fly on one engine but that still didn't remove the fear that was gripping me. My skin crawled and all I wanted was to be back on the ground again. Silly thoughts ran through my head like who would cut the grass. Was it greed and money or ambitions that had made me go to London that day? I am not a religious person but I knew maybe this was the time to start praying.

Luggage tumbled from the overhead lockers and I could hear screaming from behind me. Outside it was night and our cabin lighting seemed to be flickering. I'm sure if there'd been a door to escape from the plane people would have killed each other just to get to it but in reality there was nowhere to run. The engine, like a car out of petrol, finally died and there was a terrible silence. I could taste blood in my throat caused by fear.

The captain, Kevin Hunt, came over the intercom and

briefly explained how they had shut down a faulty engine and we were diverting to a nearby airport and all was now well. The cabin crew, who were magnificent, took their seats and the flight continued. However, after 20 minutes it all happened again: another huge bang with the same vibrations and massive turbulence.

Those passengers on the left or port side thought the remaining engine was now on fire as well. That engine finally died, leaving only the sound of the wind rushing past the unlit plane as we headed over the top of a roller coaster ride before falling through the darkness.

I could see only the bulkhead in front and the tiny lights that dotted the roads far below. Suddenly it was the incongruous sight of a church spire passing my window then the splintering trees and the crushing…

"Brace! Brace!" would have been the final words 47 of my fellow passengers ever heard as the plane crashed onto the embankment of the M1 motorway outside the village of Kegworth, close to East Midlands Airport.

I can remember a nurse looking down at me and asking if I knew what had happened and where I was. I felt guilty and stupid that I'd knocked my head as the plane was landing. I apologised; obviously the others had already got off.

I was told I'd been in a plane crash and then I gradually became aware that people were rushing around me, pulling and cutting my clothes off. Somewhere in my head a light came on and reality dawned. I was alive. My brain finally shut down and darkness followed.

I'd sustained a fractured skull, fractured vertebrae, broken legs, knees and feet. I drifted in and out of consciousness over the next few days. Different faces were there every time my eyes opened, although my dad and Liz were always there helping. The pain was terrible and I couldn't move. The nurses had nicknamed me 'The Panda' because of the huge black eyes I had from my fractured skull, although the eyes

Prime Minister Margaret Thatcher, with Northern Ireland Secretary of State Tom King on her right and British Midland chairman Michael Bishop on her left, walks among the debris at the crash site at the M1 near Kegworth

themselves were bright red with burst blood vessels due to the impact.

Initially the answers to my questions were guarded but I soon began to understand how lucky I'd been as word of the deaths all around me in the plane filtered through. Although they were strangers I wanted to know how the other survivors were faring and what had caused the crash.

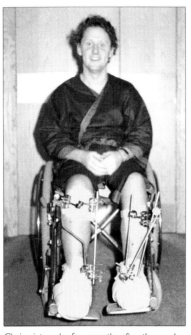

Chris pictured a few months after the crash

One morning the ward was slowly cleared of the beds and I was asked if I would like to meet Prince Charles. Of course I would. He wanted to meet me? Surely it was meant to be the other way round? We talked for a while about the scaffolding built and screwed through my legs. Known as Fixators, it's ironic they were pioneered as a result of the bombs in Belfast. A few years earlier I would have lost my legs.

An air ambulance brought me home to hospital in Belfast, where I was finally able to get my hair washed, removing the dried blood of those who had died behind me. Back in Nottingham I'd been made to feel important and special by the nurses but now I was just a patient, which was very depressing. I had to be lifted up in the morning and laid down at night. I was in hell, with even basic toilet functions requiring help from others.

The saying about learning a lot if you walk a mile in another man's shoes is so true, yet, no matter what, I knew I was lucky. No matter how bad we think we are someone else is always worse off. The weeks passed with word going round of other survivors' progress and leaving hospital. Eventually, and almost the last, I too was released.

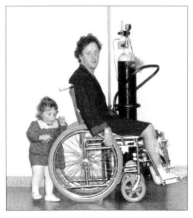

Daughter Ashley (18 months) pushes Chris in hospital

Many months followed in a wheelchair and then learning to walk again in glass fibre casts and crutches; it was all an education. The intensive work undertaken by physiotherapists was fantastic. They always smiled as they pushed you further.

Liz, of course, also made things easier with her constant help and encouragement, while the businesses continued in my absence with the help of family and the staff.

Like everyone else I wanted to know why this all had happened. I became the spokesperson of a group called the Air Safety Action Group with the aim of learning more about the crash and campaigning for greater air safety. Over the next few years, as my own condition improved, I realised how lucky I'd been – other survivors were not so fortunate.

On a few occasions local survivors were invited over to England, where we met and talked with bereaved families. Northern Ireland is so small that although initially we were all strangers some of us got to know each other well. As part of this small group I was lucky to have many good experiences. Others proved emotional, including when we were invited to visit the giant hangar at Farnborough where the investigation team worked on plane crash wreckage.

Our dissected plane was beside huge bits of the Lockerbie wreckage. Still walking on crutches I was able to sit in my plane seat again. By doing so I hoped to kill my demons. The experience of being in the hangar that day brought tears to the eyes of our entire group and some of the staff. No outsider had been allowed in there before. We understood the pain and suffering!

A small number of us were also privileged to accept an invitation to meet the fire crew at East Midlands Airport who were first on the scene. They remembered each of us and where we were trapped. Even fire crews cry!

I experienced many happier events as time passed although this was only possible due the fantastic help I received from my father, my wife and immediate family and friends who were always there for me. I was invited onto talk shows. I met rock stars like Dave Stewart from Eurythmics, actors and other famous people. Angela Rippon even came to our house.

A radio programme I was involved in won a Sony Award. I even made a training video which was used by most of the major UK airlines. As a result I was often recognised by crew members; they would sit and question me or slip

Chris Thompson today

me a few free drinks on flights. It was all a bit like therapy of some sort.

I would not wish my experience on anyone. However, I think in a perverse way I have gained so much from it. If someone is in a wheelchair, I talk to them first and not just the person pushing it. Look around and see how many people are far worse off than you, both physically and mentally.

I have met people I would never have had the luck to meet before. The Air Safety Action Group's information and safety campaign, along with the medical research arising from our injuries, has improved air safety that little bit more.

Liz and I now have three children, Ashley, Ryan and Aimee, and we still live in the area. The aches and pains I experience all the time and a few joints that don't bend properly will always remind me of my luck and optimism, along with private but irreplaceable memories. Ultimately I have gained something very special from my experience.

Sport

in Bangor in the Eighties

1980

Glenlola Collegiate and Sullivan Upper shared the Ulster Schoolgirls' Hockey Cup after drawing 1-1 in the final on 19 March. Sonia Hewitt's shot was deflected into the goal by Barbara Webb to secure the draw.

Bangor Grammar School's 2nd XV shared the Northern Ireland Schools' Second XV Competition Shield after drawing 6-6 with Foyle and Londonderry College in the final.

Ballyholme Yacht Club member Elaine Firth (21), of Ballyholme Esplanade, was accorded the honour of being Ireland's woman representative at the World Laser Championships later in the year. She qualified for the Irish squad with top marks from two provincial competitions at Galway and Malahide and the Irish Nationals at Kinsale. Ballyholme's Bill O'Hara Jr. was also awarded a place on the same team.

Martin Holmes, of Primacy Road, returned home from Dun Laoghaire after winning the All Ireland Long-Driving Championship. He set his sights on claiming the British title, held at that time by another Bangor man, Garth McGimpsey.

Bangor Hockey Club's Stephen Martin was selected for the Irish panel to play in Aberdeen against Yugoslavia, France and Scotland.

Gerry Oakley was the new Irish open archery champion following a two-day event in Kilkenny at the end of June. The Bangor man was a member of Cultra Archers Club.

Sixteen-year-old Alastair Ley, of Ballyholme Yacht Club, won the Ulster Junior Laser Championship at Killyleagh with three first places. Clubmate Kenny Loughridge was runner-up.

John McCreedy (19), a former Gransha Boys' High School pupil, left for a four-year scholarship at Pitt State University in Kansas. A 3,000m specialist, who had just won a bronze medal at the British Junior Championships, John had received offers from nine colleges throughout the USA. The course was on physical education and recreational management.

The Bangor Girls' High School squad qualified for the quarter-finals of the Northern Ireland Intermediate Netball competition in January 1980. They are pictured with the cup they won in the County Down area finals and qualifying competition. Back (from left): coach Mrs M. Mawhinney, Jacqui Crozier, Julia Wareham, Gillian Robinson, Donna Dickson, vice-principal Mr Adams. Front (from left): Ina McMurray, Linda McAuley, Pauline Steele, Linda Clint and Diane MacDonald. *116-8-9*

Cantrell and Cochrane representative Harry James presented the girls of St Comgall's Primary School with the new Glucoplus Trophy as winners of the Bangor and District Schools Netball League. Captain Gina Morrow received the trophy after the team beat Clandeboye Road Primary School 23-12. Other team members were Kelly McCabe, Stephanie Taylor, Aileen Gillen, Martine McDowell, Marie Therese Walsh and Ann Monaghan. *378-4-9*

Rathmore Primary School's five-a-side soccer team were proclaimed as Northern Ireland champions in April 1980 after beating their Larne counterparts 1-0 at the Antrim Forum. Back (from left): Ian McCann, teacher in charge, Stephen McGarry, Neil Heasley, Simon Thomson, school principal Mr H. R. Boyd. Front (from left): Ian Weatherup, Connor Aspinall and Steve Hamilton. *38-5-10*

First Bangor Old Boys won the IFA Junior Cup following a 2-0 victory over favourites Ballynahinch United at Clandeboye Park. Both goals were scored in the second half by Peter Dixon. 97-17-10

Ballyholme Primary School won a mini rugby competition hosted by Bangor Rugby Club, scoring 152 points and conceding none. Back (from left): Brian McNeilly, Christopher Reilly, Robin Flannigan, Sean Crowther, John McCutcheon. Middle (from left): Gavin Ellis, Peter Jenkins (captain), Johnathan Webb. Front (from left): Simon Cummings and Trevor Reid. 230-7A-10

Braving the elements at Pickie Pool in late July 1980 were these local and visiting children who were being taught how to swim and dive by instructor Hugh McIlduff (right). 41-8A-11

Children who availed of an opportunity to learn about sailing at Ballyholme Yacht Club in August 1980, under the supervision of Margaret Butler. *103-3A-11*

Bangor Bowling Club won the IBA Challenge Cup in September 1980, equalling the achievement of the club's 1935 team. Back row (from left): Victor McKeown, George Martin, Cecil Herron, Lenny Agnew. Middle row: Robert Pollock, David Boal (treasurer), Billy Pollock, Billy Kirkwood (team secretary), Billy Kayes. Front row: Martin Graham (secretary), Gary Boal, Bertie Cobain, Maurice McKeown (president), George Selman, Alfie Thomas and Keith Herron. Absent from picture: John Simpson. *232-17-11*

First Bangor Netball Club players who were selected for Northern Ireland squads at three different levels. Back (from left): Barbara Devitt, Pauline Steele, Liz Burnside. Front: Linda Murnin and Linda Walsh. *427-9-11*

1981

Bangor FC manager Billy Johnston was dismissed following the club's 2-1 home defeat by Newry Town in the Irish Cup. The Seasiders, without a victory in two months, had slipped to the bottom of the Irish League and had the worst defensive record.

Former Arsenal full-back Freddy Clarke was appointed temporary manager for the following week's match against Portadown, but the next full-time manager was Bertie Neill. He had previously managed the club during the mid-1970s when they secured the County Antrim Shield and the Gold Cup in the same season (1974/75).

Bangor trio Bill O'Hara, Alastair Ley and Gilbert Nesbitt headed for Florida to take part in the American Mid-Winter Laser Championships. They were members of the Ross's Water Laser squad – a group set up by the Royal Yachting Association in 1979 and initially comprising helmsmen from Ballyholme Yacht Club's Mirror and Laser classes.

Bangor Cricket Club's Chris Harte was included in the Irish panel for a tour of England and Wales. Scoring 39 runs for Ireland against Scotland in a three-day international had ensured his re-selection for the tour. Another Bangor player, John Elder, was on a six-month stay in Brisbane, where he was playing in Grade One of the Winter League.

Catherine Foote (13), a pupil at Bangor Girls' High School, received top junior angling accolade the Samuel Stevenson Award from the Ulster Provincial Council of the Irish Federation of Sea Anglers. She was rated one of the top young anglers in Ireland, having taken up the sport at the age of six.

Bangor manager Bertie Neill was sacked on 23 November, two days after the club were beaten 4-0 for the third time in five games. They had won just two games during the first four months of the 1981/82 season. A week later, and without a manager, the team was defeated 5-1 by Coleraine.

The new manager, appointed in mid-December, was former Shorts and Chimney Corner boss Eric Halliday. His tenure commenced with a 2-1 home victory over Irish League favourites Glentoran. Scorers were Gary Reid and Tom Kennedy.

Glenlola Collegiate scored a noteworthy double when the U-11 and U-13 teams took first place in their respective sections in the Ulster Region Schools' Gymnastics Championships, held in February at the Avoniel Leisure Centre in Belfast. Picture shows the U-11 team (back, from left): Louise Orr, Nichola Montgomery, Tracey Stevenson. Front: Diane Webb, Sally Ann Holmes and Alyson Cooley. *471-12-12*

The U-13 team from Glenlola Collegiate, section winners at the Ulster Region Schools' Gymnastics Championships in February 1981. Back (from left): Jayne Devenney, Zara Magill, Lorna Green. Front: Shauna McCandless, Marian McDowell, Joanne Hampton and Johanne Magill. *470-9-12*

Kilmaine Primary School won the Bangor and District Primary Schools' Soccer League in early May 1981 with a maximum 14 points from seven fixtures. With coach Mr Thompson are (back, from left): Peter Gourley, Chris Kerr, Richard Wilson, Paul Gray (top scorer with 55 goals), Andrew Plackitt, Neal Taylor. Middle: Stephen Andrews, Keith McDaid, Ian Bruce (captain), Geoffrey Spence, Alastair Law. Front: Robert Thompson and Jeffrey McNamara. *206-19-13*

Bangor Hockey Club's 3rd XI, winners of Junior League III in May 1981. *431-6-13*

Bangor Hockey Club's 4th XI, winners of Junior League IV in May 1981. *432-8-13*

Castle Bowling Club's A team gained promotion to the top tier after winning the NIBA Senior League Division Two title in September 1981. Back (from left): Norman Best, Bob Davidson, Eric Lowry, Norman Graham, William Ringland, John Campbell, Sam Mulholland, Robin Emerson, Jack Canavan. Front: Alex Stewart, Jim McCutcheon, Walter Sterrett, Alex Lightbody (president), Alan Beattie, Ralph Lynas and Carl Gibson, *577-9-14*

1982

Bangor Hockey Club clinched the Indoor League Division 2 title in February, losing only three times and achieving the best defending and attacking records along the way.

Three of the five Northern Ireland swimmers selected for the Commonwealth Games were members of the Bangor club – Julie Parkes, Simon Magowan and Moya Sloan.

Gymnast Roberta Finlay (14), a pupil at Bangor Girls' High School, was selected in May 1982 to represent Northern Ireland at the Commonwealth Games in Brisbane, Australia, that September. It was the first time Northern Ireland gymnasts had attained a sufficiently high standard to merit representation in the Games. 596-11-16

Bangor Bowling Club lifted the NIBA Senior Cup in August with a single point victory over Carrick. The club went one better the following month by being crowned All Ireland Association champions.

Rodney McCutcheon (20), from Chippendale Avenue, who played for Bangor Bowling Club, became British Isles Junior Bowling Champion following an epic victory over English international skip Tony Allcock in Ayr at the end of August. Allcock had been a gold medallist at the previous World Championships.

George Best turned out for Bangor in a friendly fixture against Scottish club Motherwell at Clandeboye Park on Monday 27 September. The former Manchester United and Northern Ireland star failed to make much of an impression on the game, which finished 5-1 in favour of the visitors. The match attracted an attendance of around 1,000. Bangor's goal was scored by centre-forward Graham King.

Bangor manager Eric Halliday resigned on 30 November after refusing to endorse cost-cutting measures that would have reduced his coaching staff. Recently sacked Ards manager Billy Humphreys took over as first team coach and was installed as manager the following May.

The Intermediate team from Bangor Girls' High School who won their league at the South Eastern Area Netball Championships, held in January 1982 at Dundonald Girls' High School. Back (from left): A. McAdam, M. Mount, A. Morgan, G. Totten. Front: P. Graham, S. Stanley and J. Poole. 556-10A-15

The PTA of Clandeboye Road Primary School presented the football team with a new skip in April 1982. The boys are pictured with coach Jim Hendry (left) and PTA chairman Lloyd Erskine. Back (from left): Anthony Bodell, David McKee, David Mercer, Jeoffrey Robinson, Gary Tipping. Front: Darren Cruise, Mark Gilmore, Paul Miskelly, Russell Cockcroft, Paul McIlwrath and Andrew Larmour. 189-2A-16

Children who attended special keep fit classes at the Bangor Castle Leisure Centre in April 1982. They performed a routine to the song *Japanese Boy*. Producer was Sandra Henry. 181-4-16

Members of Bangor's Youth XV celebrate their U-18 Cup victory at Ravenhill in April 1982, after they recorded a 12-6 win over Ballymoney Colts. Included is club president Brian McKillen (third from left). 283-16-16

The football team from Eighth Bangor (Lisnabreen) Boys' Brigade Company with the cup they received after winning the Bangor and District Junior League in May 1982. 529-19-16

The St Comgall's Primary School soccer team beat Donaghadee Primary School 1-0 in the final of the Bangor Primary Schools' Knock-Out Cup in May 1982. Included with headmaster and coach John O'Hanlon are (back, from left): John Murray, Declan Carlin (scorer of the winning goal), Jim McIlveen, Damien Bell (captain), Darren Hanna, Kieran Magennis. Centre: Kevin Lennon, Paul Keenan, Gregory Gibson, Gavin McCoubrey, John Cannon. Front: Alastair Hamilton, Paul Digney, Timothy Lennon, Martin Brannigan, Mark Weir and Michael McDowell (reserves). 440-8-16

Bangor Junior Girls' Hockey Club brought their season to a close in May 1982 with the presentation of a trophy to the most improved and most regular attender. The trophy, presented by organisers Mrs Monty Stevenson (back, left) and Mrs Pat Stewart (back, right) was handed over by Glenlola Collegiate PE and hockey teacher Miss Ann Davidson to 11-year-old Claire Samways. Smaller trophies went to joint runners-up Donna Anderson and Karen Smith. All three girls were aged 11 and attended Rathmore Primary School. 446-3-16

TV comedian Bernie Winters, having been lent a car for the duration of a tour of Northern Ireland by Bangor Mazda dealer Sammy Mellon, repaid the favour by presenting jackets and kitbags to the Gransha Boys' High School team who were preparing for a summer visit to the USA. From left: Sammy Mellon, Bernie Winters, Paul Watson, David Quee, Victor Brown, Stephen Jenkins, Darin Dunlop, Colin Anderson, Ivan Mellon. Behind them are Gransha teachers Mike McLoughlin and Bob Martin, Mayor Albert Magee and school principal Mr J. McCullough. *461-17-16*

Rathgael Gymnastics and Trampolining Club prizewinners from their Friday night championships in June 1982. Back (from left): Ian Andrews, Joanne Black, Tracy Clarke, Kerry McCabe, James Maxwell, Sharon Croft. Middle (from left): Stephen Alloway, Paul McGimpsey, Richard Skelton, Darren Crawley, Nicholas Dunn, Jason Boyd, Peter Smyth. Front (from left): Jill Smyth, Julie McManus, Lisa Jones, Claire Crawley, Rachel Armstrong, Tracy Skelton and Jenny Crawley. *107-11-17*

The Hamilton Road Gymnastics Club's A team won the Continental Sports Trophy at the Team of the Future competitions, which were held in Belfast in June 1982. From left: Alison Cooley, Barbara Smith, Zoe Bunce, Janet Smith (Coach of the Year award), Jill Gallagher, Heather Mackintosh and Kim Kensett. Catherine Roberts, not in picture, replaced Barbara Smith, who was injured at the time of the competition. *644-3A-16*

Bill O'Hara (centre), of Ballyholme Yacht Club, was accorded a civic reception in September 1982 to mark his achievement in taking second place in the European Laser Championships. He was presented with a plaque by Mayor John McConnell Auld. Also attending the function at the Town Hall were proud parents Bill and Anne O'Hara and younger sister Jane. *715-4-17*

Members of the Kilmaine Primary School Canoe Club – the only one of its kind in Northern Ireland – in October 1982. Included are teachers Carol Watt and Arnold Cousins, who instructed them in the art of canoeing at Seapark (Crawfordsburn/ Helen's Bay). *123-9-18*

Bangor Grammar School's hockey 1st XI won the McCullough Cup for the first time in December 1982. They defeated Methodist College 3-1 in the final. Back row (from left): John Smyth (master-in-charge), William Mayne, Glenn Stranex, Keith McAlister, Ian Campton, Andrew Sterritt. Front: Chris McConkey, Lindsay Rainey, Niall McAlister, Ian Dornan, Alan Chambers and Stephen Mitchell. *474-16A-18*

1983

Michael Smyth, from Shandon Drive, was Ulster's new chess champion, winning the title at Fortwilliam Golf Club at the beginning of January. It offered the former captain of the Bangor Grammar School chess team and three times winner of the Ulster Senior Schoolboys title the chance to compete in the British Championships at Southport.

Norman Drew returned to Bangor Golf Club on 1 February to take over from David Jones as the new professional. In younger days he had lived on the Bloomfield Road, close to the club from where he had embarked on a successful golfing career.

Ballyholme Yacht Club's Bill O'Hara left Northern Ireland in May bound for Los Angeles to take part in a five-month training programme in preparation for the 1984 Olympic Games. He was hoping to sail in the Olympic Finn Class at the Games.

Alastair Ley (20) was the new Irish National Laser Champion, winning the title in late August at the Open Irish Laser Championships hosted by Royal Cork Yacht Club at Crosshaven. It was three years in a row for Ballyholme as the previous two titles had gone to clubmate Bill O'Hara.

Alastair Ley with his trophy as Irish Laser Champion.
581-20A-20

Bangor Cricket Club won the Senior II title at the beginning of September, restoring the team to the top section after a one-year absence, after they beat Muckamore by seven wickets at Ward Park.

Stephen Martin was chosen in September for the Great Britain hockey squad from which teams would be chosen for a game against Pakistan in late October and for the World Tournament in Hong Kong in December. Hopes were high that the Bangor man would make the British squad for the 1984 Olympic Games.

Bangor in the Eighties

Olympic swimmer Sharron Davies attracted an enthusiastic young audience during her visit to the Bangor indoor pool in March 1983. *163-8-19*

Bangor Jogging Club coach John McCreedy congratulates Wally Gamble on his excellent time of 12.19 in the club's first annual handicap race. The club met every Monday and Wednesday at the Bangor Castle Leisure Centre. *297-3-20*

Members and officials of the St Comgall's Amateur Boxing Club, one of Northern Ireland's youngest boxing clubs, were celebrating a very successful year (1982/83), during which five of the 10 members entered in the Northern Ireland Novice Championships won trophies. They included Charlie McCoubrey (16) and Samuel Burns (15), winner and runner-up respectively at the subsequent All Ireland finals in Dublin. *687-8A-18*

Bloomfield Road Primary School pulled off a first at the 1983 North Down Primary Schools' Athletics Championships by winning the overall shields for both boys and girls. They are pictured with teacher Mr R. J. Besant. 55-7-20

Bangor Cricket Club's 1st XI who took on the ICU President's XI as the main event during the club's golden jubilee week in August 1983. The match ended as a draw. Back (from left): Brian Millar, Colin Magowan, Tim English, Michael P. Rea, Jackie Erskine, Jack Townsley (scorer). Middle: Chris Harte, Michael Rea, John Elder (captain), Sam Beckett. Front: Mark McCall and Ian McClatchey. 446-13-20

Bangor man Albert Murdock, a polio victim from birth, holds the swimming gold medal he won at the British Polio Fellowship Games, held at Stoke Mandeville Hospital in August 1983. He competed in the 50m freestyle event and also took third place in both the javelin and javelin precision events. 507-10-20

1984

Lynda Pauley, of Glenlola Collegiate, was selected to keep goal for Ulster Schoolgirls in February's inter-provincial schools hockey tournament in Kilkenny. Another student from the school, Michelle Rainey, was selected for the South Eastern Education and Library Board's U-15 team for a tournament the following month involving the five Education Boards.

Tom Dorrian, of Downshire Road, was the proud owner of Bentom Boy, winner of the Ulster Harp National at Downpatrick in March. The horse was fourth favourite in a field of 11. The following month the same horse, with odds of 33-1, won the Irish Grand National at Fairyhouse. Jockey Ann Ferris became the first woman to win the National.

Bangor won the Milk Marketing Board Indoor Cricket League with a victory over Ballymena in the final and deciding game of the eight-week tournament at the Shankill Leisure Centre in April.

Stephen Martin was selected to play for Great Britain against the USA in Cardiff on 16 June. The team then embarked on a European tour, with matches in Spain, France, Holland and Belgium. In early July it was confirmed that Martin was a member of the GB hockey squad for that summer's Olympic Games in Los Angeles.

North Down Borough Council agreed in July to provide a BMX track, adjacent to the Walled Garden in Castle Park, at a cost of £3,200.

Angela Goodall (22), a member of Bangor and District Archery Club, was selected to represent Great Britain at the Olympic Games. She was the only archer from Northern Ireland to travel to Los Angeles.

Stephen Martin returned in triumph to his Tudor Park home, complete with the Olympic bronze medal he had secured following the Great Britain team's defeat by West Germany in the semi-finals.

John Gibson (19), of Silverbirch Park, was selected to represent Great Britain at the World Student Judo Championships, which were held in Strasbourg in December.

Tanya Cooke (13), from Glenlola Collegiate, was selected in February 1984 to play for the Ulster U-15 badminton team. *609-12-21*

The Mondiale Car Company, based at the Balloo Industrial Estate, delivered its first Formula Ford 1600cc car in March 1984. The buyer, former FF champion Arnie Black, planned to race the car within days at Kirkistown. Members of the company's workforce are pictured with the first car. *22-19-22*

Eleven-year-old Nicola Patterson, from Bloomfield Road Primary School, was named Player of the Tournament in the local Primary Schools' Netball League in March 1984. *84-8-22*

Kilcooley Youth Club members Gary Armstrong (left), of Belfast Road, and Steven McBride, of Woodgreen, swept the boards at the annual presentation day in July 1984. The boys won cups and trophies for badminton, darts, snooker and table tennis. *794-4A-22*

Bangor in the Eighties

Members of Bangor Golf Club at their Lady Captain's Day in July 1984. Seated (from left): Lady Vice-Captain Mona Fox, Lady President Flo Gorman, Lady Captain Margaret Blaikie, treasurer Pat Williamson and secretary Pat Devon. *734-3-22*

Eighteen-year-old Eddie Irvine on the road to success in August 1984. *874-5A-22*

Fiona Hunter (left) won Bangor Amateur Swimming Club's annual Pickie to the Pier swim in September 1984. In second place was Clare Singleton (centre), while Kathy Reid was third. *207-17-23*

'Clones Cyclone' Barry McGuigan often stayed at Beresford House on Bangor's seafront prior to his fights in the King's Hall, Belfast. This visit, in October 1984, preceded his victory over South American (and world title contender) Felipe Orozco. Members of the Bangor Barry McGuigan Supporters Club took the opportunity of his stay in the town to present him with an inscribed cut-glass crystal bowl. Making the presentation in the Windsor Bar is club president Richard Young. Included are Barry's wife Sandra and sparring partners Andres Tena and Ricky Young. *360-6A-23*

1985

Ulster Chess Champion for 1985 was Mark Orr, who won the title following the annual tournament in Armagh in early January. Son of Mr and Mrs John Orr, of Ballycrochan Road, he was working in Scotland as a computer programmer.

Young Bangor man Keith Nicol, who had played college football for three years while living in Toronto, was behind moves to create an American Grid-Iron football team in the town. Prospective team members held practice sessions on Sunday afternoons in Ballyholme Park.

Bangor's Stuart McKinley was in fine form during the Northern Ireland Subbuteo finals – securing the junior title without conceding a goal in four matches. He went on to represent Northern Ireland at the UK Subbuteo Championships in London.

Ronnie McQuillan succeeded Billy Humphreys as manager of Bangor FC on 28 March. He had previously managed Cliftonville for four years, building up a team that often challenged for honours. He appointed Eddie Coulter, also formerly of Cliftonville, as his chief scout. The team won their next three games with a draw against Distillery breaking the sequence.

Jimmy Girvan, scorer of Bangor FC's very first competitive goal – in a fixture against Crusaders on 14 September 1918 – passed away, aged 94, in Toronto.

Thirteen-year-old John West, of Lynne Avenue, became the 'Junior Britain' Ulster Karting champion at Nutts Corner in June. He attended Gransha Boys' High School.

Ward Park tennis player David Cunningham won the Ulster Grand Prix in September, having collected the most points in tournaments during the 1985 season. Another Ward Park player, Philippa Palmer, was reigning Ireland number one junior.

Paul Gray, aged just 15, scored on his debut for Bangor FC in a 3-0 win over Carrick Rangers on 9 November. He was believed to be the youngest player ever to do so in an Irish League fixture.

The winners of the senior section in a Cubs' five-a-side football tournament held at the Bangor Castle Leisure Centre in February 1985 were from Third Bangor. Back (from left): Tony Dickson, Brian McKeown, Sandra Watson, Ian Jefferson. Middle: Ian Bleakley, Gareth Dickson (captain), Mark Johnston, Iain McKeown. Front: Shane Murray, Stuart Larmour and Christopher Jefferson. *120-12A-24*

The winners of the junior section in a Cubs' five-a-side football tournament held at the Bangor Castle Leisure Centre in February 1985 were the Seventh Bangor Hawks. They beat Craigavad 2-1 in the final. Back (from left): Terry Brown and Andrew Miller, who ran the team. Middle: Michael Gibson, Adrian Bailie (captain), Gareth Ritchie. Front: Lee McLarnon, Philip Legge and Keith Stevenson. *120-11A-24*

Gransha High School's U-12 team won the Belfast and District Cup in March 1985, beating Lisnasharragh 2-1 in the final. Back (from left): Simon Neill, Nigel Cree, Len Dugan, Geoffrey McGuigan, Mark Ashe, Peter Young, Mark Johnston, Darren Newell. Front: Simon Snoddy, Andrew Collins, Mark Noble, David Dornan, Neil McKenna, Andrew Thompson, Michael Malloy and Simon Stuart. *302-4-24*

The three teams which won through to the round-robin final of the Bangor Primary Schools' cricket competition at the Bangor Castle Leisure Centre in April 1985. At the back are the Connor House team, in the centre Towerview Primary School and, at the front, St Comgall's Primary School. Connor House emerged as winners ahead of St Comgall's. *462-5-24*

Members of the Bangor BMX display team put on a show in the car park of the Clandeboye Shopping Centre in May 1985 as part of the complex's 10th anniversary celebrations. *635-5-24*

The Percy French tennis tournament at Ward Park in May 1985 included an exhibition of Edwardian tennis, with club members turning out in costumes appropriate to the era. *640-13-24*

Pupils of Glenlola Collegiate Preparatory Department are pictured in May 1985 with the sporting awards and trophies they had won during the year. Back (from left): Judith Bell, netball; Victoria Wright, athletics; Natalie Garden, swimming; Linzy Orr, hockey. Front: Claire Gillvray, athletics; Barbara Corry, swimming; Caroline Stewart, swimming, and Jane Rainey, athletics. 732-3-24

Chief Inspector P. J. Timoney, deputy sub-divisional commander, based at Bangor RUC Station, hands over a punch bag to Project Bangor's boxing club in November 1985. Testing it out is 12-year-old David Beattie, from Bangor. Also included are Sgt. Robb, assistant trainer Victor Gibson and members of the club. 76-16A-26

Bangor Golf Club's annual dinner in November 1985 was marked by a special presentation to British Amateur Golf Champion Garth McGimpsey and the presence of Walker Cup stars Peter McEvoy and Arthur Pierce. Kneeling (from left): Gordon Stephenson, Norman Drew, Barry Crymble. Standing: Maxwell Ledlie, Roy Mullan, John Neill (captain), Alan McDade, Garth McGimpsey, Brendan Edwards, Peter McEvoy, Fred Daly, Eddie Bolster, Arthur Pierce, Bill Evans (captain, Curragh Golf Club), Hal McGimpsey and Brian Cummings. 143-12-26

1986

Stephen Martin was vice-captain of the Great Britain hockey team which beat Pakistan in Kuwait in early January. It was the first time the team had beaten Pakistan since the Helsinki Olympic Games in 1952. Great Britain was ranked number two in world hockey.

Bangor Girls' High School student Michelle Davidson was selected for the Northern Ireland U-18 netball squad for the British Isles Championships in Bradford at the end of February.

Six Bangor players were selected for the Northern Ireland Ladies soccer team against England in a UEFA Championship match at Ewood Park, Blackburn, on 15 March. Bangor Swifts supplied Nuala McFetridge, Deirdre O'Reilly, Paula McCloskey and Yvonne Fisher, while Clucas Strikers put forward Tanya Smyth and Fiona Glendinning.

Bangor Amateurs defeated Rockview United (Newry) 3-2 after extra time at New Grosvenor on 5 May to lift the Junior Cup for only the second time in their 102-year history. Goalscorers for the Amateurs were Malcolm, Galway and Tipping. The team also won the local Helmsman Cup and Section 2A of the Amateur League, ensuring the 1985/86 season was their most successful to date.

Bangor FC's first signing for the new season saw local man Peter Dornan rejoining the club in early June. He was best known as a Linfield player from 1976-1985 but had played for Bangor during the early 1970s.

Third Bangor BB became the first company in Northern Ireland, in June 1986, to win the National United Kingdom Chess Championships.

Bill O'Hara and John Simms, both members of Ballyholme Yacht Club, were selected in October to represent Ireland in the World Laser Championships, to be held in Melbourne, Australia, the following January.

National Chess Champions, from left: Howard Beckett (captain), David Farlow and Michael Cummings. *544-10A-28*

Smiles all round from the Clandeboye Golf Club team after they won the Irish Senior Cup in September 1986. From left: Joe Coey (captain), Malcolm Thompson, Colm Murphy, Ed Quiery, Colin Glasgow, Glen Kerr, David Jackson and Maurice McDaid. *191-5-30*

The West Bangor Boys soccer team, wearing their new kit provided by local sponsor Sharprint, in January 1986. Included are Roy Steele, Harry Gillespie, Maurice McCullough (West Bangor) and Nicky Henderson (Sharprint). *303-13-26*

Junior members of Bangor and District Archery Club who took part in the Bangor Winter Double Archery competition, which was held at the Bangor Castle Leisure Centre in January 1986. Gillian Venables from sponsors Agar Packaging is included. *364-3-26*

Some of the Bangor and District Cubs who took part in a five-a-side soccer competition in the Bangor Castle Leisure Centre in April 1986. *367-9A-27*

Members of the Bangor Swifts Ladies soccer team in June 1986. They played in Division One of the Northern Ireland Women's Football League. Back (from left): S. Convery, M. Gavin, M. Maguire, R. Skehin, S. McWilliams (captain), P. Hyland, U. O'Reilly, T. McCrossan. Front: P. McCloskey, Y. Fisher, N. McFetridge, D. O'Reilly and D. McMullan. Missing: M. Dunn and A. Gillen. *283-17-28*

Members of Bangor Central Primary School's Rhythmics gymnastics team took part in the U-11 section at the national championships in England in June 1986. From left: Pamela Nelson (hoop), Jennifer Kennedy (ribbon), Caroline Kennedy (rope), Victoria Branniff (reserve) and Linda Shaw (ball). *542-17-28*

Bangor in the Eighties

Young Bloomfield Road Primary School athletes who performed with distinction in the annual athletics competitions for local primary schools in June 1986. The boys won the team award and the girls were runners-up. *499-8-28*

Bangor Amateur Football Club's most successful season to date – with the Junior Cup, the Helmsman Cup and the trophy for winning Section 2A of the Amateur League in the cabinet – was marked by a reception hosted by North Down Borough Council in June 1986. Players and officials were welcomed by Mayor Bruce Mulligan. *45-19-29*

Subbuteo enthusiasts gathered at the Clandeboye Shopping Centre in September 1986 to compete in the North Down Championships for the Stewart Miller Memorial Trophy. Included with competitors is organiser Neil Hanna. *203-15-30*

1987

Herbie Barr, of Marlo Park, was selected by the Schools International Board to referee a schoolboy international between England and Northern Ireland at Luton on 27 February. Among the Northern Ireland players was former Gransha Boys' High School pupil Paul Gray, who was serving an apprenticeship with Luton Town FC.

Kim Kensett, from Bangor Girls' High School, was one of five girls from around Northern Ireland who were selected in February 1987 to travel to Scotland for a three-day training session in artistic gymnastics under the supervision of top Russian coaches.

Bangor Grammar School fell at the last hurdle in hockey's Burney Cup, with the 1st XI being at the wrong end of a 4-0 final defeat by RBAI on 19 March. However, the U-15s won the Richardson Cup on 1 April with a 3-0 victory over Annadale Grammar School.

Ballyholme Yacht Club member Jackie Patton returned from Japan at the end of March after claiming second place in the Shiseido Cup, crewing for Cathy Foster in their 407 dinghy.

The announcement of a £250,000 grant from the Football Grounds Improvement Trust paved the way for Bangor FC, along with several other Irish League clubs, to provide floodlighting before the end of the year. The first match under the new lights was a League Cup second round fixture against Ballymena United on Wednesday 4 November – with Bangor winning 2-1.

However, the club was subsequently expelled from the competition for fielding an ineligible player – former Ballymena United forward Stephen Barnes, who had already played for that club in the same competition.

Bangor Grammar School's 1st XI secured cricket's McCullough Cup on 27 June with victory over RBAI at Ballymacormick. They won the same competition two years later, defeating Foyle and Londonderry College.

Husband and wife Arthur and Elma Griffith achieved a notable double for Bangor at an international clay pigeon shooting event in Dublin on 18 July – by captaining the Irish Men's and Irish Women's teams respectively.

The Bangor Girls' High minor netball team won the South Eastern Area Netball League in January 1987. Back (from left): Karen Gorman, Tanya Kirk, Alyson Alexander (captain), Janice Douglas, Heather Allen and coach Mrs Caughers. Front: Gillian Winters, Janet Brady, Angela Hill and Debra Gault. *349-12-31*

Bangor Hockey Club won the Camera One floodlit tournament at Ward Park in January 1987, following a penalty flicks victory over Lisnagarvey at Ward Park. Back (from left): D. Shields, A. Brennan, N. Wishart, A. McClements, P. Thomas, S. Mitchell. Front: G. Blackwood, P. Corbett, R. Mairs, N. McIvor, R. Parker and G. McConkey. The trophy was retained in 1988. *338-7-31*

Boys from Towerview Primary School show the trophy they received in February 1987 for winning the Bangor and District five-a-side tournament with a 3-1 victory over Ballyholme Primary School in the final. Back (from left): David Nugent, Charles Connor, coach Ian McCann, Stewart Walker, Keith Miskelly. Front: Paul Henderson, Colin Kennedy, Stuart Farmer and Neil Johnston. *422-7A-31*

Stanley Sullivan, representing Tennent's, presents Ken Black, captain of the Ocean Boulevard Rangers pool team, with the Tennent's Cup in March 1987. The Bangor side secured the trophy with a 6-1 victory over Roadhouse Cloughey. *67-4A-32*

These two teams, representing St Comgall's Primary School and Ballyholme Primary School, contested the final of the Primary Schools' Netball League on 7 April 1987, with St Comgall's emerging as the winners. From left: (St Comgall's) Ciara Greenwood, Lucy Anderson, Joanne Fegan, Jennifer Harrison, Sarah O'Hanlon, Colette Hart, Kelly McMullan, Fiona McFerran, Lisa Connolly and teacher Mary Magrath. Ballyholme: teacher Dorothy Wyness, Claire Coates, Alyson Dunne, Julie Moore, Rosemary Stephens, Judith Robinson, Caroline Coghlin, Cathy Quinn, Caroline Cruise, Olivia Galway, M. McCord (teacher) and Gillian Roberts. *236-21-32*

Members of the Kilmaine Primary School soccer team with the five trophies they won during the 1986-87 season. With coach Peter Thompson are (back, from left): Stephen Harris, Anil Vithani, Karl Wilkinson, Steven Walker, Jonathan Chambers, Steven Dugald, Geoffrey Gillespie, Michael Keatley, Steven Barr. Front: Garry Stewart, Mark Willis, Philip Burns, Stuart Larmour (captain), Matthew Scott, Geoffrey Galbraith and Jonathan Todd. *468-16A-32*

The Bangor and District Table Tennis League held its annual dinner and presentation evening at The George on 15 May 1987. Prizewinners were (from left): Helen Gill (ladies' winner), David Addy (men's winner), Carol Miskelly (president's wife), Mervyn Scott (intermediate winner) and Michael McLaughlin (junior winner). 515-23A-32

Members of the Blackthorn Darts Club from Bangor who celebrated their 50th anniversary in May 1987. Back (from left): H. Walton, R. Fitzsimons, B. Angus, R. Turnball, I. Black, B. Beggs, D. Hamill, A. Stewart, S. Wilson, S. Walsh. Front: H. Long, E. McClenaghan, E. McMullan, N. Pickard and R. Russell. 512-6A-32

Northern Ireland and Manchester United footballer Norman Whiteside with some of the youngsters who attended a soccer coaching course he was giving at the Bloomfield Playing Fields on 22 June. The player also used the occasion to launch his fan club which was open to anyone living in the United Kingdom and included exclusive members-only functions after games at Old Trafford. 270-7-33

Seventeen-year-old Grainne Gunn, from Cleland Park North, became the first Irishwoman to swim the English Channel. She completed the gruelling 21 miles in 11 hours, 51 minutes and 27 seconds on 3 August. The A-Level student at Our Lady and St Patrick's College, Knock, was ladies' captain of Bangor Amateur Swimming Club. *101-3-34*

Bryn Cunningham, of Clifton Road, won the boys' under-10 section of the Ulster Junior Lawn Tennis Championships at Stranmillis in August 1987. Downshire Tennis Club colleague Clare McDonnell won the girls' under-10 plate. *108-3-34*

Colin Menary from Bangor qualified in August 1987 for the following year's Go-Kart World Championships at Silverstone. He earned his place by finishing second in the 250 International Non-Championship Race in the British Kart Grand Prix at the same venue. He was the reigning Ulster Champion in the Formula A 250 class. *134-12-34*

The Glenlola Collegiate 1st XI hockey team who won the National Playing Fields Tournament on 3 October 1987. The squad comprised Julie Ogilvie, Heather Walsh, Martine Nesbitt, Judith Walker, Nicola Cairns, Fiona Elliott (captain), Anthea Keyes, Alison McEwan, Julie Hampton, Claire Samways, Joanne Larkin, Cathy Hopkins, Lisa Cooper, Alison Moffitt and Joanne Weir. *374-9-34*

1988

Bangor bowler Rodney McCutcheon became a world champion on 13 February following the four-man Irish team's 27-15 defeat of the home side in the World Fours in Auckland, New Zealand.

Bangor FC manager Ronnie McQuillan left the club after his contract was "terminated amicably by mutual consent." Although Bangor had reached two semi-finals before the end of 1987, results in January and February were poor. He had been at the Clandeboye Park helm for two years.

The new manager, following a period as caretaker, was former Portadown player/manager John Flanagan, who was a regular with Bangor until breaking his leg in November 1986. He quickly signed up promising teenage full-back Mark Glendinning on professional terms.

Stephen Martin returns home to show off his Olympic medals to his family

Four years after winning an Olympic bronze medal in Los Angeles, Stephen Martin went not one but two better at the Seoul Olympics, returning home with a gold medal after the Great Britain hockey team beat Germany 3-1 in the final on 1 October.

Naturally disappointed he had played for only a few minutes in the final game – management wanted to base the team on the successful English side – he was still proud to be bringing the first Olympic gold medal back to North Down. In addition, he had played in more than 30 of the team's qualifying matches around the world.

Yachtsman Bill O'Hara, another competitor in Seoul, failed to match the 13th place he had achieved in the Finn Class at the Los Angeles Games. After breaking his rudder in the final race the reigning Ulster Laser champion fell from 12th place to 21st. He was full of praise for training partner and Olympic reserve Conrad Simpson, also from Bangor, saying much of his success was down to Conrad's encouragement.

Members of Bangor Pigeon Club at their annual dinner and prize distribution, which was held at Bangor Rugby Club in January 1988. 326-5-35

Stuart Farmer, Alan Shaw, Neal Johnston, Christopher Arnold, Christopher McDonald and David Moore, from Towerview Primary School, hold the Bangor and District Primary Schools' Sports Association 5-a-side Shield which they won in February 1988. Included is teacher Ian McCann. *407-18A-35*

Members of the Connor House mini hockey team who won the Bangor Mini Hockey Championship at Ward Park in March 1988, beating Bangor Central Primary School in the final. Back (from left): Paul Evans, David Jefferson, Andrew Slane. Front: Bryn Cunningham, Rory McMillan (captain) and Richard Harris. *153-12-36*

The team from the Bangor Castle Leisure Centre who took part in a raft race at Ballyholme in August 1988 to raise funds for the RNLI. Back (from left): Rosemary Stewart, Linda Martin, Berny McAdam, Paula Lennon. Front: Darren Potter and Douglas Skelton. *82-14-38*

Bangor Amateur Colts were playing for the first time in the Irish Amateur League in the 1988/89 season. They kicked off their season in September with a match against Larne at the Valentine Playing Fields. *431-15-38*

The newly-formed Gransha Boys' High School U-14 (Third Form) soccer team, pictured in November 1988, won four of their first five matches, drawing the other, in the schools' league. Back (from left): Nigel Snoddy, Mark Buttler, Phillip Morrow, Stuart McMillan (captain), Colin Walker, Wayne Donelan, Glen Puckrin, Thomas Taylor. Front: Neil Bond, Alan Tipping, Ian Walker, Alex Coulter and Ian Davis. Both Stewart McMillen and Glen Puckrin were selected for trials with the Glasgow Rangers Schoolboys squad. *206-7A-39*

1989

Bangor Amateur Colts accepted disqualification from the Youth Cup final, a ban on competing in Youth Cup matches for three seasons and a £10 fine. The Irish Football Association announced the penalties on 3 January following a tip-off that the Colts had competed in the semi-final against Coleraine with an over-age player on the team. The club acknowledged the player was indeed too old – by two-and-a-half hours.

Bangor golfer David Jones (41) recorded his first win in a major tournament, lifting the £11,600 prize in February's Kenya Open. Previous winners included Bangor professional Ernie Jones and Severiano Ballasteros.

David Addy regained the Open Singles title in the Bangor and District Table Tennis Championships in mid-February, while, to make it a family double, his sister Helen Gill won the Ladies' Singles.

Bangor schoolboy Keith Gillespie (14) signed schoolboy forms with Manchester United, aiming to begin a full-time apprenticeship when he turned 16. Keith, who played on the right wing for St Andrew's in the South Belfast League and had represented Northern Ireland Schools against Scotland in 1988, rejected overtures from Rangers because he was a lifelong United fan.

Bangor schoolboy signs for United

by Damien Magee

Dad Harry explained: "I was impressed with what I saw when we visited Old Trafford. Alex Ferguson took us out for dinner and we had a chat about Keith's education and then later the youth development officer showed us around the ground. I'm more than happy because I know he will be looked after."

Eddie Irvine joined the Marlboro-sponsored Pacific Racing team in February, setting his sights on the 1989 International Formula 3000 Championship – the final stepping stone to the speed and power of Formula One. He had made his Formula Ford debut at Kirkistown just five years earlier.

Bangor atoned for a Budweiser Cup semi-final defeat with a 2-1 victory over

Celebrating Bangor FC's victory in the County Antrim Shield during a special reception at the Town Hall in November 1989 are Mayor Hazel Bradford, Deputy Mayor George Green, Cllr Roy Bradford (right), along with Bangor manager John Flanagan, captain George Gibson, club chairman Gifford McConkey and Wilson Mathews. 562-9-42

Glentoran in the final of the County Antrim Shield. It was the club's first trophy in 14 years. Goalscorers were Raymond Campbell and George Gibson.

John Flanagan was named 'Manager of the Year' by Ulster sportswriters and Bangor ended the season in fourth place in the Irish League – their highest since finishing third in 1956.

Darren Nash (left, middle) from Kilmaine Drive, won the All Ireland tetraplegic bowls championship at Shaw's Bridge in May 1989.

Darren Nash. 364-18A-41

Three Bangor Amateur Swimming Club members, Claire Dorrian, Stewart Howard and Alan Officer, were selected in June for the Ulster Esso Youth squad competing in an international meeting at Oporto in Portugal. Claire was also appointed captain of the Ireland team for the Junior European Championships in Leeds.

Yvonne Fisher (left, bottom) qualified as a football coach for the Bangor Swifts Ladies team in August 1989. She took the course at Stranmillis Training College with Gillian Wylie, also from Bangor.

Athlete Noel Munnis broke the Irish triathlon record in early September at Malahide, Co Dublin, in his first attempt. His time was 10 hours and 23 minutes.

Billy Murray, from Meadowvale, won the World Kick Boxing Welterweight title at the Ulster Hall on 12 September, defeating American fighter Richard Hill in a re-match.

Yvonne Fisher. 150-11A-42

Bangor Grammar School's 1st XI won the Irish Schools Hockey Championship in November, beating RBAI 1-0 in the final.

Fourth Bangor Boys' Brigade, attached to Trinity Presbyterian Church, won the team event at the Belfast Battalion Cross-Country Championships in January 1989. Team members were David Massey, Arran Small, Graham Montgomery, Keith Jardine, Paul Frame, Andrew Frame and Stuart Harding. They are pictured with Company Captain Tommy Boal. *99-16A-40*

The Bangor District Primary Schools football team, pictured with coach David Maguire, were preparing in April 1989 to take part in the Northern Ireland Primary Schools Championships at Jordanstown. Back (from left): Richard Black, Simon McCormick, Glenn Alexander, Gareth McCullough, Gavin Campbell, Neil Coey, Robin Williamson. Front: Gareth Gettinby, Darren Adams, Steven Barr (captain), Andrew Girvan and Adam Scott. *460-8A-40*

Boys and girls from Towerview and Grange Park Primary Schools who took part in a Kelloggs-sponsored 'In the Swim' day at the Bangor Castle Leisure Centre in June 1989. Under the supervision of Olympic and Commonwealth Games gold medal winner David Wilkie, the children were shown the benefit of a healthy lifestyle through healthy eating and exercise. *407-19A-41*

The Bangor netball team won the Valley Gold tournament at the Valley Leisure Centre, Newtownabbey, in September 1989. Back (from left): manager Trixie Stewart, Karen McCrea, Lorraine Lindsay, Alison Boal, Irene Costley, Mary-Clare Taylor (PRO). Front: Lorraine Lindsay, Gail McIntyre, Liz Burnside (captain), Joanne Skehin. Absent from picture: Wenda Gray. 243-11A-42

Bridget Finnegan (11) with the shield she received for becoming Footballer of the Year at St. Comgall's Primary School. 579-14A-41

Keith Morrow, a Form 5 pupil at Gransha Boys' High School, had just signed for Second Division Hull City in October 1989 and was preparing to join the club at Easter 1990. He was following in the footsteps of brother John, another former Gransha pupil, who was playing for Glasgow Rangers. 325-1-42

These children took part in a penalty kicks competition during a 'Personality Spectacular' evening in November 1989, organised by Bangor Amateurs FC for Cancer Research. Included are Gerry Kelly from UTV and Amateurs' president Alister Scott. 483-11A-42

Ian Alexander
remembers...Golf

Ian Alexander is a grandson of D. E. Alexander, founder of the *County Down Spectator.*
  He has been golf correspondent for almost 40 years and has written light-hearted columns for the paper, firstly *Shooting From The Hip* and latterly *Our Grumpy Old Man.*

❝Tell us about golf and Bangor in the Eighties," said Terence Bowman, editor of this book. It was a broad invitation and golf, a minority sport, might not seem a likely subject for an article.

But as it happened, and if I might stretch the geographical boundary slightly to include the town's hinterland, it was the decade in which Bangor golfers thrust themselves into the sporting world's consciousness. Two men, Garth McGimpsey and David Feherty, and two clubs, Bangor and Clandeboye, were responsible for this brief period in the headlines.

Earlier decades had seen some local success. Clandeboye's Father Frank McCorry won the North of Ireland Championship in 1964 and Bangor's Brian Kissock was to win it twice in the Seventies. On the club front Clandeboye had won the Barton Shield in 1962 and 1965 and the Irish Senior Cup in 1970. But that was about it.

Garth McGimpsey and David Feherty had much in common. Both were sons of former captains of Bangor and learnt the game there but each had very different goals. Neither was particularly precocious and Garth was a few days short of his 23rd birthday when he made his breakthrough by winning the North of Ireland Championship in 1978.

Few who saw him beat Colm McGuckian 2&1 at Royal

Portrush would have guessed he would become one of the greatest ever Irish amateurs with a glittering career on and off the course. He had to wait until 1984 for his next title, the West of Ireland, but thereafter a year barely passed without another championship being added to his CV.

His finest moment came in 1985 when he won the British Amateur Championship at Royal Dornoch in Scotland. He went close again in 1989 when he reached the semi-final and by that time had acquired an international reputation. The honours flowed: he was to play in the Walker Cup in 1985, 1989 (winners for the first time in America) and 1991; the Eisenhower Trophy in 1984, 1986 and 1988 (winners), and against the Rest of Europe in the St Andrews Trophy in 1984, 1988, 1990 and 1992.

Garth McGimpsey plays his second shot at the eighth hole in the afternoon round at Royal Dornoch. Three holes later he had won the competition 8&7. *164-10A-22*

Family members and other supporters who had travelled many miles to witness Garth McGimpsey's success in the British Amateur Golf Championship at Royal Durnock in June 1985. From left: Nigel Woods, Peter Barry, Brian Kissock, Alan McDade, Marilyn McGimpsey, Kevin McGimpsey, Garth, Jack Kissock, Gillian McGimpsey, Malcolm McMorran, Nell McDonald (caddy and a 13-handicapper from Royal Durnock), Clive Thompson, Ian Sanderson and Hal McGimpsey. *166-16A-22*

Garth's statistics speak for themselves; in addition to his British Championship he won 12 provincial titles, the Irish Close in 1988, and represented Ireland a record 226 times.

His competitive days over, it was no surprise when he was asked to captain the GB and Ireland Walker Cup team twice. In 2003 his team beat the USA 12½-11½ at Ganton and in 2005 the score was exactly reversed in another thriller at the Chicago Golf Club.

He never had any intention of turning professional, a fact he made clear at the press conference following his British victory at Royal Dornoch, and he has gone on to develop a very successful sports agency business.

David Feherty, very much his own man, even as a teenager, was of exactly the opposite opinion. His parents were appalled but accepting when he announced he wanted to leave Bangor Grammar School before his A-Levels and turn professional. He was 16, a skinny youngster, a big-hitting, rather wild, five-handicapper with no obvious extraordinary talent for the game.

Fred Daly took him on as an assistant at Balmoral. Work in the gym improved his physique and a year in Florida being coached by Phil Ritson sharpened up his game. Still his breakthrough victory was a complete surprise.

David Feherty (22) with the Rank Xerox trophy he received after winning the Irish Professional Golf Championship at Royal Dublin in late September 1980. *362-3-11*

The Irish Professional Championship has been won by all the great names in Irish golf and the 22-year-old Feherty would not have been considered a likely winner when he travelled to Royal Dublin for the 1980 event.

His caddy was a Bangor member, Jack McCloskey, and between them they conjured up a victory. It was a feat he was to repeat in 1982 at Woodbrook but by that time he had established himself on the European Tour. However, he had to wait until 1986 before actually winning and he had to do it the hard way, beating Ronan Rafferty in a play-off to win the Bell's Scottish Open. A few weeks later he collected his second title, holding off Severiano Ballesteros 'down the straight' as they say, to win the Italian Open.

Although he won five times on the European Tour, played in the Ryder Cup at Kiawah Island in 1991, when he beat Payne Stewart 1 up, and captained the Irish team to victory in the Dunhill Cup at St Andrews in 1990 (a sublime four iron to the 17th sticks in the memory), after a brief foray onto the US Tour (second in the New England Classic was his best finish), he retired from the game.

I was not surprised as he told me early in his career he would not play in his 40s. And so it proved; instead he

Bangor Golf Club won the Senior Cup, Ireland's premier inter-club competition, for the first time in September 1981, defeating Douglas Golf Club, Cork, 3½ to 1½ in the final at the Grange, Dublin. Back (from left): Nigel Woods, Brian Blaikie, Alan McDade, Brian Kissock, Garth McGimpsey, Bertie Wilson. Front: Desmond Hillen (team captain), Geoffrey Henderson (club captain) and John McInerney (president of the Golfing Union of Ireland). *561-5-14*

has established himself as a columnist, novelist, after-dinner speaker and TV personality. He is, as they say, "huge in the States," and his quirky, sometimes outrageous, sense of humour has made him a household name.

However, golf here in the Eighties was not all about our dynamic duo. For a time in that decade Bangor and Clandeboye vied with each other to be the number one club in Ireland.

Bangor did it first when it won the Irish Senior Cup, the blue riband of inter-club golf, at the Grange in 1981 and repeated the trick at Tramore in 1984. Then it was Clandeboye's turn, winning in 1985 at Kilkenny and at Galway in 1986.

And we shouldn't forget Carnalea's contribution to the game here. It was in the Eighties when a few wise men like Joe Crozier, Jimmy Kennedy, Harry Graham and Charlie Kyle re-imagined the club and started the changes that transformed it from a modest municipal track to the successful club it is now.

Oh and one last thing. In 1981 Bangor's Ted Guthrie and (ahem) Ian Alexander won the *Belfast Telegraph* Foursomes, having earlier, in 1976, lost the final in humiliating circumstances.

Yes, the Eighties. A wonderful decade for golf.

Jeff Hearst

remembers... Squash

The 1980s, particularly the first half, was a golden period for squash in Bangor. It was very much in fashion throughout the country and local clubs provided a great environment to safely enjoy sport and social events.

There were several clubs in North Down, including Crawfordsburn and Kiltonga, which contributed much to the sport. However, a reflection on squash in Bangor in the 1980s is for me synonymous with a history of Bloomfield Squash Club – then the biggest club with nine courts. It was led by John Magrath, an Irish Men's champion renowned for his shot playing, with Irene Hewitt as club coach.

At its busiest, Bloomfield ran a full schedule of events – ladies' morning leagues, club nights, junior club sessions, club tournaments, etc. – and had a strong social side. The membership included many 'larger than life' characters, whose energy and efforts on the courts was often matched at social events. There was also a great family feeling with several families providing a backbone

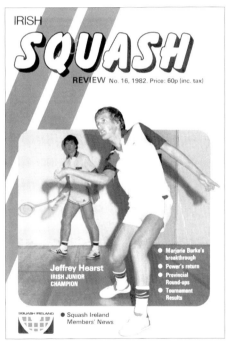

Jeff Hearst on the cover of *Irish Squash* magazine in 1982

Born in 1965, Jeff Hearst is the son of Peggy (née Lewis) and John Hearst and spent his childhood growing up in Bangor with brother John. He was first a pupil of

Groomsport Primary School and then Bangor Grammar School.

He went on to attend Cambridge University to complete a degree in Engineering and captained the university squash team. This was followed by an MBA at Manchester Business School.

Jeff enjoyed a successful squash career, including 129 caps for Ulster and 39 caps for Ireland.

He first met his wife Eileen whilst they were both teenagers, marrying in 1988. After living in England for a few years they moved back to Northern Ireland in 1991.

Jeff qualified as a civil engineer, working for local firms before moving into operations management with several international companies.

He and Eileen have two daughters, Cara and Amy, and a son, Stephen.

of players, volunteers and supporters – Fulton, Orr, Roycroft, McCormick, Robinson, McCabe, McKeown, Lowans, Getty and Warden, to name a few.

Teenage memories include a 24-hour squash marathon by the juniors (the first and only time I played at 3am in the morning), New Year events, summer training on nearby playing fields, the ever-present 'chicken in a basket' from the bar kitchen, my first experience of video games such as Galaxian, snooker, Dunlop Green Flash shoes, Black Tower and Blue Nun wine, wooden rackets and more.

With Bloomfield's success attracting new members and developing juniors, the club gradually became more successful in the Ulster leagues, which at that time had an amazing number of squash divisions (25-plus). This included winning the overall Ulster Division One League and Cup competitions several times in the 1980s.

There were many memorable league matches with rivals such as Windsor, Belfast Boat Club, Rosario and Ballyearl, when over 100 spectators would cram in behind the main glass back court and it sometimes felt more like a

The Bloomfield team were Men's Ulster Club Champions in 1984. Included are John Wright, Ian McClure, Graham Hull, John Magrath and Jeff Hearst, along with Guinness representatives Robert Blackburn and John Kinahan.

boxing venue. A notable highlight was winning the Division One League on the last match of the season against Rosario in 1984. The team included myself, John Magrath, the incredibly fit Ian McClure, the skilful John Wright and the talented shot player Graham Hull. With scores level at two matches each, John Magrath mixed outrageous skill with determination to win the deciding match 3/2 and we won the overall division from Rosario by 353 to 350 points. The women's teams, which included Irene Hewitt, Frances McCreanor and Linda Orr, also enjoyed success.

A mixed Bloomfield team consisting of seniors and juniors reached new heights by winning the National

Squash Federation British Club Championships at Derby in 1981. Bloomfield went on to compete in European Club events, including a memorable trip to Amsterdam. In 1989, as the decade ended, Bloomfield also finally overcame some of the strong Leinster clubs to become All Ireland Champions over a great weekend in Sligo, with a youthful team including Graeme Stewart, Ian Eldridge, Jimmy Moffat, Shaun McKee, John McKeag and myself.

The Bloomfield Men's team were All Ireland Club Champions in April 1989: Graeme Stewart, Ian Eldridge, Jimmy Moffat, Shaun McKee, John McKeag and Jeff Hearst. *Spectator* picture

Throughout the 1980s many more players loyally supported the club in league competitions – including Ian Houston, Billy Bell, the Blayney and Gardner brothers, Jim Bowers, Brian Kelly, Brian McKeown, Maurice Lorimer, Nicky Henderson, David Aumonier, David Shaw and John Campbell, again to name a few. Often you could tell who was playing on a court long before reaching it by the shouts and arguments going on. Some continue to play today – slower but just as competitively, still arguing over lets and strokes. Volunteers from Bangor also took active roles in Ulster and Irish squash. Paddy McIlroy and Jim Fleming, for example, were well known as referees and administrators throughout Ireland.

At schools level, both Bangor Grammar School and Glenlola enjoyed success as a result of the juniors playing at Bloomfield. BGS headmaster Tom Patton was a great supporter, with Irwin Bonar taking charge of the team.

Bangor Grammar School's All Ireland Schools Champions in 1981 with coach/ master-in-charge Irwin Bonar. From left: Ian Eldridge, Scott Fulton and Jeff Hearst. *377-13-16*

The school went on to win several Ulster league and cup

Bloomfield juniors competed for Ulster at the 1980 Inter-provincial Championships, held at the Bloomfield club. Included are Ian Eldridge, Linda Orr, Barbara Lowans, Ian McKeown, Gary McCormick and Jeff Hearst.

competitions, along with two All Ireland Schools titles, first with a team including Ian Eldridge, Scott Fulton and myself in 1981. This was repeated in 1984 with a new wave of players, including Keith Walker, brothers Colin and Graham McCabe, and Derek Rothwell.

Bloomfield during this period hosted numerous junior and senior events such as inter-provincials, Ulster and Irish championships, and was ahead of its time in attracting international events. With John Magrath's support, Bloomfield was first to host an international junior squash event with players from the mainland, Pakistan and other countries.

This was followed in 1981 by the World Masters Championship featuring all the top 32 players in the world. Legendary Australian Geoff Hunt and upcoming teenage sensation Jahangir Khan from Pakistan competed in an historic final at Bloomfield. Even though Geoff Hunt won, it marked the beginning of a switch in dominance, with Jahangir Khan going on to become the greatest player ever. To put this into context, it was equivalent to running Wimbledon at Ward Park and watching the battle between Borg and McEnroe. Further events followed, including hosting the Junior Home Internationals in 1984.

As to my own story, sporting genes were definitely in there somewhere – my mum Peggy had been a regular badminton player at Ballyholme, my dad had in his youth played football with the Boys' Brigade, including representing Northern Ireland at youth level. The reason for my family joining Bloomfield was quite by accident but possibly not unique given our weather. A touring holiday down south in the summer of 1977 was cut short after three days of constant rain, and my mum suggested we instead join the new squash club. My older brother John and I joined and immediately took to the game.

Following initial coaching from Irene Hewitt, John Magrath proved to be a great mentor who regularly took time out to play me and encouraged me to challenge all the top players. I was also surrounded by other talented Ulster juniors at the club such as Ian McKeown, Gary McCormick, Linda Orr, Barbara Lowans (future Irish International) and the especially talented Ian Eldridge. Most importantly, I had the full support of my parents as we travelled all round Ireland and the mainland.

I was fortunate to enjoy early local success and joined in the first Ulster U-14 team ever to play against a Leinster team. This was followed, over the next few seasons, by several Irish Junior titles and success at British and European competitions, including reaching the final of the British U-16 Championships and being ranked amongst the top three in Europe for my age. I joined the Ulster Men's

Jeff Hearst (left) with fellow members of the Irish Men's team who finished 10th, their highest position, in the 1983 World Team Championships in New Zealand. Also included (from second left) are John Young, Paul O'Brien (manager), David Gotto and Willie Hosey.

team at 16 and international senior representation also came early as the youngest representative for Ireland at 17.

Jeff Hearst today

There followed some great experiences at European and World Championships, with highlights including reaching the last 32 at the 1983 World Men's Individual Championships in New Zealand when aged 17, and the last 16 at the World Juniors in Canada, losing out to future five-times world champion Jansher Khan. As a student, I also enjoyed some great times competing in England, winning the British Universities Individual Championships and other team events.

Apart from the playing side, squash and Bloomfield provided the backdrop to many events in my life. I first met my wife Eileen there during schools games afternoons, organised by teachers from both Bangor Grammar (Irwin Bonar) and Regent House (Ivan Webb). My three children all now play to some degree – Cara competing successfully in the British Transplant Games, Amy enjoying success in the local youth games and Stephen currently on the Ulster U-13 team. And after an absence of several years, I am again involved as a member of the Ulster Squash Board and had the privilege to travel out to the Commonwealth Games in Delhi 2010 as coach to the NI squash team.

By the end of the 1980s participation in squash had passed its peak. Other sports became fashionable, snooker tables took over space for courts, a gym was introduced and so on. However, looking back it was a privilege to play squash in Bangor during that decade. It led to many great friendships, both locally and further afield. It remains one of the best sports in the world, for both exercise and good old-fashioned competition, and there are some great young players out there, including from Bangor. Hopefully there will be a new golden period for squash in Bangor in the not too distant future.

Tom Henry
remembers… North Down Cycling Club

In the early summer of 1977 Ian Henry had the idea of establishing a club to cater for the area's undoubted cycling talent. The accuracy of his vision and forethought has been demonstrated over and over again, as a stream of talent has benefited from being part of what became known as 'The Leading Team'.

Most of the forefathers were already members of other clubs around Northern Ireland. Eric and David Dunne were active members of Kings Moss CC, Ian and Tom Henry belonged to East Tyrone CC, and Jack Watson was a member of the Northern Cycling Club in Belfast – yet Ian convinced them all to break their existing ties and establish the new outfit.

Always with an eye to business, Ian soon coerced local entrepreneur Jim Irvine to join the steering committee. Others, including master butcher David Burns, insurance broker James Newberry, cycle dealer Percy Marshall and funeral director John Shields, were soon associated with

Some of the original members of North Down Cycling Club (from left): Eric Dunne, Jim Irvine, Heather Henry, Ian Henry, Rea Watson, Betty Irvine, Olive Freedman, Laura Henry, Jack Watson, David Dunne and Tom Henry

Tom Henry is Vice-Principal of Ballyholme Primary School. He's an active cyclist, having had a lifetime involvement in the sport.

He comes from a cycling family, where his father was President of the Northern Ireland Cycling Federation, and his two sons are also active cyclists.

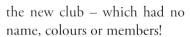

David Burns sponsored the Burns Bonus League for a number of years. Here he meets the emerging talent in the form of David Gore, Raymond Brownfield and George Pickford.

the new club – which had no name, colours or members!

That was quickly to change. Firstly, 'North Down' was chosen to associate the club with the wider locality, rather than be tied simply to Bangor. The number of members drawn from a wide catchment area has demonstrated the wisdom of this decision.

The choice of pink was equally evocative, controversial and successful. In an era when the majority of club colours were blue or red, to pick such a colour was quite mind-blowing. Yet it was not the policy of North Down Cycling Club to follow but, rather, to set trends. With that in mind, it was decided to adopt the pink race leader's jersey associated with the Tour of Italy.

Amazingly, within weeks of its formation the club was picking up medals – Alistair Irvine and Tom Henry won silver medals at the Irish Roller Sprint Championships in the schoolboys' and senior events respectively.

The undoubted jewels in North Down's 1980s crown were the Irvine brothers, Alistair and Gerald. As is still the case, the first road race of the season took place at Annaclone, near Banbridge. Wearing the distinctive colours of pink and black for the first time, Alistair won the schoolboys' race. Thus began an illustrious career – amongst his most celebrated achievements was selection, at 19, for the full national side in the Tour of Europe. In 1986 Alistair won the Irish Road Race title and in the same year he secured selection for the Commonwealth Games, becoming part of the team that won Northern Ireland's first Commonwealth Games medal, bronze in the team time trial.

Multi-Irish champion Alistair Irvine

Four years later, in Auckland, Alistair became the first Northern Irish cyclist to win an individual medal, with bronze on the track in the points race. In the same year he also won the prestigious Tour of the North International stage race. In all, Alistair represented Northern Ireland at four Commonwealth Games and then coached the cycling team at a further two.

Younger brother Gerald was an equally gifted athlete, going on to win Irish titles and represent Ireland on numerous occasions, including the 1983 Nations Cup when three North Down riders were on the team, Alistair, Gerald and Paul Watson.

Gerald won his first Irish cyclo cross championship in 1986 and went on to win a further seven Irish titles. Indeed he dominated cyclo cross racing for over a decade, finishing in the first three in Irish championships on 12 occasions, as well as picking up Northern Ireland titles in 1985 and 1988. In addition to representing Ireland at two world championships, Gerald was on the Olympic panel for the 1984 and 1988 Games and competed for Ireland at world level in various one-day classics.

In all, he achieved 63 career wins, 11 Irish championship medals (including two firsts), 13 Northern Ireland championship medals (including three firsts) and represented Ireland on 48 occasions.

North Down became a conveyer belt of emerging talent in the 1980s. A long list of young riders quickly dominated youth racing in Ireland, including Anthony Mitchell, Brendan Kirk, Alan and Paul Watson, Steve Enderby, John, Alwyn and Robert Orr, David Stanfield, Geordie Pickford, Norman McLeer, Maurice Ambrose, Alex Taylor, Gavin Barnes, Gary Boyle, Neill Moore, Ian Carlin, Mark O'Hara, Phillip Shields, Andrew Shields, Alastair Brogan, Gary Boyle, the Gore brothers (Davy, Alan and Colin), Colin McGivern, Colin Bell, Dougie Lennie, Phillip Marshall, Michael Hamilton and Ross Blayney.

A major financial breakthrough had occurred in 1979 when Toyota agreed to sponsor the club. Initially the contract was for three years, but such was the relationship between Toyota and the club that it was re-signed on numerous occasions, lasting an incredible 25 years, with the name Toyota North Down becoming synonymous with all things cycling in the Bangor area.

The list of activities taken on by the club was legendary. For example, on the Saturday before Christmas it traditionally organised a fancy dress 'race'. During the 1980s the venue was Castle Park, with the race being preceded by a parade through the town.

Strong emphasis was placed on the club's charity work with thousands of pounds being raised through sponsored cycles and events such as the Charities Race during Bike Week. Also noteworthy was the work it did with the visually impaired. Tandems were purchased and those with visual handicaps rode pillion with sighted club members piloting. Several visually impaired riders became involved with the club; Michael Beggs, for example, as a very active committee member.

Irish Cyclo Cross champions Gerald Irvine, Alistair Irvine and Paul Watson being congratulated by Mayoress Hazel Bradford and club president David Burns

Given the experience and calibre of Ian Henry and Jack Watson, it was obvious from the start that North Down would promote more that its share of top-class events, including roller racing, cyclo cross and road races. One such event was 1983's Centenary Classic. Bangor had been due to promote the finish of a Ras stage but at the last minute the organisers changed their plans. North Down Borough Council had already ring-fenced finance for what was the biggest cycling event in Ireland, but by coincidence it was also the centenary of the island's first organised bike race. So with the Council's permission, Jack Watson organised the Centenary Classic over 100 miles for a first prize of £100, a sum unheard of in 1983. The race, over the Rathgael to Newtownards circuit, was won by Liverpool Century's Les Westwood, then an upcoming star.

Three years later North Down promoted the Irish Senior Road Race Championships, using the Ring Road, Newtownards, Six Road Ends circuit. It attracted widespread television coverage and was won by local hero Alistair Irvine.

Perhaps the event which attracted most attention was Bangor Bike Week. Initially, Jack organised a very successful two-day three stage race. Then, after he passed the reins over to Ian Henry, it became a hugely successful week-long event, involving recreational cycles, time trials and even international road races such as the Dale Farm Ulster Games event.

North Down Cycling Club was a trendsetter in so many ways. For example, the club actively encouraged female participation, with many becoming active in club and open cycling events. The most successful was undoubtedly Noreen McArthur, but there were others, including Laura Henry, Julie McLeer and Katrina Gillespie. Many more were active supporters and facilitators, for instance Rea Watson and Heather Henry who served the club diligently as timekeepers.

Committee members in 1980. Back row (from left): Tom Henry, Alistair Irvine, Eric Dunne (treasurer), John Orr (secretary), Winston Price, John Orr (Jnr.). Front: Sam Bell, Jack Watson (chair), Brian McMullan (race secretary) and Ian Henry.

Heather, in fact, became the first and only lady to hold the position of chairperson and she also held the office of race secretary for a lengthy period. She even became a qualified commissaire, officiating at races all over the country. There were others, however, such as Irene Dunne and Vi Jones, who marshalled at events, not to mention the ladies from Rathgael and Lisnevin schools who catered for the club and participated in numerous fundraising activities.

Unfortunately, like all families, North Down also has had its difficulties. One undoubtedly occurred in 1987 when the club had to decide to re-align with the All Ireland cycling body or remain within the Northern Ireland Cycling Federation. The majority of members voted to remain with the NICF but a number left to join other clubs.

It was a sad time as friendships were splintered and in many respects the harmony that characterised cycling was lost. Many, in fact, questioned whether the club, or

The Eighties ended on a high note for North Down Cycling Club with continued support from Toyota and burgeoning membership

even the sport, could survive this unwelcome fracture. Amazingly, however, like a phoenix North Down Cycling Club rose from the ashes and in the closing years of the decade enjoyed its largest ever membership.

As the decade ended, those involved in the club could only marvel at what had been achieved. Organised cycling in the Borough had provided its inhabitants with a channel to develop their sporting potential and to achieve success, which surpassed even the most enthusiastic observer's ambitions at the club's formation.

Some NDCC members from the 1980s who are still involved in the club. From left: Eric Blayney, Michael McMullan, John Hunter, Noel Munnis and Tom Henry.

Perhaps more importantly, the club had become an integral component in the local community, offering opportunities to socialise, raise finance for charities and provide a healthy pastime for everyone, regardless of age. Given this backcloth it is not difficult to understand why North Down Cycling Club looked forward to the Nineties with enthusiasm.

Alan Kernaghan
remembers... Soccer

I've always played football, mainly, I think, because my dad Bill was so enthusiastic about it and would often tell me stories about how good he had been! When we came to Bangor from Leeds in the early 1970s I attended Towerview Primary School and right away got into the school team. Jim McCarthy and Gordon Whittle were the teachers in charge of the team and we did quite well in our games.

When I was 11 I moved to Gransha Boys' High because Bangor Grammar didn't play football, so maybe I already knew that was what I wanted to do. My football really took off there – I must say again with the help of the teachers, this time Billy Bell and Lex Hayes, who gave me both confidence and encouragement.

Fifteen-year-old Alan Kernaghan after he was capped for Northern Ireland Schoolboys

They looked after our team pretty much right through to me leaving Gransha and had a big influence on how my career panned out. We had a good team with Andrew Montgomery in goal, Allan Smith as central defender, Neil Bruce in midfield and Phillip Stanley along with myself in attack. I must admit Phillip was a better goalscorer than I was, but I think I made a lot of his goals for him. We had a decent record and managed to win the odd trophy.

I was around 13 when I got spotted by Middlesbrough.

Alan Kernaghan was born on 25 April 1967 in Otley, West Yorkshire, moving with his family to Bangor when he was four. He attended Towerview Primary School and Gransha Boys' High School, where his skills as a central defender came to the attention of Middlesbrough FC.

He joined the club as an apprentice in his early teens, going on to make 212

The Gransha Boys' High School team with the Belfast and District Cup in 1981, including teachers Lex Hayes (left) and Billy Bell, with Alan Kernaghan (back row, far right). *53-7a-13*

Members of the Gransha Boys' High School team who won the Belfast and District Cup in 1983, including Alan Kernaghan (back row, sixth from left), teachers Billy Bell (left) and Lex Hayes (right), along with headmaster J. McCullough. Back row also includes: A. Cockcroft, A. Montgomery, J. McAteer and A. Smith. Middle: P. Douglas, L. Curran, N. Morrow, A. Neill, P. Stanley, K. Walker. Front: S. Ferris, G. Bennett, N. Bruce (captain) and D. Scott.

appearances during an eight-year period, scoring 16 goals in that time. He also spent a spell on loan at Charlton Athletic in 1991, making 12 appearances.

Despite playing for Northern Ireland Schoolboys when he was 15, Alan was deemed ineligible to play for the senior

I had a friend called Connor Gallagher whose dad Jackie was a coach for the IFA and instructed budding coaches on courses to get their badges. Connor and I would go along and join in where needed and at the end of the session we would have a game. It was after one of those games that a man called Bobby Macauley came up to me and invited me to go to Middlesbrough for a trial. That's how it all began – with that little bit of luck we all need in life.

Although football was a big part of my life, I enjoyed myself in other ways around Bangor. Every Saturday night my pals and I would go to BJ's on the Seacliff Road for a night of dancing and meeting girls; it was where I met my wife Gillian (née Burns). The music was a big factor as you were either a Mod or a Rocker or a Rude Boy – I think I had a spell as both a Mod and a Rude Boy! Roller discos were big at that stage and Rollerama on Queen's Parade was another big draw as it had amusements as well as snooker to keep us entertained.

I reckon we were very lucky to have such places in the 1980s as I don't think there is anything similar for the present generation of 12 to 16-year-olds.

I spent much of the time during our school holidays in Groomsport where we had a caravan. I know it sounds a bit daft as we only lived about three miles up the road but it was a completely different world there. We had different friends, mainly from Belfast, and we had different ways of spending our time – mostly in the play area or down on the beach. We were very fortunate to have a speed boat and my dad, my brother and I would be out water skiing at every opportunity off Groomsport, Ballyholme or Bangor seafront itself. We would use the beach at Queen's Parade, right where the car park is now, and go off around the bay by Pickie Pool. I helped to teach my friends Roger Spence and Steven Yeates how to water ski in and around Bangor; since then Roger has always been around boats and now jet skis.

Through the winter I really liked to mess around on motorbikes but my mum's brother – I'm named after him – was unfortunately killed on one when he was young so I was not allowed to have my own but would beg a go on my friends' bikes. We never went on the roads but would use any spare bit of ground we could find: usually the lead mines, the Balloo Industrial Estate or, as Ballycrochan was being built then, any field around that area.

Sometimes there would be around 10 of us, Roger and Chris Spence, Gary Higginson, Michael Arbuthnot, Gareth and Marcus Dunlop, Ian and David McEachern, Clive Hunter and a couple of others. Chris Spence and his dad Ted would go to proper races and I would make every effort to go along and watch, especially if it was at Clandeboye. The race used to take place where the Blackwood golf course is now; it was a really good track and would attract many of the best riders from not only Ireland but England and Scotland as well.

So my 1980s were certainly action-packed from start to finish, from going to school in Bangor to making my first team debut for Middlesbrough at the age of 18. I'm still

Alan achieves world cup dream

By John McCreedy

Alan Kernaghan is off to the States with the Republic squad

ALAN Kernaghan made history last night by becoming the first footballer from Bangor to reach the World Cup finals – and he did it the hard way playing for the Republic of Ireland at Belfast's Windsor Park.

The former Northern Ireland schoolboy sensation, who wasn't eligible for the Province at senior level, reached the pinnacle of his career with a hard earned 1-1 draw against Northern Ireland in what was a make or break match for Jack Charlton's Republic team.

Before kick off the men from the South needed to win outright to qualify for next year's glamour tournament in the USA. Fortunately for Alan and his teammates, a draw proved to be enough due to Spain's win over Denmark in Seville, leaving the Republic to scrape through on goal difference.

In what was a night of excruciating drama, Alan's American dream hung in the balance for most of the game – especially when Jimmy Quinn hammered home what looked like a killer goal 17 minutes from time. However thanks to a late equaliser by the Republic's Alan McLoughlin, Kernaghan who lived at Ballycrochan Road, with his parents before moving to English league football, will now achieve what in every footballer's dream – to take part in the the World Cup finals.

Alan and the rest of the Republic lads were whisked off to Dublin directly after the match.

Proud father Bill who has been a constant source of encouragement throughout Alan's playing career was thrilled to bits with the qualification. "Considering the atmosphere was electric and the general

consequences which were at stake I thought he played really well. Even when Jimmy Quinn scored I didn't think it was all over us up until then the Republic had looked like scoring themselves." He also added: "It was a great occasion and I'm glad Billy Bingham went out on a good note." Asked would he now be saving a few pounds to go and watch Alan's World Cup debut he quipped, "It looks like I will have to get the wife another job, but yes I think you can bank on it that we will be there next year."

Also attending last night's sporting showdown was former Gramsha High school vice-principal Gifford McConkey. He was delighted that his former pupil had qualified for next year's finals and attributed the achievement to Alan's determination and character, Mr. McConkey,

who is also chairman of Bangor F.C., commented: "I thought Alan had a super game and there is no doubt he has been a great loss to Northern Ireland. Indeed I tried very hard to enlist him for what he views as his home country, but the rules wouldn't allow it." He added that he was pleased with Alan's progress and in particular that he hadn't forgotten his roots as a pupil at Gramsha.

There is no doubt that the towering, fair haired defender, who recently signed for Manchester City, having previously played for Middlesborough is currently experiencing the greatest period of his football life. Not content with a World Cup place Alan is off to Norwich on Friday with his new club for Saturday's league game, before appearing live on Monday night's Sky TV match against premier side Chelsea.

team as both his parents were English-born. However, as he had a grandmother who was an Irish citizen he was approached by the Republic of Ireland, whose criteria he did meet. He subsequently played for Jack Charlton's side on 26 occasions between 1993 and 1996 – including a call-up for the 1994 World Cup – and scored one goal.

In September 1993 Alan joined Manchester City for a fee of £1.6m, playing 63 games for the club. In addition he went out on loan to Bolton Wanderers (11 games), Bradford City (five games) and St Johnstone (12 games).

He left Manchester City in 1997, playing the final nine years of his career in Scotland, firstly with St Johnstone (60 games), Brechin City (three games), Clyde (63 games), Livingston (four games) and Falkirk (nine games).

Alan Kernaghan following his arrival at Brentford FC in 2012. *Picture © Mark D Fuller/obfcp.co.uk*

He was player/manager of Clyde in the 2003-04 season, assistant manager at Livingston, player/coach at Falkirk, and then manager of Dundee for seven months during the 2005-2006 season. In that same year he became the first former Republic of Ireland player to hold a coaching role (with the U-17s) at Rangers, remaining at the club until the beginning of 2012.

In February 2012 he joined League One side Brentford as coach under manager (and former Manchester City colleague) Uwe Rösler. Five months later he was appointed assistant manager.

in touch with some of my friends but I must admit that, having been away for more than 30 years, I would most likely not recognise them. That could soon change, however, as Gillian and I are looking to move back to the area in the near future.

Tribute from Alan's former teacher

It was obvious that Alan Kernaghan was going to make it as a professional footballer. He listened to all that you told him and gave 100% in every match, practice and training session, always working hard to improve any weaknesses in his game.

He was that rare pleasure to coach – a talented player who had the humility to bend to team needs and he tried to do all that you asked him to do with an overwhelming desire to win.

Lex Hayes, principal, Glengormley High School,
October 2012

Colin Loughead
remembers... Rugby

The Eighties proved to be a very special decade for Bangor. Not only did the town's 1st XV produce, arguably, some of the finest performances in any club rugby in Ireland, but Bangor also celebrated its centenary, in 1985.

A plethora of players represented both Ireland and Ulster in this remarkable era of the club's history. Davy Morrow, Jimmy McCoy, Kenny Hooks, Don Whittle and Ronnie Elliott all played at full international level, Terry McMaster and Mark McCall turned out for Ireland 'A' and Ireland U-21s respectively, and the same players were joined, in different games, by such notables as Ashley Armstrong, Garth Maxwell, Sandy Todd and John Rogers, who all represented Ulster at senior level. In the early Eighties Michael D. M. Rea was Ulster rugby's number one referee and he represented the club as the only international referee in its history.

Many other Bangor players also played representative rugby while members of other clubs.

There were few seasons in the Eighties when Bangor did not have some of its members playing representative rugby; with such experience in the side it was little wonder the less well known players always gave of their best and ensured the Seasiders were clearly the team of the decade.

Obviously competitive games, namely the Senior League,

Colin Loughead was born in Bangor in 1956. His interest in rugby started at the age of nine or 10 when he was taken to Ward Park (where the all-weather pitches are now) to watch Bangor, and in particular his uncle Roy.

He started playing the game after moving to Bangor Grammar School in 1968, and was a ball boy at the newly opened Upritchard Park the following year.

Colin also became extremely interested in music around this time and was fortunate enough to be offered a place playing the bassoon in the Ulster Youth Orchestra, and consequently the Irish Youth Orchestra. Rugby of necessity had to take a back seat!

Bangor in the Eighties

Bangor's 1st XV celebrate winning the AIB Ulster Challenge Cup for the first time in April 1980. *498-15-9*

A place at Trinity College of Music, London, followed in 1974, and he was in the right place at the right time to be offered a job with the musical *Oliver!* at the Albery Theatre in London's West End, from the end of 1979 until the show closed in late 1980.

Colin returned to his native Bangor, eventually being offered a peripatetic woodwind tutoring job with the South Eastern Music Service, a post he still holds today.

In 1981 he resumed playing rugby for Bangor Sevenths (!), eventually working his way up through the other teams until a 1st XV debut in 1985. Colin thoroughly enjoyed his playing career at Bangor and went on to become club president in 2008.

Fortunately he was able, quite successfully, to juggle his musical commitments, occasionally playing with the Ulster Orchestra (along with his good friend Greg Morgan, the then principal trombonist with the orchestra, who also appeared occasionally in Bangor colours), and with most of the local operatic

the Senior Cup and the Bass Boston Cup (later the Smithwicks Boston Cup), were the most important, but in that era 'friendlies' were quite the norm. It was not unusual, early on a Saturday morning, to see a coach set forth from (or arrive at) Upritchard Park for an encounter involving the best opposition in the country.

Such was Bangor's reputation that teams like Wanderers, Blackrock, Monkstown, Trinity College, Garryowen, Lansdowne, Skerries and Old Wesley always showed due respect by fielding their strongest possible sides.

On St Valentine's Day 1984 Dinamo Bucharest visited Bangor, with the hosts proving too strong for what was virtually the Romanian national team. The teams kicked off in front of a healthy crowd and entertained everyone with a fine attacking game. Bangor won comfortably by 23-6 in what proved a great experience for one and all.

Two main tours took place in that halcyon period, namely to South Africa in 1981 and to Canada in 1988. The former involved an invitational tournament in which top teams from England, Wales and Scotland, as well as the host nation, were all represented. Bangor, something of an unknown quantity, opened everyone's eyes with their skill, enthusiasm and style of rugby, and rounded off the trip successfully by winning the plate competition in Pretoria.

The 1988 tour was more informal, with the team playing four friendly matches in the blistering Canadian heat. As well as a very close defeat at the hands of British Columbia, there were fairly straightforward wins against Calgary Irish, Calgary Canucks and Cowichan RFC on

Victoria Island. A breathtaking journey by coach through the Canadian Rockies was a highlight of the tour, and one that most of the party would love to revisit!

There was only one barren season (1983/84) when Bangor did not win any of the major

The victorious Bangor 1st XV following their 20-16 defeat of Queen's University which secured the Section One League title in April 1981. 316-12A-13

senior trophies. Apart from that, the Senior League title came to Upritchard Park on no fewer than four occasions, with the club finishing runner-up in two other seasons. The Senior Cup was secured on four occasions, the Bass Boston Cup four times as well and the Smithwicks Boston Cup twice, plus the Smithwicks Floodlit Challenge Trophy and the Pretoria (SA) Plate.

Several seasons spring to mind as being particularly special. In 1981/82 the club achieved unprecedented success. The Senior League was won at Ravenhill in April after the team defeated Collegians 13-9. Ten days later the Senior Cup was Bangor-bound following a well deserved 26-7 victory over junior opponents Carrick, the club having, between those two matches, lifted the Carrick-sponsored Holmes Salver seven-a-side tournament.

Earlier in the year the side had made that notable impression on the international stage by winning the Pretoria Plate in South Africa, while nearer to home they had defeated local rivals Ards 15-6 in the Bass Boston Cup.

The centenary year, of course, was particularly memorable. Although not overly successful on the pitch – the sole trophy being the Bass Boston Cup at Christmas 1985 – the team played all the major Irish sides. Two matches stand out as being very special, the game against the Wolfhounds and then a very prestigious encounter with Cardiff, hailed in those days as the best team in

societies, eventually conducting the Banbridge (now in his 20th year), Bangor and Newry Musical Societies.

Some of his fondest, and proudest, moments in recent times have involved watching his two sons playing their own rugby, at school and latterly at university.

Bangor's multi-trophy winning team of 1987/88. Back row (from left): William Trimble, Norman Gault, John McNabb, Jeff McMaster, Niall Johnston, John Henderson, John Rogers, Davy Morrow, Colin Loughead, Terry McMaster, Jimmy McCoy, Noel Scott, William Preshaw. Front row: Ronnie Elliott, Richard Kennedy, Mark McCall, Roden Ward, Garth Maxwell, Jack McMaster, Victor Dougan, Dick McCullagh and Ricky Huddleston.

Colin Loughead demonstrated what a player would have worn in the 1880s when he joined club captain Sandy Todd (left) to help launch Bangor Rugby Club's centenary year in 1985. *Spectator picture*

Britain.

The very next season, 1986/87, saw Bangor being welcomed as the first Ulster visitors to Cardiff Arms Park for 81 years. It was a rare privilege to grace that hallowed Welsh turf. An epic display from all concerned, in front of a 5,000-strong crowd, saw Cardiff struggle to emerge victors. They scored in the dying minutes to win by 21-14. In the same year Bangor also won the Senior Cup.

Another particularly noteworthy year was 1987/88, with the team winning the Senior League and the inaugural Smithwicks Floodlit Challenge Trophy, retaining the renamed Smithwicks Boston Cup, plus the Sportability senior sevens, the Omagh sevens and the Collegians 15-a-side competition. They were narrowly beaten 6-3 by Malone in the Senior Cup final.

The *Irish Times* named Bangor the Digital Club of the Month for January 1987, while the side was also acclaimed as Irish Club of the Month for March 1988 by *Rugby World* magazine.

The Eighties tapered off for Bangor with the introduction of the All Ireland League. The Seasiders hadn't enjoyed

Attending Bangor Rugby Club's centenary dinner in May 1986 were (from left): Victor Hazlett, chairman of the Northern Ireland Sports Council; Joe Upritchard, president of Bangor RFC; Sir Ewart Bell, senior vice-president of the IRFU; former Welsh captain and broadcaster Cliff Morgan; D. T. McKibben, president of the IRFU; Roden Ward, chairman of Bangor RFC; Dick Milliken, Bangor RFC; C. Gibney, Lombard and Ulster; John West, international referee; J. M. Simms, Bass Ireland; and Roy Loughead, Bangor RFC centenary committee chairman. *180-6A-28*

quite as much success nearing the end of the decade and they were therefore placed in the second division of the inaugural AIL. The arrival of that new era is a very appropriate point to wrap up what was probably the best 10 years of Bangor Rugby Club's existence.

I was very privileged to have been a member of the 1st XV during this era, playing against, as already documented, the best Irish sides from both North and South, and also playing in that epic encounter at the Arms Park.

The spirit and camaraderie evident in that 80s team, not to mention the great skill among the players, contributed to the overall success of the side. On top of that, the post-match craic cemented off-the-field friendships that have lasted to the present day. Meeting old adversaries at an Ulster or Irish match, a current Bangor match, or, more interestingly, at school games in which sons are playing, always evokes magical memories of past days. That, I think, is something unique to Rugby Football.

Still an ardent Bangor supporter, I was privileged some years back to become its president, following in the footsteps of my late uncle, Roy Loughead. He had served as one of club's presidents in those heady days of the 1980s and became IRFU president in 2001.

Outstanding decade for Bangor Grammar School
by Dougie Rea

Without doubt the 1980s was the most successful decade in the history of rugby at Bangor Grammar School. Following the Schools Cup win of 1978, BGS reached the final again in 1979 and 1981, and the semi-final in 1982, in the process building a reputation as a formidable cup team.

In advance of one of the biggest fixtures on the local rugby calendar, North Down Mayor George Green welcomed captain Mark Tinman and members of the Bangor Grammar School 1st XV, who had reached the March 1981 Schools Cup final, to the Town Hall. Included are team coaches, headmaster Tom Patton and members of the Council. The team lost 12-3 to Ballymena Academy at Ravenhill on St Patrick's Day. *39-7-13*

Although the 1983-84 cup campaign ended with a first round defeat, the team, captained by Peter McFall, went on to share the Subsidiary Shield with Belfast High. The valuable experience gained from this final at Ravenhill contributed greatly to the run of success for the next four seasons.

The 1984-85 season was particularly successful, with the school winning both the Schools Cup, under the captaincy of Michael Webb, and the Medallion Shield (Sean

Bangor Grammar School's 1st XV celebrate their success in the 1985 Schools Cup final at Ravenhill. *358-3A-24*

Crowther). Michael was an outstanding leader and represented Irish Schools on the wing, although he played at wing forward for BGS. He is still involved in rugby as a doctor with the IRFU and, in particular, the Ulster side.

Two other notable members of that school side were Mark McCall and Stephen McKinty. Mark subsequently captained

Ulster and Irish Schools, as well as the Ulster team which won the European Cup in 1999. He went on to play for Ireland and is presently director of rugby at Saracens. Stephen also represented Ulster numerous times, including the European Cup triumph, and was a stalwart of Bangor RFC for many years.

Under the captaincy of Mark McCall, BGS retained the Schools Cup in 1986, defeating RBAI in the final. The Medallion side, captained by Stephen Mann, again reached the Shield final but lost narrowly to MCB. The 1st XV played a very attractive brand of rugby, especially in the Cup final, and at season's end was judged to be the Schools Team of the Month by *Rugby International* magazine, all schools in the British Isles being considered. The side also defeated the full Ulster Schools team 18-4 in a floodlit game organised by Bangor RFC as part of its centenary programme.

The Bangor Grammar School team celebrate success in the 1986 Schools Cup final at Ravenhill. *Spectator* picture

The 1986-87 season was one of mixed fortunes for the 1st XV. Although results overall were average, the team had another excellent Schools Cup campaign and were only denied a hat-trick of wins after conceding a very late score to lose 10-9 to MCB in the final. Darryl Flanagan was an inspiring captain and representative honours were achieved by Sean Crowther and Gavin Ellis, who both played for Ulster Schools and were members of the Irish Schools party which toured Australia. Gavin had an outstanding school rugby career, playing in three successive Cup finals.

Sean Crowther was captain of the 1987-88 side and led the school to a third Cup win in four years, with a 13-4 victory over Coleraine Inst. in the final. Sean thus had the distinction of captaining both Medallion Shield and Schools Cup-winning sides and represented both Ulster and Irish Schools for two years. He captained the latter

The jubilant Bangor Grammar School 1st XV celebrate their Schools Cup success – their third in four years – in March 1988. 165-18-36

on one occasion. Jonathan Mawhinney played for Ulster Schools, while Simon McKenna and Chris Kerr joined Sean and Jonathan as members of the Ulster Schools party to tour Zimbabwe.

Finally, a further honour was bestowed on Bangor Grammar School when *Rugby World* magazine judged the 1st XV to be the Irish Club of the Month, an outstanding honour since all schools and clubs in Ireland were considered. During this period the team was coached by Dougie Rea, assisted by Duncan Macpherson, while strong support from the staff for senior rugby in the school was provided by Jimmy Welch, the master in charge of rugby, Vic Swain, Stephen Blake-Knox, Eric Cardwell, Bob McIlroy, Ray Mowat and David Napier.

Valuable contributions to coaching were also made by Jimmy McCoy, Terry McMaster, Davy Morrow, Roger Clegg and Dick Milliken.

In this remarkable era for the school the interest and the support shown by the board of governors, old boys and parents were very evident. Receptions at the Town Hall became an annual event and on one occasion the team was invited to Stormont by then local MP and Assembly member Jim Kilfedder.

To conclude, a team drawn from all those who played in this period would have been a match for anyone. Hard though it is to choose, this would be my personal selection: C. Jackson; M. Webb, M. McCall, G. Ellis, R. Blackmore; S. McKenna, K. Woods; J. Mawhinney, D. Flanagan, W. Johnston; R. Wilson, D. Cooke; S. McKinty, N. Johnston, S. Crowther. Would you agree?

Andy McAvoy
remembers... Karate

It was while living in South Africa in the 1970s that I witnessed a demonstration of Goju Karate and was greatly impressed at the speed and flexibility of the participants. It heralded the beginning of 40 years of training, practise and teaching karate.

Principal training was with the Japan

Andy McAvoy in a late 1980s encounter in Bangor with Masao Kawasoe, now one of the most highly respected karate teachers in the world. *Spectator* picture

Karate Association of South Africa (SAJKA) under various instructors, Nigel Jackson, Duncan Player and Robert Ferrier, with the latter inviting me to attend his elite Friday night classes. This involved some of the most brutal training to be experienced anywhere – with many injuries, as well as blood and broken bones. If you survived you were mostly relieved but also proud of your achievement.

On returning to Northern Ireland in 1980 I looked around Bangor and district for a Shotokan club but without success so I went back to weight training at Joe Scott's Eagle Barbell Club.

Born at Shore Street in Holywood, Andy McAvoy moved with his family to Church Street, Bangor, in 1948. He recalls how the Bangor of his childhood, then a much smaller town, was a safe place for children who played happily in the street after school and during the holidays, from breakfast until teatime.

According to Andy, that freedom of the 1950s and early 1960s allowed his generation to develop their independence – with less traffic on the roads they walked or cycled everywhere.

Boyhood friends of Andy and his brother George included Raymond and Paul Rea, Eddie Reid and Ted Oliver. They could all be found playing football in the street or cricket in the field behind the Reas' house on Belfast Road. Popular haunts included the Tonic Cinema, especially for the cowboy movies and serials on Saturday mornings, and the Queen's Cinema in the afternoons or evenings.

Andy attended Trinity Primary School, which headmaster Hugh McComb ran with a firm grip. When

Lindsay (left) and Lisa Adair in the late 1980s

Clandeboye Road Primary School opened, Andy was among the many neighbourhood children drafted into "this very large and intimidating edifice". He concluded his education at Lisburn Technical College, where boys were prepared for industry and girls for office work.

Employment was easy to find in the 1960s and he

As I was training there three times a week, with a lot of stretching techniques as part of my routine, some of the bodybuilders and power lifters became curious about what I was doing. They encouraged me to hold some classes and teach karate. Initially I was reluctant to start a club as others were opening for a few months, gathering up deposits, etc., and then disappearing off the face of the earth. In truth, very low-graded instructors, with a limited interest in developing students' potential, were running many karate clubs back then.

After much thought I enquired into the availability of decent training space and the Bangor Shotokan Karate Club, after being advertised in the *Spectator,* commenced on Tuesday nights in Hamilton House. I was a little unsure of the public response but to my amazement there were some 52 potential students on that first night, all keen to find out what the new karate club was about.

There is usually a very low retention rate in karate as would-be exponents expect to quickly turn into Bruce Lee! When they realise the work and effort required of them to make even modest progress, they quickly turn to other pastimes. Within a few months numbers had levelled out at about 20 and the real work began. In those early days students like Michael Legge, Jim and Mary McNabb, Peter Sangster and, later, Anne and Kevin Adair with their hugely talented children Lisa and Lindsay, got down to serious training. Many later became instructors in their own right but only after a lot of hard effort and repetitive practise.

The club became affiliated to a British Shotokan organisation so we could invite senior instructors over to run courses and gradings. However, when we tried to arrange this no one was prepared to come to Northern Ireland. It was the 1980s after all and they must have thought it wasn't safe. We then became affiliated to the Karate Union of Ireland and travelled to their courses in Dublin and Letterkenny, followed by annual trips to Crystal Palace to train with the top Japanese instructors who were being invited to London by Keinosuke Enoeda. That was when we first met Masao Kawasoe, one of the most highly respected karate teachers in the world today and currently chief

Members of the Bangor Shotokan Karate Club, which met at the Valentine Playing Fields, are pictured after a training session in December 1985. *179-8-26*

instructor of the United Kingdom Traditional Karate Federation and holder of the grade of 8th Dan (Japan Karate Association).

The Bangor Shotokan Karate Club had two venues for its meetings – the Bangor Castle Leisure Centre on Tuesday evenings and Saturday mornings and a hall we rented on a permanent basis from the Council at the Valentine Playing Fields. Anyone training at the latter needed to be a hardy individual. North-facing with a concrete floor, stone walls and corrugated iron roof, it would have made a fine fridge!

Nevertheless everyone trained in bare feet and we even went for the odd 'warm-up' run around the park, also bare-footed, in both winter and summer. Occasionally we would decamp to the beach at Ballyholme to train... ah, such fond memories! It involved difficult training in difficult situations but surviving the ordeal gave one the confidence to deal with hardship and adversity. So there was method in the madness.

As time went by we travelled to Dublin to train and have the junior grades assessed by Tommy McGrane; Tommy also visited Bangor regularly to train and grade students. By 1984/5 we'd got most of the original students through the exacting black belt gradings in London. Later Lisa and Lindsay Adair graded to first Dan (black belt), becoming

eventually settled into work in the dyehouse laboratory at the Berkshire factory in Newtownards.

It was workmate Leslie Dowie who introduced Andy to training with weights in Joe Scott's Eagle Barbell Club off Croft Street. Also training there were Eric and Alan Dowie, Michael Legge, Mike Gabbey, Trevor Harvey, Norman Woodman, John Carson and many others.

After marrying local girl Valerie McGimpsey, and with the couple looking for adventure, they decided to travel to South Africa in 1971 for a working holiday, but opted to stay. Three of the couple's four children, Paul, Peter and Michael, were born there, while Sarah arrived after they had returned to settle permanently in Bangor in 1980.

After attending College and University in Jordanstown, Andy took up a post teaching in the Belfast College of Business Studies. Now retired, he continues to teach Shotokan Karate and organises the NI branch of the Traditional Karate Federation (www.facebook.com/NITKF)

the youngest to achieve that level in their particular year.

We had some high achievers in the mid-1980s. John Donaldson showed great promise, while Richard Beattie was a formidable Kumite (free fighting) exponent. Richard was selected for the Ireland squad to travel to Australia to compete in the JKA World Championships, where the standard of competition was incredibly high. He managed to qualify for the individual and team Kumite events, fought well but unfortunately did not achieve a podium position.

Richard Beattie (right) pictured in August 1987 following his selection for the European Karate Championships in Sunderland that November. On the receiving end of his karate kick is fellow Bangor Shotokan Karate Club instructor Jim McNabb. *399-14-34*

Valerie did her nurse training at the Ulster Hospital before going to South Africa. On returning, she completed a degree with the OU and began teaching in Bangor FE College. During this time she became very interested in yoga, gained her yoga teacher's qualification and since retirement has continued teaching yoga.

All four children subsequently tried karate and achieved high brown belt standard with Paul continuing to black belt level. They each attended University, Paul in Glasgow, Peter in Manchester, Michael in Coleraine and Sarah in Lincoln. Currently Paul and Peter live in England, while Michael and Sarah live in Belfast.

However, Richard was not disappointed for long and set about examining the possibilities of a more permanent move to Australia. I was greatly touched when he declared: "Training in karate and having Andy McAvoy as my teacher opened up opportunities I would never have had otherwise."

Richard certainly made the most of those opportunities, living in Australia for eight years before returning to live in Dublin and, for several years, the Isle of Man. He spent a further year in Australia and South East Asia. During that period he continued to compete and teach and train in JKA Karate, Shukokai, Escrima and Mixed Martial Arts.

John Donaldson, who was also highly talented, was later invited to the World Championships with Mr Kawasoe's UK squad but that was in the 1990s.

Ever keen to attract the best instructors, I agreed with Tommy that we should invite Japanese instructors to Ireland and the possibility of training, one day in Dublin and one in Belfast, over a weekend was provisionally agreed. Time passed though and we continued to travel to London each year.

It was during one of those visits I asked Mr Enoeda

The senior class circa 1986, including John Hogg, Linda and Elizabeth Glenn, George McAvoy, Jim McNabb, Michael Legge, Richard Beattie and Arty Speight, along with some of the students from the Belfast Shotokan Karate Club.

(sadly since deceased) if he would be willing to visit Ireland and he was positive if a little reserved. It was the Japanese way. Mr Enoeda sent Yoshinobu Ohta to 'test the water'. Mr Ohta is a very friendly and warm instructor (he is now chief instructor to JKA England) and we had several edifying weekend courses with him. The visits proved a great success and plans were made to welcome Mr Enoeda to Northern Ireland. Unfortunately some of the 'politicians' within the Karate Union of Ireland were not best pleased with these developments and objected to Bangor SKC hosting Japanese instructors. One thing led to another and the club split away from the KUI towards the end of 1989.

It was actually a stroke of luck because at this time Mr Kawasoe was creating the United Kingdom Traditional Karate Federation. I contacted him by telephone and explained how the club wanted a JKA chief instructor. He was surprised, saying he had been in Bangor the previous weekend. When I pointed out it was probably Bangor in North Wales and not Northern Ireland, Mr Kawasoe laughed and invited me to train at his next course. Again

Pictured after a training session with visiting instructor Daniel Bradley, chairman of the English Karate Council and vice-chair of the British Karate Federation, are some of the children from the 1980s. Many familiar faces, too many to name. Can you find yourself?

positive if a little reserved!

A few weekends of hard training and discussions resulted in the club winning Mr Kawasoe's approval and an invitation to set up the Northern Ireland Traditional Karate Federation. Since that time (1990) Mr Kawasoe has been visiting Northern Ireland three times each year and has made many strong friendships here.

Lynda and Ray Phillips
remember... Rathgael Gymnastics and Trampolining Club

Rathgael Gymnastics and Trampolining Club started life in 1976, based in the gym hall of the now long-closed Rathgael Training School.

It was there a PE teacher at the school, Colin Skelton, together with other teachers in the Bangor area and like-minded enthusiasts, opened a gymnastics club which drew its membership mainly from the Bangor area, but also included some of the pupils who had originally formed the nucleus for gymnastics in the school within the curriculum.

Contributors Lynda and Ray Phillips pictured in 2012 with Arlene Hunsdale (Senior Coach and Manager of the club), and young members Caitlyn Montgomery, Emma Lowey and Hannah Gourley.

Although headmaster Tom Baxter was very generous in allowing the use of the school's facilities, as the membership grew it was not long before the club turned its eye towards owning its own facilities.

Following a trawl of suitable available premises, the club eventually (in 1983) bought the former Bangor Building and Hardware premises in Bank Lane, just off Holborn Avenue, and set about extending it to create its

Lynda and Ray Phillips are Life Members of the Rathgael Gymnastics and Tumbling (previously Trampolining) Club, having been involved with the club through two of their sons, Ryan and Simon, since 1984.

Both Lynda and Ray were active members of the club committee for a number of years. Lynda was also Club Secretary for a period as well as becoming, latterly, the

Enjoying a break during a busy Friday night at the Rathgael Gymnastics and Trampolining Club in the school gym back in January 1981. 326-9-12

The Bank Lane Gym (off High Street), new home of the Rathgael Gymnastics and Trampolining Club, was officially opened by Cllr Mary O'Fee on 1 October 1983. It was described as Ireland's first gymnastics facility. Cllr O'Fee receives a bouquet at the opening from club captains Claire and Darren Crawley. 56-9-21

own purpose-built gymnastics club, complete with changing and showering rooms, and a viewing / social area, together with limited catering facilities.

In those days its state-of-the-art equipment, foam pits and sunken trampoline bed led the field, due largely to the efforts of the committee and its members through extensive fundraising and a grant from the Department of Education.

Add to that the generous professional help of committee members and parents, among them a builder, electrician and solicitor, all with their own up-and-coming young gymnasts in the club. Nor should we ever forget the magnificent support given to the whole project by Mary O'Fee, a well respected Bangor Councillor who eventually became one of the club's four trustees.

RGTC provided men's, women's and recreational gymnastics, as well as trampolining, under the guiding hand of Colin Skelton and a team of dedicated coaches whose vision, drive and enthusiasm was supported by an active committee drawn from parents and gymnasts. It was also the first club of its kind to provide Kinder Gym, a concept which proved particularly popular amongst busy mums.

Although primarily a gymnastics club, the mix of young people of all ages, along with adult coaches and committee members, created a wider family social environment, with barbecues, dinners and other associated events. These included days away in the Mournes, not-to-be-missed foam pit parties, family discos (who could ever forget groovy DJ Tim Clifford, another trustee), and the introduction of birthday parties, which proved a great success.

In those early years many hundreds if not thousands of young people benefited from the club, not only through formal participation in gymnastics but also through the youth club aspect and 'taster sessions' which became an ancillary part of the club's activities and attracted a variety of youngsters from all walks of life.

Members of the Saturday training group, including 27 Ulster national squad gymnasts, at the newly-purchased Bank Lane premises in March 1984. Back row (from left): Cheryl Gibson, Jill Clough, Rachel Armstrong, Claire Crawley, Catriona Hudson, Lisa Jones, Sarah McGuiggan, Jenny Crawley, Jill Smyth. Fourth row: Grace Smyth (coach), Harry Allen (coach), Paul Coulson (chairman of the Northern Ireland Amateur Gymnastics Association), Ruth Croft (coach). Third row includes: Matthew McKnight, Nicholas Dunn, Peter Smyth, Glen Skelton, Jeffrey Allen and John Walker. Second row includes: Michael Revie, Paul McGimpsey, Kenton McKnight and Geoffrey Gillespie. Front row includes: Paul Henderson, Rory McIlroy, Darren Hanna, Ryan Mowett, Dowie Hollie and Stephen Alloway. 844-18-21

Indeed many past gymnasts will remember with great nostalgia how RGTC became the focal point for their social activities, either before or after clubbing in the town!

Growing from strength to strength, the club undertook exchange visits to Falkirk, Toxteth (home club of Beth Tweddle MBE, Bronze Medal Olympian and three times Women's Artistic World Champion), Hinckley, Shantallow, Limavady, Letterkenny (which forged very close links through the Rooney family) and Coolmine, not to mention an ill-timed visit by fishing boat to an Isle of Man gymnastics club when bad weather forced a rather expensive flight back home again!

As RGTC gymnasts became more proficient, success came in a variety of ways. RGTC girls formed the basis of the Ireland team, with one girl in particular representing Northern Ireland at the Commonwealth Championships.

But it was the boys who were to dominate gymnastics in Northern Ireland. RGTC had members who competed

Northern Ireland Amateur Gymnastics Association (NIAGA) Administrator and Secretary, and indeed both were members of the Management Committee of NIAGA (now Gymnastic Northern Ireland) until recently.

They continue their close association with gymnastics through British Gymnastics, where Ray is the current Deputy President and a member of the Board of Directors. Their grandson Lukas, child to Alan, their other son, carries on the tradition at RGTC, with granddaughter Autumn also showing early signs of being a gymnast.

at World Championships (Colin Close and Nicky Dunn) and others who represented Northern Ireland in the Commonwealth Games. One of that number (Colin Close) had the distinction of representing both Canada and Northern Ireland in his career.

Season 1989-90 trophy winners, including, amongst others, Richard Sproule, Richard Barr, Darren Dinsmore, James Rooney, Nicholas Dunn, David Waites, Dowie Hollie, Richard Croft and Ryan Phillips

At the lower level, RGTC boys took part in British gymnastics competitions and the four-nation Celtic Cup, together with competitions throughout Ireland, North and South! Hardly a week went by without RGTC gymnasts featuring in the *Spectator,* having achieved success not only in Ireland and Northern Ireland, but also in Great Britain. RGTC even had one up-and-coming youngster invited to trial for the Great Britain men's national squad.

These young people today continue to achieve success, building on the solid foundation their gymnastic training gave them. Many have taken their place in society as teachers, IT consultants, managers, world class ballet dancers and even one as an airline captain. Most continue to keep in touch with each other despite being scattered throughout the world in places as far apart as Paris, New York, Australia and, of course, the UK.

The T in RGTC today stands for 'Tumbling', as interest in the trampoline has declined over the years. However, the club continues to grow and develop with a current membership of approximately 800 and a waiting list. As in the early Eighties the current premises are no longer meeting its needs, so the club has once again taken the initiative, through an active management committee, and is about to move into purpose-made state-of-the-art premises in the Rathgael area – thus closing a circle that began over 35 years ago!

John Savage
remembers... Motorcycling

Back in the Eighties Joey Dunlop was at the peak of his prowess as a motorcycle racer, with the maestro winning all five of his Formula One World Championship titles during the decade. But Bangor could also boast two road racing heroes: Sam McClements and Steven Cull.

They were distinctly different individuals. Sam was enigmatic and shirked the limelight; Steven was more outgoing and occasionally outspoken. Both were consummate masters of their chosen sport.

While the rivalry between the pair was evident, there was a mutual admiration, friendship and respect that was not publicly perceived.

Sam, the elder of the two, inspired Steven to follow in his tyre tracks, when he brilliantly won the 1975 Senior Manx Grand Prix. Steven went on to score a brace of Isle of Man TT victories: the 350cc Historic race in 1984 and the 250cc TT two years later.

Added to that, Steven enjoyed three wins at the Ulster Grand Prix, he notched up six wins at the North West 200, including a brilliant hat-trick in 1988, and just a few weeks later he set a new outright lap record at the TT. Indeed he was leading Joey Dunlop in the blue riband Senior race until his 500cc Honda caught fire during the closing stages.

Despite his prolific performances, Sam was denied an

John Savage today

John Savage is acknowledged as one of the most respected motorcycle racing writers in the UK and Ireland, and has been a recipient of several major awards.

For many years he wrote the highly popular motorcycle racing pages in the *Newtownards Chronicle*, and he has contributed to many books, magazines and publications. In 1986 he compiled a history of the Motor Cycle Road Racing Club of Ireland.

He contributed annually to the *Rothmans Grand Prix Motorcycle Yearbook*, was Irish correspondent for *Motor Cycling Weekly* and also contributed to *Motor Cycle*

Steven Cull at Bell's Crossroads, Tandragee, aboard the 500cc Honda on which he scored a Superbike double at the North West 200 and set a new outright lap record at the Isle of Man TT

Steven Cull with a sample of the silverware he won during his illustrious racing career

News. Additionally, he was involved as a consultant in the launches of *Road Racing Ireland* magazine, *Irish Bike* and *Irish Racer,* and contributed extensively to all three titles.

He has also worked in a public relations capacity and as a ghost writer for a number of leading motorcycle racers over the past 30 years.

As one of the longest serving journalists in Northern Ireland, 2012 marked 40 years of John's career; he was Editor of the *Newtownards Chronicle* from June 1985 until August 2012.

international road race victory, most cruelly in 1982 when his Suzuki was stricken by mechanical gremlins with an Ulster Grand Prix 500cc victory in sight, and he lost out to Dungannon man Paul Cranston.

The 1986 Carrowdore 100 brought the Bangor duo head to head in a duel that will long be remembered by those privileged to witness it.

Dubbed the 'King of Carrowdore', Sam led the main race from the start and upped the lap record to 107.52mph on his second lap. But after he was forced to make an unscheduled pit stop in the village to replace a wayward plug lead, Sam lost the lead to Steven, arguably the most under-rated Irish rider of his generation.

Sam set off in pursuit and became the first man to lap the five-mile course in under three minutes, as he hoisted the lap record to 108.97mph.

When, three laps from the finish, Sam overhauled Steven, the packed Main Street echoed to cheers of delight and Sam was wished on his way by hundreds of waved programmes.

It truly was unforgettable – a remarkable performance, fit to grace the Diamond Jubilee Carrowdore 100.

Sam set the lap record at 106.81mph in 1984, and he smashed it four times during that nine-lap race in 1986 – indeed such was his pace that the official programme's lap speed table was inadequate to deal with the new heights he was ascending.

Sam led at the completion of the opening lap and by lap two he was out on his own, becoming the first man to lap the course at over 107mph.

On lap three the real drama began. Sam exited New Road with a healthy cushion, but that rapidly evaporated as he pulled into the village pit area to replace a plug lead that had come adrift.

Steven took over at the front, while Newtownards man Davy Cowan, together with Belfast's Michael Swann and Bill McCormack from Waterford, had also crested the village by the time Sam rejoined the fray, in fifth position, with all hopes of victory apparently gone.

Sam McClements rounds New Road Corner in Carrowdore, during his final tragic race

Lap four saw the commencement of his comeback, as Sam dipped within his old record to lap and moved ahead of McCormack and Swann.

He passed Cowan as they screamed through the village on the fifth lap, with Sam lapping in exactly three minutes to become the first man to navigate the course at 108mph.

With the crowd urging him on, Sam slashed Steven's lead on the sixth lap, which brought a new record of 108.97mph. Steven still seemed to have the situation well in hand, but on lap seven he slowed dramatically, dropping 19 seconds, and Sam dived in front on the run along New Road.

Steven stopped at the pits, where his helmet visor was frantically cleaned, and he rejoined the race as Cowan blasted through – it later emerged Steven had been covered in oil from a backmarker's machine.

Sam now had the race in the bag and went on to score a remarkable victory, with Steven back ahead of Cowan to secure second.

Tragically, three years later at Carrowdore Sam lost his life when he crashed after he was baulked by a touring rider on the approach to Ballyboley Corner – he was leading rising star Phillip McCallen at the time and was posthumously awarded the race win.

Steven went on to ride for the JPS Norton team.

Born in Bangor in 1955, John spent his formative years in his home town, before his family relocated to Craigantlet and subsequently to Newtownards. Following his marriage to Bangor girl Dawn Boyd in 1975, the couple briefly resided in Newtownards before returning to Bangor.

John and Dawn have a son, Jonathan, and two daughters, Sara and Rachel, together with two grandchildren, Faith and Alex.

Steven Cull with his son Richard (left), Sam McClements's son Ryan, and Ryan's son Sam

However, his racing career was prematurely ended when he suffered a life-threatening crash while competing at the Oliver's Mount parkland circuit in Scarborough in 1990.

Sam won 57 Irish national road races, while Steven won 44, both remarkable figures in themselves.

The heady days of Cull and McClements are fondly remembered. How I wish I could turn the clock back.

Sam McClements (43) died in hospital after crashing at Carrowdore on 2 September 1989.

Hundreds of friends and fellow racers – including Joey and Robert Dunlop and Steven Cull – packed Trinity Presbyterian Church for the funeral service three days later, and to pay their respects to Sam's wife Anne and their four children, Paul, Tara, Adele and Ryan.

Sam's brother-in-law Peter Harris was organist and the service was conducted by the Rev. Dermot McMorran, assisted by the Rev. W. J. Wharton, Newtownards Non-Subscribing Presbyterian Church, the Rev. R. S. G. Gilmore, Helen's Bay Presbyterian Church (retired), and the Rev. Desmond McBride, Second Saintfield Presbyterian Church, who delivered the address.

"He died as he would have wished, at the peak of his career and competing in the sport that was his life," said Mr McBride.

The coffin – covered in a wreath of red and white flowers and bearing one of Sam's racing helmets – was carried out of the church to lead the funeral cortege towards Clandeboye Cemetery.

Gillian Weir
remembers... Athletics

N orth Down Athletic Club was formed in 1974 by Arthur and Hilary O'Neill and through the 1980s was building on experience and gaining skills in coaching, officiating and administration. I joined the club in 1976, at the tender age of 12.

To celebrate the commencement of the decade, 40 of the young members organised a New Year party in the old cricket pavilion at Ward Arras Park, which was the club's home until the opening of the Sportsplex at Ballykillare in 2001. The pavilion was our regular Saturday night haunt, where we enjoyed games of darts, table football and air hockey.

Throughout the 1980s there was a very strong veterans cross country team coached by Billy Brannigan. Billy was the originator of cross country and road running at North Down Athletic Club; in fact most of the early training runs started and finished from his home in Somerset Avenue. In 1980 Billy became a veteran along with teammates ex-boxer George Graham and Terry Mallon, father of Roma McConville (Belfast Marathon winner in 1983) and grandfather of Commonwealth Games decathlete Brendan McConville. Alongside the slightly older vets, John Dawson, Vince Elliott and Ken Hawtin, they were never to lose a team race for at least 10 years.

Girls throwing dominated the early Eighties. Coached by

Gillian and Geoffrey Weir on a recent trip to Half Moon Bay, California

Gillian Weir (née McPherson) was born in Bangor on Sunday 24 November 1963, whilst the world was reeling from shock following the assassination of President John F Kennedy two days previously.

She is the eldest of three children of parents Norma and Houston (Houstie or Hooky) McPherson. Sport always played a large part in the McPherson household as Houstie was a footballer for Cliftonville and Bangor, former boxer, keen golfer and talented darts man and, in later years when arthritis struck, fondly known as 'the armchair critic'.

Five North Down athletes who did their club proud in 1982 at the All Ireland Championships and the Northern Ireland heptathlon championships respectively. From left: Alison O'Neill (16), Anita Kane (15) and William Burnside (16); Alison Moffitt (12) and Sharon Magowan (14). *256-3-17*

Noel Kane, the outstanding throwers were Anita Kane, Lisa Kane, Alison Moffitt (Javelin), Jackie Crawford and many others.

Training was held on Tuesday and Thursday nights at the cinder track at Ward Arras Park from April to September. Every member had the signature marks from the wet cinder track ingrained into their clothes that no washing powder could remove. In the winter we moved into the Borough Gym at Hamilton Road on Tuesdays for circuit training and then St Columbanus' High School. There were other specialised groups who met outside normal training sessions. The more serious athletes had membership of the Mary Peters Track to enhance their skills. Add travelling together in groups of cars to Belfast and breaking records for how many could fit into a Mini or Cortina! Afterwards they enjoyed tea and sticky buns to recover from a hard training session.

The camaraderie of the club was second to none. We went around together in groups, always welcome in each other's homes. There was always a friend available to go to the swimming pool, beach or cinema.

The early Eighties witnessed marriages for three couples who met at the club: Duncan Emerson and Maureen Patton, Geoffrey and myself (24 June 1983) and Mike McCann and Sarah Hamill (3 September 1983).

There was a great family atmosphere which emanated from the coaches and officials, namely Arthur and Hilary O'Neill, Daphne and Ian Hamill, Davy Bennett, Billy Elliott, Noel Kane, Billy Brannigan, Claire and Barry Scarth, Brian Smith, Pat and Michael Moffitt, David Seaton, Eddie Wilson and Steve Enright. Our coaches and officials not only gave of their time freely to our club,

Gillian was educated at Clandeboye Road Primary School and Bangor Girls' Secondary School. She joined North Down Athletic Club in 1976, two years after its formation, at the age of 12. Her brother Peter was also a talented sprinter at the club until he became part of the 'brain drain' of students who left Northern Ireland to study in England and established their homes there.

Geoffrey and Gillian met at North Down Athletic Club and they married on 24 June 1983 in Bangor Abbey.

Houstie was often to remark to family and friends that "Gillian ceased being an athlete when she caught hold of Geoffrey". However, those who know of Geoffrey's running talent would know that Gillian would never catch him!

The couple still live in Bangor and sport remains a large part of their lives. Gillian is Club Secretary and a coach at North Down Athletic Club and North Down Special Olympics Club, while Geoffrey

but also to officiating at athletic events, coaching national squads and travelling as team management with youth teams to National Championships. Some were also heavily committed to progressing athletics in Northern Ireland by serving on committees of the NIWAAA (women's association) and NIAAA (men's association). We followed our coaches' advice and from them we learnt not only the skills of our sport but also the skills that would carry us forward into our adult life.

In 1983 the athletes of North Down were really starting to shine through at competitions. We won 19 gold medals, 10 silver and three bronze at the Ulster Sports Council Championships. Alison O'Neill broke the Northern Ireland record for 3,000m and Alison Moffitt won the Junior Javelin at the AAA Championships at Crystal Palace.

When Arthur O'Neill retired as chairman in 1984 he stated that "after 10 years North Down AC has developed to such an extent that it now has a depth of coaching and administrative ability that will carry it forward for the next decade".

I started to coach in 1985, under the mentorship of Claire Scarth, travelling from Ards by bus to Ward Arras Park on Tuesdays and Thursdays, coaching the young members of the club and giving them an introduction to all disciplines of athletics. We used all the facilities available around the Ward Park area and I would be regularly spotted running through the park along with 30-plus athletes, doing fartleks through the rose arch and bounding up the steps of the war memorial.

Towards the mid-Eighties, as the skills, depth and knowledge of our coaches developed, the club began to produce excellent multi-discipline athletes (coached by Claire Scarth) and sprinters (coached by Steve Enright), as well as good cross country runners and throwers. GB

has been Club Treasurer since 1977 and currently chairs the North Down Sports Advisory Council and North Down Special Olympics Club.

Gillian also volunteers as chairperson of Camphill Community Glencraig, as well as having a full-time career with the Northern Ireland Health Service.

In August 1983 Alison O'Neill (left) achieved a personal best in the 1,500m and twice broke the Northern Ireland native record in the 3,000m within a week at different venues, while Alison Moffitt won the Junior Javelin at the Women's AAA Championships at Crystal Palace. *391-8-20*

Junior Internationals of the 1980s included Alison O'Neill (Middle Distance), Roger Sexton (Sprints), Darragh Murphy (Jumps) and Alison Moffitt (Javelin). Alison went on to have full Senior International representation and was the holder of the NI Javelin record for 13 years. Others who had international representation included Andrea Ramage (multi events), Anita Kane (throws), Stephen Murphy (walk) and Paul Fleming (sprints).

There was a great rivalry amongst our young middle distance group (coached by Brian Smith). Mark Weir, Barry Kelly, Scott Symington, Colin Smith, Gareth Jones, Sean Crowther and Keith McClure would battle it out at every single race, juggling for best finishing position; they never knew when they were beaten.

We were always a club which promoted events – the Bank of Ireland Young Athletes Meeting, the Castle Park Road Races and Bangor Road Races, to name but a few. However, our flagship event was the Bangor Classic 10k (described by *Irish Runner* magazine as "the best 10k in Ireland"). This was an international 10k road race through the streets and roads of Bangor. The first Classic took place in 1985 and had high profile sponsors, i.e. Kodak, Manx Airlines, Brooks, Nike and the *Daily Mirror*. The most high profile athlete to compete in the Bangor Classic was Zola Budd in 1987, but the race attracted many other famous athletes to Northern Ireland, including Kenyan competitors.

BUDD BRAVES BLUSTERY BANGOR FOR KODAK VICTORY

The club welcomed these athletes to Bangor as members of their own families; some keep in touch to this day. Members of the organising sub-committee were fondly known as "the back room boys". The whole club was involved in marshalling the course and providing assistance in some way. The club clearly demonstrated we had the skills, knowledge and commitment to organise successful international events.

I was elected as Honorary Club Secretary in 1987 (a position I still hold today). Taking over the helm from Pat Moffitt, I remain just the third club secretary in the club's history, the first having been the late Hilary O'Neill.

Taken in 1988, this picture shows the organising sub-committee – or 'back room boys' – of the Bangor Classic 10k Road Race. Back row (from left): Michael Moffitt, Geoffrey Weir, David Seaton, Brian Smith, Barry Scarth. Front: John Craggs (*Daily Mirror*, sponsor) and Gillian Weir. *Spectator* picture

Geoffrey, a founding member, has been Honorary Treasurer since 1977 (a position he still holds today). Hence our home has long been the 'hub' of the club.

North Down AC always catered not only for the very talented athletes, but also for the committed club athletes who came to enjoy the sport of athletics.

Throughout the Eighties we travelled as a club, from the youngest to the oldest, to Gateshead each November to take part in the Gateshead International Cross Country Festival. Some of our more mature members even sampled the night life of Newcastle upon Tyne.

The cross country season in 1989 ended with athletes taking part in races

North Down Athletic Club members at the presentation of their end of the winter season cross country awards in April 1988. Back row (from left): Tom Milne, John Dawson, Ian Lyle, David Dunne, Ken Hawtin, Brian Smith, Noel Munnis, Barry Scarth, Gareth Jones, Stephen Murphy, Peter Nugent, Ian Jamison, Richard Wilson, George Dowling. Seated (from left): Mark Weir, Barry Kelly, Keith McClure, Keith Esdale. Kneeling: Stuart Harding, Gareth Freeman and Simon Munnis. 338-18-36

North Down officials and athletes who competed in the 1989 Club Handicap Race around Ward Park. Back row (from left): George Dowling, Tom Milne, David Seaton, Colin Smith, George Bell, Mark Weir, Jonathan Gettinby, Paddy McGrattan, Claire Scarth, Brian Smith, Ian Lyle, Ean McClure, Huib Baauw, Ken Hawtin. Front (from left): Peter Nugent, John Quiery, Stuart Harding, Fra McWilliams and Billy Brannigan. *Spectator* picture

in Banbridge from ages under 10 to veteran age groups, whilst two members, Sandra Gawley (12th) and Julie Carlisle (35th), were representing Glenlola in the All Ireland Schools Cross Country Championships in Dublin. Next came the road running and marathon season with athletes all set for the track and field season, following good preparation all winter.

I can honestly say the club shaped my life and I have thoroughly enjoyed my time as an athlete, coach and official. As Geoffrey and I always remark, sport gives many opportunities and opens many doors. We have made many long-lasting friendships over the years and have fond memories of the 1980s. We have always been proud to say we are members of North Down Athletic Club.

Culture
in Bangor in the Eighties

Dianna Boullier
remembers... Folk Music

The beauty of folk and traditional music is its simplicity. That's the reason why it has endured for hundreds of years. You don't have to be an expert to play a few jigs on the tin whistle. You don't need to read music or know any musical theory!

Dianna and Nigel Boullier perform for RTE's *The Pure Drop*

In the 1980s it was easy to obtain fiddles, flutes, banjos, concertinas and accordions for a very meagre price, although as you continued to play and practise, a more expensive instrument became very desirable. I started off on the tin whistle and then tried my hand at a fiddle which cost the princely sum of £10. Incidentally there is a very nice Shetland tune called *The £10 Fiddle,* so my experience was not unique!

County Down has a very rich heritage of traditional music, dance and song. County folk, especially in remote areas, had been singing, dancing and making music for years, largely unnoticed, until the folk music revival of the 1960s, when folk and traditional music spread into urban areas and Bangor was no exception. Very soon everyone

The Skillen family have lived in Bangor for generations and Dianna Boullier (née Skillen) is now the only one left in the town. She inherited her love of music from her grandfather who played the flute and the concertina. After experimenting with various instruments she eventually took up the fiddle in her early 20s.

Dianna has spent many years playing and meeting with musicians in sessions and at music festivals all over Ireland. She has played on television and radio on numerous

had heard of groups like The Dubliners, Planxty, The Bothy Band and, especially, The Chieftains since their harpist, Derek Bell, actually lived in Bangor.

Downpatrick Folk Club was the venue in 1980 for this session featuring (from left): Sam McCaughey (fiddle), Dianna Boullier (fiddle), Nigel Boullier (banjo) and George Russell (bodhran)

But, of course, you don't have to be famous or in a group to play folk music. You may just play at home for your own enjoyment or venture out into one of the public houses in Bangor where music has been played on a regular basis. I chose the latter!

occasions, along with husband Nigel on banjo and good friend Davy Graham on mandola. They have also played at gigs in Scotland, England, Toronto and Amsterdam.

She has taught fiddle workshops at folk festivals and travelled around Northern Ireland bringing traditional music to schoolchildren as part of the Arts Council/ Department of Education *Jigtime* programme.

Dianna has written *Exploring Irish Music and Dance*, published by The O'Brien Press, while Nigel has written *Handed Down, Country Fiddling and Dancing in east and central Down*, currently under publication by the Ulster Historical Foundation.

The couple have two sons, Jack and Patrick.

Wednesday and Saturday night 'sessions' in Fealty's Bar (aka The Ormeau Arms) were thriving in the 1980s. It was hard to get a seat. There were songs from Denise McCutcheon, tunes from Johnny Muir on tin sandwich (mouth organ) accompanied by himself on bones (two cow ribs played like castanets in one hand), recitations by Crawford Howard and sea-shanties and songs from Bill Oliver. I especially remember Bill singing *The Liar* by Tommy Makem:

> *It was during World War 2 I met them all,*
> *There was Roosevelt and Churchill and De Gaulle*
> *Then one day I nearly fainted, I was having my house*
> *painted*
> *There was Hitler hanging paper in the hall!*

With a rousing chorus, when everyone sang along:

> *Singing rightful too-ra-laddie too-ra-lee*
> *There is no one who can tell a lie like me*
> *You can search until you tire,*
> *You won't find a bigger liar*
> *I've been lying since the dawn of history.*

We, that is myself and husband Nigel (banjo), Davy

Graham (guitar and mandola) and George Russell (bodhran) enjoyed the songs but wanted to play more tunes, so we started a music session in Fealty's on Friday nights and later on Tuesday nights as well – you can never get enough tunes!!

We were joined by various other local musicians – Geordie McAdam (fiddle), who played both traditional and American old-timey music, Stanley Mooney (accordion), Julian Friers (flute and whistle), Sam McCaughey (fiddle), Willie Coyle (accordion) and, occasionally, by harpist Janet Harbinson, as well as lots of visiting musicians from all over Ireland and beyond.

Recalling early days in the Bangor folk music scene (back from left): Charlie Ferguson (flute), Davie Wylde (fiddle), Nigel Boullier (banjo), George Russell (bodhran), Davy Graham (guitar), Dianna Boullier (fiddle) and Julian Friers (whistle)

The session moved for a few years in the 1980s to The Windsor Bar, where we were made exceptionally welcome by publican John Donegan. The Windsor Bar was also home to the Down Coast Folk Society. It had begun life in The Tivoli Bar in Donaghadee and was run by Downtown Radio's Jackie Dixon. Eventually it shifted to the quaint thatched upstairs bar in The Windsor.

This was a very popular venue for local singers, songwriters and musicians. Traditional music, acoustic blues, comedy, folksong and ballads could all be sampled every Wednesday evening. Unlike the more informal setting of the pub session, you had to plonk yourself on a stage and 'perform' to a hopefully appreciative audience.

Mainstays of the Folk Society were accomplished Bangor musicians David Lennon (Belfast's first Busker of the Year winner in 1984), Marcus McAuley and Ian McKeown, collectively known as Finvarra. They played

Folk music in Bangor – a programme for a traditional night held during the Percy French Festival in 1984

Finvarra performing at the Belfast Boat Club circa 1982. From left: Marcus McAuley (mandolin), Ian McKeown (bouzouki) and David Lennon (guitar and vocals).

an interesting mix of traditional songs and tunes, alongside contemporary songs and some of their own compositions. Their arrangements included guitar, mandolin, tin whistle, bouzouki, Northumbrian pipes and hurdy gurdy. They played at the Belfast Folk Festival and also toured Europe.

Another Bangor duo who regularly took to the stage at the Folk Club was Föhn – Philip O'Connor (flute) and Bart Lyons (guitar). I remember them playing a bit of Jethro Tull and some Horslips tunes and songs. Of course, anybody could get up and sing or play, so there was never any shortage of performers – both good and bad.

Playing in 2006 at Áras an Uachtaráin, in Dublin's Phoenix Park, are (from left): Davy Graham, Dianna Boullier and Nigel Boullier

And then there were the well-known musicians who were booked to play at the Folk Club. Those nights were very popular too. The legendary Martin Carthy, Andy Irvine, Kieran Goss, Tommy Sands, Vin Garbutt and Archie Fisher all appeared at the Down Coast Folk Society.

One of the most memorable concerts we ever played at was held in the Bangor Castle Leisure Centre in May 1984 as part of the Percy French Festival – billed as 'a County Down Night of instrumental music, song, dance and chat'. It certainly was all that.

Tracey Cree
remembers... Dancing

I had just turned 14 in l980. How was I to know that in the next 10 years I would leave school, go to college, dance professionally throughout Europe and meet and get engaged to my future husband!

I was actually born in Toronto, Canada, and accompanied my parents, Harry and Joan, when they returned to Northern Ireland in 1971. Dad, being a native of Bangor, and Mum, from Belfast, were both glad to settle in the town I'll always regard as home.

I'd attended Ballyholme Primary School and at the turn of the decade was a pupil at Glenlola Collegiate. Needless to say my favourite subject was music and my favourite teacher was Miss Lorna Watton. I still remember some of her now legendary musical productions.

My life back then seemed so simple with never a dull moment. I started to dance at the age of five, being taught ballet and modern by my Aunt Jeanne who ran a ballet school. A bit later Mum began teaching tap and, all told, I attended lessons three times a week in Hamilton House. I was very lucky as most of my friends were also dancers.

As well as working for exams I also danced at Bangor, Portadown and Holywood Ballet Festivals, which

Tracey Cree, then 16, with some of the 20 trophies she had won for dancing during 1982/83. 538-11-19

Tracey Cree was born in Toronto, Canada, and moved to Bangor in 1971. She attended Ballyholme Primary School and Glenlola Collegiate.

She began her dancing career at the age of five, being taught by her aunt Jeanne Cree. Tracey entered her first festival in Bangor at seven and began to win awards by the time she was 10. During the following years she won an assortment of medals at competitions in Bangor and Portadown. Her teacher also took a team of dance students to Edinburgh where she won a first in ballet and modern dance.

As the years progressed, as well as studying for ballet exams Tracey knew dance was the career she wanted to follow. She became quite a

Tracey displays the skills that made her a formidable festival competitor in the 1980s. *Spectator picture*

formidable festival competitor, being acclaimed All Ireland Intermediate Ballet Champion at 14. A year later, while studying for her GCSEs, she auditioned successfully for the Doreen Bird College of Performing Arts.

In her final year of competition she won a total of 23 trophies, including Most Promising Dancer at Holywood and Portadown Festivals.

In 1983 Tracey began her

attracted competitors from all parts of the Province. At 14 I was lucky enough to be awarded the title of 'All Ireland Intermediate Ballet Champion'.

Also for two years I attended the Edinburgh Festival so I could compete with dancers from the rest of the UK. That's how many lasting friendships were formed. Indeed, most of my local friends were also dancers and we hung around together at weekends and during the summer holidays. I just felt life couldn't get any better!

Summers always seemed to be sunny with no rainy days. We spent the days sunbathing on Bangor's pier, occasionally jumping into the freezing water! On other days, armed with a packed lunch, we would cycle to either Groomsport or Donaghadee, laze in the sun and swim.

It's funny how you always tend to remember the good weather and never the bad!

On Saturdays we danced the night away at the disco in the Royal Hotel. The last dance was always to *Careless Whisper* and this was followed by a pastie supper from Paul's on the seafront. The other place where we would go on Saturday evenings was the youth club on Hamilton Road, attached to the Presbyterian church – it was called 'The 109'.

Our home was an open house for all and sundry – tea and toast being our favourite dish!

While we were all aware of the Troubles, life remained mostly calm and peaceful in Bangor and Belfast was very much the place to shop. However, the warning was always drummed into us: in the event of a bomb scare leave the area and make our way home! How times change. As I write this my eldest daughter is 15 and we live the same distance from the centre of London as Bangor is from Belfast – yet I would be reluctant to let her travel there with her friends.

I'd decided by then to pursue a career on the stage and,

with very welcome encouragement from Mum and Dad, realised the only possible route was through one of the stage schools in London. After completing my O-Levels, Mum and I travelled to the Doreen Bird School of Performing Arts in Sidcup, Kent, where I was granted an audition. Although I had to wait until the post brought me the news a week later, I was lucky enough to be successful. I had made it!

Tearful goodbyes followed and then I was off from idyllic Bangor to the bright lights of London for a three-year course that ran from 1983 to 1986. I was very homesick but was lucky enough to be able to return to Bangor every six weeks.

Until my college friends got to know me better they believed we all lived in wee thatched cottages and were amazed to discover we actually had TV with BBC1! A number crossed the water and all were quite amazed at how beautiful Bangor, and indeed the rest of Northern Ireland, was. What particularly surprised them was the friendliness and how welcoming people were – not at all like the place appeared to be on TV and in the press.

After I graduated in 1986 my career took me to all parts of Europe, where I danced with 'The Hoff' in Germany, with East 17 at the MTV Awards in Paris, and with Peter Gabriel at the Brit Awards in London. I even managed to body-double for Andie MacDowell in *Four Weddings And A Funeral.*

Always managing to return home during breaks between assignments, I kept in touch with friends and family. Christmas was a bit hard though as there was always a panto somewhere which kept me away from home – but such was the nature of the job.

There were also modelling assignments for Playtex (I worked for the company for seven years), including a visit home when the Wonderbra

stage training at the College, where she qualified as a teacher of dance and in her final year (1986) she was presented with the prestigious 'Best All Rounder' award.

She spent the next four years performing all over Europe and the UK. In 1990 she became engaged to her husband Graham (also a dancer) and was married in Bangor in 1991. They live in London and have two daughters who are also dancers.

Tracey now works as a teaching assistant in a primary school but still has a hand in dancing with a school 'Dance Club' and also assisting with her daughters' training.

22-year-old entertainer Tracie Cree from Bangor has just become engaged - to a member of the cast she is currently touring with. Tracie, and fiance Graham Gilmore, are both performing in West Side Story, Tracie as Consuela and Graham as Action, which is touring Great Britain for six months. The pair first met at the Doreen Bird College at Sidcup in Kent and Graham's proposal was accepted on Sunday. Tracie, whose parents Harry and Joan live at Windermere Drive, Bangor, was trained in Bangor by her mother in tap and aunt Mrs. Jeanne Cree in ballet. She has recently qualified as a teacher from the Doreen Bird College. Tracie spent last summer in Cannes with Dougie Squire's Second Generation and has appeared in major pantomimes and television shows in London and nationally. Although she works mainly in Great Britain Tracie returns home as often as possible and will be back during the summer.

Tracey's progress – a *Spectator* story from 1989

Tracey today

was launched on UTV's *Kelly Show*. Another great opportunity to visit home and show fellow cast members where I came from was when Marks and Spencer toured the UK and Dublin with its fashion shows.

At the end of the Eighties I was lucky enough to work in Cannes, in the south of France. Twelve weeks of dancing on an outdoor stage at Palm Beach and a company of wonderful dancers who still keep in touch. The group also included my future husband Graham. Following Cannes I was in the touring company of *West Side Story* and he also had a role. At the end of the tour we became engaged and married a year later, in 1991.

Even though I have now spent more years in North London than in Bangor, I still consider the latter to be my home town and it is with immense pride that I show my family where I grew up and introduce them to the friends I made during my time there.

Michael Ievers

remembers... Bangor Drama Club

For Bangor Drama Club the 1980s was a glorious period: by 1987 they had beaten the best in Britain and represented Ireland on the world stage. But the story leading up to these glory days began some years earlier, when two people in particular were to significantly influence the future of the club.

From the early 1970s Peter LaGrue had been directing drama at Bangor Grammar School and by the early 1980s

Principals in the Bangor Drama Club production of *The Roses Of Eyam*, which was staged in the Little Theatre in February 1982. From left: Alan Huffington, Tony Ablett, Judy Boal, Michael Ievers, David Marshall, Don Ritchie, Cherrie McIlwaine and Bill Murphie. *745-8-15*

this meant a core group of his ex-pupils were well-trained, inspired and looking for new opportunities; at the same time Patricia Irvine was producing a wealth of talent from her speech classes in Bangor.

These two sources combined in the early 1980s to lay the ground for some of the most outstanding productions in the club's history. Among a number of notable highlights, in 1984 Walker Ewart and Isabel Eaton directed Noel Coward's *Hay Fever* and won the Ulster Full-Length Finals. In the same year, Patricia Irvine directed Laura

After leaving Bangor Grammar School with a scholarship to train at Shorts Plc., Michael Ievers qualified with a Masters in Aeronautical Engineering in 1986; he completed a Post-Graduate Certificate in Education in 1988 and was appointed as a teacher of Physics at Strathearn School in Belfast, then as a Head of Department in 1994.

The Bliss family at breakfast during a scene from *Hay Fever* at the Little Theatre in February 1984. Seated (from left): Di Neill, Geoffrey Miller, Cherrie McIlwaine, Alan Huffington. At rear: Patricia Irvine, Carol Graham, Peter White, Johnny Gwynne and Marie Gildea. 697-3-21

He was awarded a Ph.D in 2004 and two years later took up a position as a Senior Lecturer at Stranmillis University College, where he is currently both a researcher and Advisor of Studies.

Michael lives in Bangor with his three children and his wife, Mags.

Michael Ievers today with his wife Mags

Hughes, Michael Ievers, Patricia Burns and Max Reid in Brian Friel's aptly named *Winners*. The team won not only the Northern Ireland One-Act Finals and then the British Finals in Cardiff, but went on to represent Ireland at the World Festival in Tokyo in 1985.

Two years later the club mourned the death of her most famous son. Colin Blakely began his stage experience with Bangor's Amateur Operatic Society before moving to Bangor Drama Club. He made his professional debut in 1957. Along with many stage plays and regular television appearances, his film appearances included *A Man For All Seasons* (1966), *Young Winston* (1972), *The National Health* (1973), *Murder On The Orient Express* (1974), *The Pink Panther Strikes Again* (1976), *Equus* (1977), *The Dogs Of War* (1980) and *Evil Under The Sun* (1982).

Colin died of leukaemia at the peak of his career, aged 56. An anecdote was told by his contemporary, Anthony Hopkins: during rehearsals involving the two actors in a production directed by Sir Laurence Olivier, Hopkins asked Sir Laurence for advice about how he should approach a particular role. Sir Laurence replied that he should just watch Blakely and he would know all he needed to know.

In 1987 Patricia Irvine was again the director, this time for a production of Brian Friel's *Philadelphia, Here I Come!* which won both the Ulster Finals and the Glasgow International Festival; in the same year Di Neill directed James McLure's *Laundry And Bourbon* to victory at the Northern Ireland One-Act Finals. In 1988 Kenneth Irvine directed Frank McGuinness's *Observe The Sons Of Ulster Marching Towards The Somme*, again winning the Ulster Full-Length Finals, but this time narrowly losing out at the Glasgow International Festival.

And of a hundred stories that could be told of the Drama Club in the 1980s, one of the most memorable occurred in the *Sons Of Ulster* production at a festival in Strabane. Backstage in the town's theatre there was a labyrinth of corridors, with loudspeakers at every turn to relay the sound of voices from the stage. Johnny Gwynne and Mark Mawhinney left their dressing-room to make for the stage when they heard from the loudspeakers that their entrance was coming up in a few pages.

Cast members from *Observe The Sons Of Ulster Marching Towards The Somme* just after coming off stage at the Glasgow International Festival in 1988. Back (from left): David Cree, Mark Mawhinney, Geoffrey Miller, Jim Wolstencroft, Johnny Gwynne, Jeremy Glover. Front: Billy Rea and Michael Ievers. Missing is Walker Ewart.

However, their problems began when they tried to find the stage. With loudspeakers in every corridor they couldn't work out where the source of the sound was coming from; and they quickly realised the stage wasn't where they had thought it should have been. Very soon Mark and Johnny were running very fast through the corridors trying to find the stage. Meanwhile, on the stage and with the performance in full swing, Geoffrey Miller and Jeremy Glover were playing characters who were in the middle of introducing themselves to each other, but they were also quickly approaching the cue for Mark and Johnny to enter.

That moment arrived. There was a very heavy silence for two very long seconds. Geoffrey and Jeremy looked at each other; Mark and Johnny stopped running through the corridors and listened to hear what might happen next. After another long second of frozen silence, Geoffrey said to Jeremy: "So what part of Enniskillen are you from?" In a panic, Jeremy stared at Geoffrey and desperately tried to work out a suitable line to continue the improvised script. "High Street," he replied, praying fervently that such a street existed in Enniskillen, and realising immediately

A reception was held at the Town Hall in August to acknowledge the various achievements of Bangor Drama Club during the 1983/84 season. The event was hosted by Mayor Hazel Bradford and those honoured included (seated with the Mayor, from left): Di Neill, Walker Ewart and Patricia Irvine. Back row (omitting some names where faces are obscured: Charlie Browne, John Knipe, Laura Gilbert, Kit Gilbert, June Browne, Marie Gildea, Margaret Wylde, Carol Graham, Alan Huffington, Geoffrey Miller, Johnny Gwynne, Laura Hughes, Patricia Burns, Michael Ievers, Peter White, Kenneth Irvine, Irene Cairns, Dan Gilbert and Harry Williamson. There had been success for the club at the one-act play finals in Cardiff (with *Winners*) and at the Ulster Drama Festival (with *Hay Fever*). 62-4-23

that the Strabane audience in front of him would probably know!

"And what do you do for a living?" asked Geoffrey. "What?!" said Jeremy, now in abject terror. "What do you do for a living?" repeated Geoffrey. "I'm a farmer," said Jeremy, immediately realising this might be unlikely if he lived on High Street! For over a full minute Geoffrey and Jeremy continued one of the most heroic improvisations ever witnessed on the festival circuit, while the other 'Sons of Ulster' (Walker Ewart, Billy Rea, Jim Wolstencroft, David Cree and Michael Ievers) broke land speed records running through the corridors to find Johnny and Mark.

Such is life in live theatre, particularly on tour. Tragically, David died some years later and Johnny lost his battle with cancer in 2007. For those of us privileged to be a part of it all and share wonderful times, these were indeed heady days for Bangor Drama Club, on both the national and international stage, filled with many good memories – some sad ones too, for our friends now departed, but with so many unforgettable moments of theatrical magic.

Brendan Monaghan
remembers... Music

My mother was from County Donegal and my father was from County Fermanagh. When they got married they moved to County Down to start a new life together. My parents settled in Newtownards and I attended St Finian's Primary School in the town, as did my brothers and sisters.

Growing up at home I was influenced by many different types of pop music on the radio and television. I would also hear my mother sing old Irish numbers and some country songs. Little wonder I had a very broad range of musical styles running through my head and that much of this music would go on to influence my writing in later years.

After sitting my 11-Plus exams I attended St Columbanus' High in Bangor. As a child I'd always enjoyed going over to Bangor for the day, earlier with my mother, sometimes on my own or with my older brother Gerald, then later with the new Bangor mates I met at the so-called big school.

We would go to the Queen's Cinema on Queen's Parade and, of course, Barry's Amusements. This was all very strange to me as I was around 12 or 13 and had never been on a ghost train or at a fun fair, though it was pretty exciting at the time.

The journey from Ards to Bangor on school days was

Brendan Monaghan today
Picture by Ursina Baitella

Brendan Monaghan performs his material at home and in many different countries around the world. He has shared the same bill with numerous top international artists and has written material for several recording artists.

He has released four albums, *precious time, no more words, look no further* and *flicker of hope*, on Brambus Records. The singer/songwriter's release in the early part of 2012, a five-track EP entitled *I love how you love me*, reached Number One on the international Celtic Music Charts.

Bangor in the Eighties

Brendan started his musical career in the 1980s with his band Dogmatic Element, performing their own brand of New Wave music. He developed his songwriting in the 1990s with the Cattle Company, leaning towards New Country music. Both outfits achieved relative success both at home and overseas.

He has received very enthusiastic reviews for his music as he continues to progress in his art form. Belfast singer/ songwriter and journalist David Ballantine has praised the Bangor man and his music, saying: "Brendan is one of Ireland's unsung songsmiths who writes straight from the heart. He is also a performer of electrifying energy and enthusiasm."

Irish journalist and RTE radio presenter John O'Regan adds: "Brendan Monaghan's music evokes the best elements of classic folk rock, singer/ songwriter artistry and Irish folk sensibilities in an attractive, listenable package."

Brendan's fifth solo album is also scheduled for release in 2012. Visit www. brendanmonaghan.com for further information about him.

never particularly enjoyable. Not being that academically inclined, I didn't really look forward to going to school, plus doing or copying my homework on a bus was never an easy thing to accomplish!

If I was unlucky enough to miss the school bus and needed to get public transport, and as a result was pretty late arriving at school I, like so many other unfortunate fellow students, had to face our headmaster Mr McWilliams and six of the best! This was our punishment for being late.

Mr McWilliams, who kept his trusty cane up the sleeve of his jacket, was a dab hand at caning. I must admit here and now – as I am sure would any other poor soul who received his punishment – the pain was so excruciating it would bring more than a little tear to the eye after the initial shock wore off. Yes, folks, this was the 1970s and corporal punishment was alive and well!

I was in my mid teens when I started playing on a guitar my older brother had bought. I was always listening to music and generally loved it. Some of my Donegal relations were musicians and my mother sang. I would use guitar beginner books, learning chords and simple songs.

I struggled at first, especially with the tuning. I used pitch pipes – and how I would have loved back then to have the guitar tuners we have today. I was pretty good at writing poems and stories at school, so I started putting my own words to some chord structures I had been working on. Very soon I had completed my first few songs which I thought were pretty decent, so you can imagine how happy I was at the time.

I was socialising in Bangor quite a lot after I left school. I would usually go to the Savoy Hotel with my mates from football. The 'Savoy' was the place to be in during the late Seventies and early Eighties. On Saturday nights Downtown Radio hosted a roadshow disco which was great. It was also the place where I met my wife-to-be Valerie McDonnell, a Bangor girl. After we married in 1980 Bangor became my home.

In the early Eighties I decided to put a band together and we called the outfit Dogmatic

Element. I was very serious about my music and we all looked very moody so the name just seemed to fit. I had some songs, played a little guitar and never thought of being a front man; I just wanted a vehicle to showcase my material.

With my good friend Graham Stannage playing bass, I was told about a female singer, Alison Gordon, who was at Glenlola Collegiate. I

Dogmatic Element (from left): Graham Stannage, Brendan Monaghan, Dave Lynas and Alison Gordon. *Picture by W.A. Carson*

approached her about doing lead vocals for the band and, thankfully, she was delighted to get involved. Then I found an excellent drummer in Dave Lynas, from Glengormley, and that completed the band.

We rehearsed non-stop at St Patrick's Hall in Newtownards. These were very special times as we'd no idea where we were going with the band and that seemed to add to the excitement. Our music grew from the New Wave, Punk, New Romantic feel at the time, plus I was a big David Bowie fan.

THE IMPERIAL
CENTRAL AVENUE, BANGOR
COMING FRIDAY, 23rd AUGUST
DOGMATIC ELEMENT

I experimented with chords and sounds on my guitar and effects pedal. It was an exciting time in Bangor in the early years of the Eighties with several other bands around the scene. Our first show was at The Sportsman's on High Street (now Wolsey's). Then it was on to Project Bangor, a youth club at Dufferin Avenue, in a building that has since been knocked down.

Both venues were crammed with people and the gigs went very well. John and Tommy McDowell, who had a shop in King Street called Ampec, which sold musical instruments and had a PA system hire service, did our sound and made a great job of it.

Colin Bateman, a very successful writer now but who

Brendan Monaghan (left) developed his songwriting in the 1990s with the Cattle Company. From second left: Brian Murray, Niall McClean, Richard Murray and Matthew Fleming. *Picture by Gavin Roberts*

Brendan in 2012 with his children Sarah, Daryl and Michael. *Picture by Ursina Baitella*

then worked as a journalist at the *Spectator*, showed an interest in the band and assisted with our first two single releases on his Cattle Company label. First single *Just Friends* is included on an Irish Eighties New Wave compilation, which was released in 2012.

Dogmatic Element continued through most of the Eighties with relative success and several line-up changes. However, I decided the band had run its course as I was moving on in my musical journey.

Bangor now, very much as it was in the Eighties, is a good place to live. I have so much to be very grateful for: my children Daryl, Sarah and Michael, who are true Bangorians having been born and raised in the town, and my faith and the pastoral care provided to myself and my family through the St Comgall's (Ballyholme) and Brunswick Road churches.

Spectator Reporters

Have Their Say

All Change
AT THE SPECTATOR

In much the same way that the Eighties represented a period of considerable change for Bangor, so too the passing years witnessed no fewer than 16 new reporters joining the editorial department at the *County Down Spectator* and not one but two changes at the top.

The decade had commenced with legendary Editor Annie Roycroft still very much at the helm, with Joy (now Jo) Bannister her able deputy and a reporting team that included the recently recruited Colin Bateman, along with Paddy Price, Peter Russell, Maxine Mawhinney and Sports Editor Peter Gibson. Details about their respective roles at the paper can be found in *Bangor in the Sixties* and *Bangor in the Seventies.*

During the 1980s (and indeed beyond) the *Spectator* maintained its unmatched reputation for providing a direct route for its young reporters, having served their apprenticeship, into the newsrooms of the top Belfast papers as well as TV and radio stations, including the expanding Downtown in nearby Newtownards.

Reporters who filled the gaps as they arose in the *Spectator* editorial department during the first four years of the decade included Paul Flowers, Ann-Marie Hillen (now Foster), Chris Capper, Karen English and Adrian Beattie (now in Australia).

However, the main news headline occurred in October 1983 when, much to the surprise of everyone at the newspaper, not least Annie herself, she brought to a close a career that had commenced more than 40 years earlier, prior to marrying cousin Joe Stephens that same month and moving in retirement to Cork.

Joy maintained the high standard set by mentor Annie, adding new reporters Clare McGinn and Patricia Fox to the team. However, within three years her own burgeoning career as a highly respected science fiction writer saw Joy tendering her resignation with longest-serving reporter Paul Flowers, her equally able deputy,

Directors and staff of the *County Down Spectator* and *Newtownards Chronicle* bade a fond farewell in October 1983 to Annie Roycroft. She was presented with a silver galley tray and six crystal goblets to mark a career that had spanned 42 years. Among those present were Messrs Ian Alexander (front, second left), John Alexander (front, third left) and David Alexander (right), directors, Norman Boal (second right), Editor of the *Chronicle*, along with Joe Cairnduff and Jimmy Connolly (on Annie's left), printers, whose years with the *Spectator* rivalled those of their departing friend and colleague. *53-21-21*

taking over as Editor, a position he holds to this day.

Paul's innate ability to spot a talented young reporter saw a further nine new members of staff joining the team at various points during the remaining years of the decade. They included a trio of future household names because of their work for the BBC: Yvette Shapiro, Colette Wilson (now Maguire) and Karen Patterson.

Further additions to the *Spectator*'s unending 'roll of honour' included Paul Connolly (Group Managing Editor at Independent News & Media NI), Damien Magee (senior news and current affairs producer with Radio Ulster), Fiona McCarney (now Rutherford, Editorial Manager with the *Community Telegraph* series in Belfast), Ruth O'Reilly (co-founder of the *Below The Radar* TV and film production company), Richard Sherriff *(News Letter)* and current *Spectator* Deputy Editor Helen McDowell.

A number of the above-named reporters elaborate on their career paths while sharing some memories of their *Spectator* years in this section of *Bangor in the Eighties*. Others, who joined the paper in late 1989 and didn't hit their stride until the beginning of the 1990s, have indicated their intention to contribute to the next book in the series.

Footnote – Printer Jimmy Connolly (included in the above photograph), whose passing at the age of 97 took place just before this book went to press, surpassed Annie's length of service by at least a decade.

"He had already served his seven-year apprenticeship before I joined the *Spectator* at the end of 1941," Annie recalls. "In the journeyman tradition he had gone to Belfast to join a printing firm there, but returned to the *Spectator* in the 1940s. In the ensuing years he had embraced massive changes in printing processes and even after retirement he was often to be found at the printing works, watching the *Spectator* roll off its modern presses."

Sympathy goes to Jimmy's son Mervyn and daughter Marlene and the family circle.

Ann-Marie Foster

(née Hillen) remembers...

The Council Chamber at Bangor Town Hall must be one of the most beautiful in Northern Ireland. The stained glass windows and oak panelling give it a church-like air. It would have been a magnificent music room when the building was still owned by the Hamilton family.

Many residents of the Borough have probably never crossed its parquet floor – which is a shame – but the room was to become a significant part of my life in the 1980s. Unfortunately, there was rarely anything musical about the accompanying soundtrack.

As a cub reporter with an interest in local affairs and fairly good shorthand it was perhaps inevitable that I would be invited to join Joy Bannister at the press table in the centre of the room. It was an intimidating place to sit, surrounded as we were by the Councillors' heavy desks – all polished wood and leather insets – with no visible exit point once proceedings had started.

All eyes were on us during the debates – the Councillors were always keen to see if their bons mots were significant enough to make our notebooks. A quick confession here – sometimes I wrote out Clash lyrics instead of recording their contributions; Joy practised her Hebrew script.

The nights were long – very long – and for the most part quite boring, filled with the mundane administration that

Ann-Marie, eldest child of fanatical BGC golfers Des and Ann Hillen, has lived in Bangor all her life. After school she completed a journalism course in Belfast and considers it a huge stroke of good fortune to have served her apprenticeship at the *Spectator* under Annie Roycroft.

She also spent some time helping to run her family's business at the Ava Bar on Main Street before eventually moving back into journalism via DTR/Cool FM and now the BBC in Belfast, where she works as a broadcast journalist and newsreader on Radio Ulster.

Married to Campbell, she has two girls who amaze her every day... and a novel that will probably never get finished.

takes up most of a local Council's time. Every so often a more contentious issue would emerge and tempers and voices would rise. In truth however, because of the make-up of North Down Borough Council there was a lot of indignation and condemnation but it was one-sided.

Sometimes the highlight of the evening for all of us was the tea trolley and if things got desperate, then those in the know could nip into the Mayor's parlour and help themselves to a little glass of draught beer or puff a quick ciggie in the corridor. No names, no pack drill.

MASTERING MY LITTLE BLUE BIKE

By Ann-Marie Hillen

Buying your first motor-bike and taking it out on the road can be a nerve-racking experience for you and your parents. Whether it's a mere moped of 49cc or some-thing more powerful, it's still quite a step from riding a push bike about town.

When I bought me Honda Express Deluxe (the same as Twiggy rides in the TV ad-vertisement) I was aiming for simplicity, convenience and economy and so far I seem to have made the right choice. However it was my first motorbike and although I've been driving a car for 2½ years I'd never been on a motorcycle before.

With this in mind I followed the good advice of the Holywood dealer I bought my bike from and arranged to take a Bronze Star Award course at Scrabo High School a few Saturdays ago.

The Bronze Star Award is the first of three courses in the

The Silver Star intermediate course is arranged in six 2-hour sessions of 'on the road' in-struction which takes the rider up to and beyond the standard required by the L test, and an advanced 12-hour course in-volving both theory and practical riding requires those gaining the Gold Star to attain a very high level of riding ability.

Normally the dealer delivers the bike to the centre for the new rider and it is there they learn the basics about control and maintenance before the wheels even meet a proper road surface. However, my moped had been in my hands for about a week before I ventured over to Newtownards, and although I had mastered simple things like starting, moving and stopping, there were some points I wasn't sure of and felt needed more clarification.

My instructress, Mrs. Veronica McCall, arrived on a Kawasaki 250 which com-pletely overpowered my little blue bike, but as soon as the noise of the engine had died away we were able to get down to business.

An early story (from 1981) by Ann-Marie about learning to ride a motorcycle

Time rolled on and I forsook the pages of the *Spectator* for the life of a publican – many would say the ideal progression for a journalist – but it wasn't enough. So in a different local pub one night I allowed myself to be persuaded to stand in the 1989 Council elections.

We were a disparate group in the North Down tradition – the Better Bangor Campaign (or BBC). Comprising a few ex-politicos, traders and ordinary people, it was quite amazing how such a fledgling organisation managed to pull it all together to get me elected for Bangor West in the early summer of that year.

Canvassing had proved a real eye-opener. On the doorstep a proportion were keen and interested in what we had to say. Others wanted to know if I was a true 'Bangorian'. It was a loaded question then and I hope it's not asked today because to be a true 'Bangorian' you're supposed to have at least three generations buried in the Abbey churchyard. That rules out me and so many others – it belongs to the Church of Ireland.

Time for a new definition.

Even many of those born in the quaintly-named beds

of the old Bangor maternity ward overlooking Ward Park wouldn't have qualified (including the 'Barry's Amusements' bed, which I always liked to imagine was provided out of the profits from *What The Butler Saw At Expo Tokyo).*

We gave up canvassing in Helen's Bay after so many doors were closed in our faces: "We're voting Conservative" they smiled in relief.

Six Conservatives were elected along with me that year when I took my place at one of those heavy desks. The next four years passed by quickly. Committee meetings, Council meetings, site meetings, charity committee meetings, Council events, community events – I don't know how I fitted everything in around being part of a family business but thanks to the support of my then partner (now husband) Campbell, my parents and siblings, I did.

It wasn't easy, being an independent on the Council, when you were up against party machines. There was much negotiating each year when the time came to elect a new Mayor and committee chairs with no room for individuals, but sitting at the top table didn't interest me. What mattered was the opportunity to try to improve everyday life for the people of North Down in everyday ways that affected their lives.

My finest moment in that hallowed hall? Well, I got married there – the only sitting Councillor ever to do so at that time.

Women's Aid in Bangor

By the early Eighties a number of voluntary organisations inspired by the previous traumatic decade were maturing. Stronger and surer of themselves, they began to spread out from their bases in Belfast to other towns around Northern Ireland.

Among them was Women's Aid – the organisation that provides support and shelter for female victims of domestic abuse and their children.

Early in the decade, in one of those serendipitous moments, a few women from North Down happened to be

Support for Women's Aid – The Ava Bar and Dufferin Rooms made their annual cheque presentations in November 1985 to three charities chosen by the staff. Picture shows (from left): Kate Fleck from North Down Women's Aid with Phillip Hayes (public bar); Janette Giltrap and Pamela Hillen (Dufferin Rooms) with Doris Mackey, chairman of the Belfast and District branch of Guide Dogs for the Blind); and Wilma Faulkner (saloon bar) with Sister Alison Kearney of the Clark Clinic at the Royal Belfast Hospital for Sick Children. Included are working and retired guide dogs Gemma and Topaz. I 45-4-26

attending a workshop where they met Karen McMinn, the Northern Ireland Women's Aid Federation co-ordinator at the time.

The discussion turned to the work carried out by the Federation and Karen confided they were particularly concerned by the number of women seeking help from North Down. A public meeting was organised and a tiny band of volunteers took on the task of setting up North Down Women's Aid.

For most of the Eighties the group worked hard to provide an advice centre in Main Street – pleading with funders, spreading the message and being there for any women who needed them. By the end of the decade their first shelter opened in Bangor.

It's still there.

Chris Capper

remembers...

I t was an act of journalistic vandalism. Well, just vandalism. My name and the date carved into a desk, close to my dad's name and a considerably earlier date. Government property too – the Press gallery of the Stormont Assembly.

Chris Capper at the Assembly

I can confess now, because the evidence – and the Capper family record at Stormont – was destroyed in the 1995 fire. Dad had etched his name during his time on the *Belfast Telegraph* – mine was added as the *Spectator's* reporter on events at Jim Prior's Rolling Devolution Assembly, which first sat in November 1982.

Chris Capper began working at the *Spectator* from the age of 17 – and stayed there until 1989. He left to join the BBC in Belfast where he still works.

What was the *Spectator* doing there? It was just about on the edge of our patch. I suppose the paper had a sense of duty, and in a way, although it was never going to work, saw the Assembly as an attempt to do something its originators at least thought was constructive. But there, among the seats labelled BBC, UTV, Downtown Radio, *Belfast Telegraph, News Letter, Irish News* and more, was one right on the end with our name on it.

Chris Capper today

North Down's representation in the actual chamber that day contained the elements of the story of the constituency's politics in the Eighties. The Ulster Unionists had three seats, with the DUP and Alliance Party on two each. The eighth, of course, was occupied by Jim Kilfedder, the maverick leader of the Ulster Popular Unionist Party. As in quite a few elections at the time, he had topped the poll.

It was always hard to define exactly why he enjoyed such electoral appeal. It was said it was because he was a hard-working constituency MP who worked diligently on local issues. Another explanation was that he appealed to both wings of unionism – or at least didn't alienate them, by avoiding comment on any really difficult political issue.

Jim did manage to convert his support into a few seats on North Down Borough Council, but he never built much of a base for his party. There were some cynical interpretations of his announcement at later elections that he would not be putting up any posters because of "concern for the environment".

He was elected Speaker of that experimental and doomed Assembly – and no man ever enjoyed the role more.

Among the Ulster Unionist representatives from North Down was another maverick who was to succeed Jim as (again, a more or less independent) MP for North Down, Bob McCartney. One of his witheringly sarcastic denunciations of the Assembly from its own benches always enlivened an afternoon on the Hill. The one about the members being astronauts sitting in a broken rocket with no engines was laugh out loud (it was the way he told them and, like SDLP and Sinn Fein members, there weren't many jokes about).

The Campaign for Equal Citizenship he led a few years

later was yet another example of North Down's ability to wander along a different political path from the rest of the country.

That was also evident in the relative success – again compared to elsewhere in Northern Ireland – of the Alliance Party. Another charismatic leader, John Cushnahan, had chosen North Down to build a substantial electoral base – but the 1985 Anglo-Irish Agreement and the appearance of Bob McCartney hardened attitudes and any hopes of challenging Jim Kilfedder for Westminster evaporated.

That's not to say there was an atmosphere of harmony in an oasis of peace. I had reason to be very grateful to another of North Down's representatives in the Assembly chamber. When the Third Force rallied in Newtownards in November 1981, I was one of several *Spectator* reporters and photographers who went to cover it. A group of masked men didn't like it when I took their picture and pinned me against a wall by the throat. Bad things were just about to happen, when the DUP's Simpson Gibson ran up and vouched for me.

As only a cub reporter on a weekly, it was great to be involved in the Northern Ireland political story – even the North Down version of it.

If Stormont was the peak of the political range, the foothills were the meetings of the political parties. They were much more fun. Especially when it was the DUP and Beryl Holland was involved. Not a week went by without a 'Letter to the Editor' from the elderly Beryl. Her enthusiasm for, and unblinking support of, her party leader would put the tweenie fans of a boy band to shame.

No opinion other than Dr Paisley's could ever be right. He was right up there with the best political leaders in history. As was obvious from her other hero – and she would frequently produce her tea-towel printed with

Reporter survives Ballyholme dip shock

by our saltwater correspondent CHRIS CAPPER

Up to your neck in freezing seawater at 2.30 p.m. on a Tuesday in May is a good moment to reflect on just how your career in journalism has placed you in such a position.

It had seemed, like these things often do, a good idea at the time. Was Ballyholme Bay too dirty to swim in? Go and find out, and at the same time make a twit out of yourself for the amusement of readers and the benefit of circulation (mine stopped for about 10 minutes anyway).

The Mayor, Alderman Bruce Mulligan, had given off about the beach's failure to come up to EEC standards, one of three in Northern Ireland to fail to make the grade.

Dr. Roy Ramsey, at the DoE's Environment Protection & Control Division, made reassuring noises about all faults having been repaired in the sewage system, just not in time for the 1987 sampling. Latest tests had shown that the water did come up to scratch.

Like I said, testing it out for myself seemed like a good idea at the time, in the best traditions of have-a-go (be-a-twit) reporting.

I sat in the car waiting for the "Spectator" photographer to turn up to record this remarkable event, and I have to admit to second, third and even fourth thoughts on the advisability of making decisions about exposing oneself to the great outdoors during coffee break in a warm office. The two windsurfers in the bay were travelling at 120mph in the wind, falling off, and taking two hours to remount. Spray was whipping off the waves to mingle with the windblown sand. It was cold.

Unfortuantely, the photographer arrived and I reluctantly stripped down to my trendy swimwear, pulled in the stomach and sprinted to the waterline. Turning to camera briefly (very briefly), there was a quick turn, wade, and then short crawl in on a wave - a distance that wouldn't win a six-year-old a five metre badge. A quick "after" shot, sprint to the car, and an awkward change in the front seat. All over.

What did I elucidate from my examination? The water was v. cold, v. green and v. wavy. I did not feel ill, but then I didn't feel very well either. In my opinion, however, it was far too cold for any bacteria to multiply and if you don't believe the DoE, it should be safe to swim from

November to May, though why you'd want to.

The cause of all the heroics (total ridicule) was a statement from the Northern Ireland Office, revealing that 11 out of the Province's 14 designated bathing beaches were 'clean enough according to EC rules. Helen's Bay, Crawfordsburn, Groomsport awnd Millisle were among those that made it; the failures, apart from Ballyholme, were Newcastle and Ballycastle.

This is the first time Ballyholme has officially failed; last year, however, the DoE tested Ballyholme Beach in a sort of trial run and found that it did not come up to the required standard.

According to Dr. Ramsey, faults in the sewage system had meant that the water coming from the Cottown river (also known as the Ballyholme river) on to the beach was too dirty. The faults had been identified and repaired, but not in time for the 1987 season.

The Mayor was "very annoyed". He said, "The beach hasn't come up to standard for the second year running. The government has not bothered about North Down while they're fixing up all the other beaches.

"I'm very disapointed the DoE haven't kept their word. They got the warning last year and

thought they would put it right this year, but it still hasn't passed the test.

"The Minister is coming very soon to North Down. We bring him along and show it to him," he said.

There had also been dark rumours from the Town Hall about threatening to close the beaches - and you know the fuss that caused in "Jaws".

Dr. Ramsey said that the repairs to the sewage system had been made, and that a further survey of the water in January had shown the levels of faecal coliforms on the water conformed to the EEC rules. Faecal coliforms come from warm-blooded animals, including human beings.

"Hopefully that improvement will continue and that 1988 will conform. I can't give any guarantees, but there certainly have been major improvements and I am confident thay can be sustained," he said, adding that sampling for the 1988 season had already started.

He also said that the problem was entirely due to the stream that poured on to the beach, and had nothing to do with the sewage outfall at Briggs Rock, the bane of Orlock residents.

Personally, if you can ignore the cold, I'm sure a few faecal coliforms won't be any trouble.

Overweight, over-cold and over-apprehensive at the prospect of weeks of abuse and banter: Chris Capper does something stupid in pursuit of a story.   Seefoto

Chris Capper suffers for his art in 1988

Winston Churchill's words of appreciation for Ulster. You could never win an argument with Mrs Holland (never Beryl to her face). One of the many surreal moments that came out of our encounters was being branded "a so-called Protestant" in one of her letters to the paper.

Different times in many ways, the Eighties. I've often wondered what Beryl would have made of politics today. If she were still with us, she'd be the first to tell me.

Karen English
remembers...

Two life-changing events shaped the Eighties for me – literally falling head over heels in love for the first time and my foray into journalism.

I think I was born to be a reporter. Besides being restive, enquiring and curious, I've always had a love affair with words. The dictionary is still my favourite read. Why say leadership and not hegemony?

Landing a job on the *Spectator*, then a broadsheet, when aged just 18, was a dream come true. Eyes blazing with enthusiasm, I happily pounded the keyboard revelling in the black words on crisp white paper spooling up before me. The clanking of the carriage-return brought sheer joy too.

It's a hard life but someone has to do it...
Karen meets pop star Marti Pellow

And I'll never forget the deafening but glorious noise of the printing presses as they thundered overhead. Back in the day social media meant editorial staff and compositors (those who set type) meeting up in the pub once the paper had gone to bed (to print)!

Under the wing of inspiring journalistic mentor Annie Roycroft, I covered a slew of stories spanning many genres. Crime was part of my reporting remit, catapulting me to the big league – that of a serious journalist!

Karen English has been in broadcasting for 25 years, having joined Downtown Radio in 1987 as a roving reporter after spending her formative years in journalism on the *Spectator* in Bangor.

Criss-crossing the Province, she covered the Troubles extensively; on one occasion finding herself at the centre of a story after being knocked off her feet and cut by flying glass and debris when a massive IRA bomb detonated in Belfast.

With a ferocious work ethic and seemingly ubiquitous at a time when Northern Ireland was a hotbed of terrorist-related news, she was nicknamed 'Downtrodden' by one high-ranking NIO government aide.

As a news anchor she has broadcast many monumental events – for example, Downtown Radio/ Cool FM scooped the world by breaking the Provisional IRA complete ceasefire declaration in 1994.

At the softer end of the news spectrum, Karen has interviewed probably the most famous ice dancers of all time, Jayne Torvill and Christopher Dean, and got up close with pop pin-up Marti Pellow of Scottish group Wet Wet Wet fame.

Such is her passion for the immediacy of radio news, Karen turned down a television job offer from Sky News in the Eighties.

At Downtown/Cool FM she has climbed the career ladder, notching up a hat-trick of female firsts in the process. In May 2012 Karen was appointed Downtown/Cool FM's first female News Editor, overseeing all daily news output from breakfast time to lunchtime. She was also their first and only female Duty News Editor and then Deputy News Editor.

Off-air life is exigent too. Karen is a dedicated mum to Sarah-Jane and Joshua, born in December 1999 and July 2002 respectively.

She is married to Brian McEneny and the family live in Bangor.

When not pumping out court copy on the penalties imposed on the perpetrators, I was flushing out the facts to expose the 'Rat of the Week'.

My fledgling career was a pastiche of journalistic types, from gut-wrenching hard news (the Troubles were still raging then) to opinion-based reviews. Peppering interviewees – from pundits to politicos – with probing questions was thrilling.

Some of my text was headline-grabbing and made the front page; other narrative came under the band of niche reporting (education was my speciality); and then there were the touching human interest features.

But my tongue-in-cheek fun fillers drew most response. Notably, my anti topless sun-bathing stance fell as flat as my chest among the breast-beating décolletage divas. No cover-up was their collective cry!

A high point was my first by-line, for a story on a house hunt with a difference. With a bunch of Canadian tourists in tow, this cub reporter turned dwelling detective tracked down their family's ancestral home – and all from an ancient faded sepia photograph.

Like intrepid war correspondent Kate Adie I never shied away from danger and had a close to the action approach! Pitching out of an airworthy plane above the Ards Peninsula at over 2,000ft was all in the line of duty. Parachute jumping only got the chop when this thrill-hungry amateur embarked on another high impact endeavour – karate. This was designed to make me fighting fit – and capable of taking part in two major assignments.

I've always admired the valiant frontline journalists who push the envelope in battle reporting and risk death to bring us living history. While no combat reporter, this greenhorn in khaki got a crash course in surviving war-like conditions on a TA military exercise in Denmark in 1984. Digging in with the audacious and indefatigable 74 Engineer Regiment (Field Squadron 112) as they prepared for a simulated attack from the communist bloc, tested my mettle to the limit.

Trekking over muddy terrain, kipping in filthy malodorous water-soaked trenches, building and blowing up bridges, minefield construction and hand grenade practice, all required single-mindedness of purpose. With a mixture of anxiety and adrenaline coursing inside us, we were always on heightened alert fearing a coup de main.

This realistic war game, code-named Bold Gannet, was an off-shoot of the vast NATO exercise Operation Lionheart, which involved the largest UK transportation of troops overseas since the 1939-1945 war.

I'll never forget my journey to Denmark in a Hercules, a beast of a military aircraft with no creature comforts – the toilet was a bucket shielded by a curtain. Windowless, dark and sparsely insulated, the ear-splitting noise which roared from this troop and tank carrier was hellish and unremitting.

My flight to Gibraltar earlier that year to meet up with infantry battalions the 4th (Volunteer) Battalion and the 5th (Volunteer) Battalion of the Royal Irish Rangers was more conventional, but not without drama. Our approach to the Rock was petrifying as our passenger plane had to sharply manoeuvre to avoid Spanish airspace. Surrounded by the Mediterranean Sea, as the craft dipped shaking violently from side to side I felt like I was aboard a capsizing ship about to be swallowed up by the crashing waves.

Spectator reporter Karen English followed the Royal Irish Rangers to Gibraltar in May 1984, meeting some of the island's renowned Barbary Apes along the way. *276-15A-22*

Gibraltar, a British colony, is disputed territory and remains a diplomatic sore point between London and Madrid. There, not all of the TA operation was make-believe – the part-time soldiers had to guard Gib's frontier with Spain for real.

There was plenty of 'pretend' combat action too. I joined the heavily-armed soldiers as they engaged in a FIBUA exercise (fighting in a built-up area). Loud war zone noises permeated the hilly terrain, including gunfire, smoke grenades and thunder flashes.

Looking back I realise how lucky I was. As a young reporter, trusty notebook and pen in hand, it was a huge adventure to travel to far-flung places. It was also revelatory and made me extremely defensive of the TA. These training exercises and conflict scenarios are not junkets. Played out with precision and professionalism they require commitment, endurance and pluck.

Ultimately they shape these brave spare-time volunteer soldiers to meet any military challenge, like that in Afghanistan today where TA recruits are deployed alongside regular troops. We all know, due to the blanket news coverage, that this remains a perilous and bloody combat zone where many soldiers have paid the ultimate sacrifice.

So what became of my other intense Eighties passion? My rakishly handsome first love fancied himself as king of the roller disco craze, which peaked around 1980.

Karen with her children Sarah-Jane and Joshua

Being catastrophically calamitous, the wheels came off this teenage romance when, like Prime Minister of the day Margaret Thatcher, this lady was not for turning! Truth be told, I couldn't even stand upright, let alone execute manoeuvres in motion!

As the wheeled whizz skated off with my heart leaving me in a heap, I felt as ridiculous as my gargantuan shoulder-pads – the epitome of Eighties excess. And all this played out as the tragic Dire Straits track *Romeo And Juliet* hauntingly reverberated round the rink.

Personally the Eighties was a defining and character-forming roller (!) coaster decade, synonymous with TA trips, hack highs and love lows – all part of my own unique life story.

Clare McGinn
remembers...

So what's the connection between Los Angeles and Bangor? And what has it to do with me and this book? The answer is *Lou Grant.*

I was around 13 when the fictional *Los Angeles Tribune* appeared on our television screens and made me think that journalism was the calling for me. The programme starred Ed Asner as the irascible Lou Grant and was set in a busy newsroom where everyone was screaming and shouting at each other.

Grant's team included young general assignment reporters Joe Rossi and Billie Newman who were always in competition with each other. Joe, deep down, was an ambulance chaser and, to my mind, on the cusp of

Clare McGinn in the late 1980s

sleaziness. Billie, in contrast, was the intelligent, incisive female reporter trying to make it in a man's world on her merits. I saw a lot of myself in Billie.

Then there was the avuncular Managing Editor Charlie Hume, who had brought Lou to 'The Trib' and was frequently baling him out of trouble or buying him time as a controversial front page story was brewing; the photographer 'Animal' who was brilliant but unhinged, and the tough, autocratic publisher Margaret Pynchon

After the *Spectator* Clare McGinn worked for *The Belfast Post* and freelanced for both the *Belfast Telegraph* and *The Irish News*. She then worked as a press officer with the Northern Ireland Tourist Board.

In 1987 she went to the University of East Anglia to study English and American Literature but was a freelance reporter for the *East Anglian*

Daily Times and The Irish News.

1991-1992 – Attended the University of Kansas to study American Literature and Journalism.

1992 – Became a BBC Network Radio Production Trainee in London and worked on a range of programmes for BBC Radio 4 and Radio 5, including Woman's Hour, The Johnny Walker Show and All In The Mind.

1994 – Producer, Kaleidoscope, Radio 4 daily arts programme.

1995-1997 – Radio documentary producer, including the award-winning Secret Theatres Of The Mind with Michael Ignatieff and Don't Fence Me In with Michael Palin.

1997 – BBC Education Executive Producer. Devised and launched The Learning Curve on Radio 4 and ran the non-schools radio output, including documentaries and features.

2000-2002 – BBC Northern Ireland's Editor of Popular Programmes. Ran non-news Radio Ulster speech output, including Your Place And Mine, Gardeners' Corner and On Your Behalf, as well Radio 4 output, and produced Country Times and Fair Play for BBC Northern Ireland Television.

2002 – Editor of BBC Radio Production in Bristol. Responsible for Radio 4

who had blue hair, blue blood and reminded me of another blue Margaret who was around at the time.

In each episode you saw Lou assigning Rossi and Billie to cover various news stories which invariably involved tough choices or moral dilemmas. You followed them as they wrestled with ethical questions around plagiarism, entrapment, chequebook journalism, door stepping and conflicts of interest. It was heart in mouth stuff.

They lurched from one mighty issue to another – prostitution, child abuse, fires, earthquakes, mental illness, drug abuse, pollution and political corruption but, however bad it got, Lou was always there to offer moral guidance and direction to Rossi and Billie.

What was clear to me was that journalism was a way to change the world. Words were your shield and your weapons. I was only 13. Six years later I slid into my seat in the *Spectator* as a trainee reporter and the rose-tinted glasses were unceremoniously ripped off and thrown into the "get over yourself" bin.

Joy Bannister was the Editor who hired me and I think I was the first reporter who had not known or been chosen by Annie Roycroft, but she cast a long shadow over the office.

My credentials were completion of the NCTJ course at the Belfast College of Business Studies (much to the shock of my parents who really wanted me to go to university), the Esso prize for Young Trainee Journalist of the Year in 1983 for something I wrote on how computers were transforming the workplace, and my unblinking belief that I could be the next Billie Newman.

But the *Spectator* was not 'The Trib', Joy Bannister was not Lou Grant and Bangor was not Los Angeles. Of the reporter intake at that time I was the baby and therefore sat facing everyone else like a toddler on a high chair. Joy sat to my left, while Chris Capper, Ann-Marie Hillen, Karen English, Paul Flowers and Adrian Beattie were the other more experienced ducklings.

It was made pretty clear to me on that first day that

making teas and coffees, two or three times a day, for the other reporters was a key part of my job until someone more junior was brought in. That could be more than 21 cups a day! I was shown the kitchen, the kettle and then told to get on with it. What?

So I didn't get to cover the earth-shattering stories that 'The Trib' reporters managed every week or have regular moral guidance sessions with Joy. Instead, over the next few years I cut my journalistic teeth on court cases (North Down Magistrate's Court with Resident Magistrate Wishart Mills), where I soon discovered that a lot of people in Bangor and Holywood did not understand the speed limit, the point of traffic lights or the need to pay their television licence.

I sat through interminable Council meetings, eyes glazing over as the minutiae of planning applications were debated intensely. There were fiercely contested dog shows and Bangor Music Festival to report on. Numerous school events, church events, sports events and charity events took me all over North Down. I learned to take pictures and write snappy copy. I dealt with very happy and very grumpy members of the public and I met Frank Carson, Princess Anne, Princess Michael of Kent and Thereza Bazar from Dollar.

I remember the embarrassment of being sent down to go on exercise with the Bangor RNLI while wearing a red dress and white stilettos because I'd got my days mixed up. I can still hear Joy's words "an appointment is an appointment" ringing in my ears.

I also remember Paul Flowers going to great lengths to take a picture of a creepy-crawly discovered in a meal he'd ordered from a local Chinese restaurant, which I think appeared in the paper that week with the headline 'Fried Lice'.

There was the nameless reporter who went to cover a story about a Royal National Institute for the Blind event and assembled everyone together for a picture afterwards, asking them to "look at the birdie" which, thankfully, they all found hilariously funny. Not long after that the same reporter went to interview a man who had lost both legs in

output including *A Good Read, Poetry Please, With Great Pleasure, Great Lives* and *Word Of Mouth*, as well as documentaries, drama, readings and features for BBC Radio 3, 4 and World Service. 2012 – Head of Network Radio Production, Bristol. Responsible for existing Bristol output plus *Farming Today, The Food Programme, Open Country, Ramblings, Costing The Earth, On Your Farm*. Also director of *More Than Words*, BBC Radio 4's first ever listening festival.

Clare McGinn today

an accident and tactlessly started the interview with: "So, what's it like to be in your shoes?"

For me there was nothing quite like the satisfaction of receiving the little brown envelope with your payslip and money in it every Thursday once the paper had been put to bed. We had earned it, staying late on a Wednesday night writing up our stories frantically to hit the deadline and then getting in really early on a Thursday to proof-read reams and reams of copy to watch out for mistakes. I have to hold my hands up and say I was responsible for a court report where someone was assaulted with a 'clenched fish'.

A few hours later the bundles of published papers would arrive and you'd see what you'd written in print with your by-line. And then we started all over again. By the time I moved on from Bangor and the *Spectator* I had grown up a lot. I was editorially a lot sharper than when I started and much more street-wise and I finally saw *Lou Grant* for what it was – a great TV programme but not the real thing.

Patricia Fox

remembers...

Thirteen thousand miles away from my home town of Bangor, in my other home town of Bairnsdale in rural south-east Australia, over the ether comes an email asking for memories of Bangor in the 1980s.

I'll have to admit I've spent some energy trying to forget the white high heels, the canisters of Elnett hairspray for the obligatory big hair, the nights at BJ's, Rollerama…

The *Spectator* was my first job as a junior reporter. You couldn't do a journalism degree back then so we passed through the fearsome tutelage of Joan Fitzpatrick for one year at the College of Business Studies in Belfast, learning shorthand and arguing the finer points of

Patricia Fox in the 1980s

proportional representation with another lecturer, North Down Councillor Brian Wilson.

Joy Bannister then had the dubious pleasure of drumming in the difference between *its* and *it's* and making a real reporter of someone who had effectively returned to Bangor after seven years at a convent boarding school in Portstewart.

Patricia Fox worked for the *Spectator* for 10 years. She started the first regular environmental page in a Northern Ireland weekly, and left to study ecology at Queen's University Belfast.

She moved to Australia in 1998 to study at the University of Western Australia and since the early 2000s has worked in woodland restoration in south-east Victoria. Some of her best friends, she points out, are Protestants.

The old *Spectator* office and its printing presses were in upper Main Street. Beauty board walls, the constant smog of cigarette smoke that hung over the journos who hung over their typewriters, the late night Wednesdays. I loved every bit of it, although I'm not sure if my liver and lungs would agree.

Catholic. Lapsed. I'd feel like putting it on a badge sometimes, not that that would have made any difference. It didn't make any difference to me or many around me, but there were interesting undercurrents that my children certainly don't have to navigate. I was under strict instructions not to let a boyfriend's granny know "what I was". When it was felt she could be told without the shock killing her, her immediate response was: "But she's such a nice girl."

Patricia Fox interviews Paddy Ashdown, leader of the Liberal Democrats, during a visit to Bangor. He was a former pupil of the town's Garth House school.

After what he saw as unfavourable coverage in the paper, one local minister began to circulate pamphlets advising people "this fox will not unearth us".

Royal visits were always fun. I loved that marking. Tracking down the obligatory North Down person who'd had a millisecond with said royal, who'd received the invitation to the garden party, who had to be photographed. "Not much bloody use sending those two," was muttered as I and another 'Catholic' reporter left to cover a royal visit. I was totally confused. Elizabeth was my queen too, or so I thought. At primary school the Irish dancers had put on a show for her silver jubilee. I wasn't involved. I'm not bitter but you can stop mentioning it Debi.

"I am bigotry. I'd kill you if things got bad here," someone slurred to me at a drunken Christmas works party where we were discussing the rise in paramilitary groups. I feel curiously disloyal writing this down but it was the way it was.

There was only one time I recall actually being scared in Bangor. Around the Twelfth of July one of the housing estates had been barricaded off. A photographer and I were dispatched to interview those manning the barricades. They turned out to be children, probably none even in their teens. They had no idea what they were doing it all for.

"What would you do if a Catholic came along now?" I asked. I'd kill them, this young girl answered. Then she noticed I was writing down what they said in shorthand. What was that code, she demanded. She could be writing anything. She could be writing lies about us. I showed them how shorthand worked and the moment passed. The

Another string to her bow – Patricia helps to hand over a prize to competition winner Robert McKinley in January 1988 after he won the top prize in the Grand *Spectator* Christmas competition. Robert's name was drawn from a large number of correct answers for the quiz and he was presented with his prize – a stereo cassette recorder – by Billy Mitchell of Mitchell's electrical retailers, Main Street. Looking on is Robert's sister Carolyn.

photographer (he could have used one of those badges too) and I did not hang around.

It is a natural disaster that stays most in my mind though. The great storm of 1987 had a local casualty, a ship's master went down with his ship and I was dispatched to interview his widow. It never fails to amaze me why people will let journalists into their homes at times like that but she did. She had lost the love of her life and I hope I did him justice.

I returned to Bangor last year

MISSING CAPTAIN'S WIFE STILL WAITS

"I NEVER thought I would lose him to the sea", said Mrs. Elizabeth Birch, wife of the Newtownards sea captain who is missing, presumed dead, after his ship sank during the violent storm off south east England last week.

By Patricia Fox

Mr. David Birch, 35, was captain on board the Sumnia, which was on its way to Germany when it was caught in the hurricane that caused deaths and widespread damage in Britain. His photograph has been circulated in all the ports off the English Channel.

Mrs. Birch heard from her husband on Tuesday last week and first knew that he was missing when the police called to see her at work on Friday. "Our house was burgled in February and I thought it was about that", she said this week from her home where friends and family were keeping her company while she waited by the 'phone.

She believed that the ship got into difficulties in the early hours

said that Davey had sounded the alarm and he told them to be prepared to abandon ship. They said he had a lifebelt and lifejacket on". She added that two lifejackets had been found in the sea.

Mr. Peter Warrington, regional controller of the Coastguard, was not optimistic about Mr. Birch's chances of survival, said Mrs. Birch. "That man said that in all his years he had never seen weather like it. I said to him that maybe my husband was under the ship and he said I'm being very brutal but I wouldn't say that, he couldn't possibly be under the ship.

"You know he probably is dead but I'm still hanging on until they tell me officially. Then I can try

Mr. Birch is originally from Ballywalter where his family still lives. Mrs. Birch is from Belfast and she explained that they had settled in Newtownards because it was 'half-way for both of us'. She said that her husband loved the sea. That was all he ever talked about".

She pointed out a large model of a ship which he loved. "He used to be able to tell what the weather was going to be like from the stars. From when he was a boy he loved the boats, he was always down at the shore in the village. There were that many things that remind me of things he did".

WEEKEND

Her husband was last home about two weeks ago when he

Patricia's story in the aftermath of the violent storm that swept across southern Britain on 15/16 October 1987

after 14 years away. My children developed Bangor accents within weeks and charged along the coastal path

Patricia Fox with husband Stewart and children Holly (10) and Finn (8) at their home in country Victoria, Australia

just as I had done, trying to skip stones and find blackberries. Queen's Parade still wasn't finished (what's going on, people?). It felt good to leave Bangor but it felt even better to come home.

Paul Connolly

remembers...

They say the best grounding in journalism is with a great local weekly paper. And it's true. Mine was with the *Spectator*. But I nearly didn't end up in Bangor. In fact, if it hadn't been for the *Spectator,* I wouldn't have ended up in Northern Ireland at all.

What happened was this. Fresh from the Belfast NCTJ journalism course in 1987, I applied for whatever jobs were going at home and across the water. Within a few weeks an interview letter arrived for a reporter's job in the town of Goole in the East Riding of Yorkshire.

As I travelled over my eyes widened at the grim post-industrial landscape that dominated the journey from the airport. To a Glens of Antrim boy the place was scarred, brutal and ugly. My conclusion that Goole was an uninspiring backwater, to put it politely, was confirmed by a pre-interview scoot around the town. When the Editor confided that even he lived 25 miles away, my mind was made up.

I headed home, praying I wouldn't get the job. I did; my heart sank. It was the Thatcher era and unemployment was stubbornly high. Thankfully, the next day word went round that the *Spectator* was recruiting. Myself and Colette

Paul Connolly in the late 1980s

Paul Connolly is Group Managing Editor at Independent News & Media (NI), publishers of the *Belfast Telegraph, Sunday Life* and the *Community Telegraph.*

He has also worked for the *Ulster News Letter* and *Sunday News* and has freelanced in the past for a range of publications including *Time Magazine.*

Bangor in the Eighties

Paul is a member of the board of directors of the Society of Editors and a member of the accreditation board of the National Council for the Training of Journalists.

Wilson, now the BBC's Colette Maguire, got the jobs and started on the same day.

There followed 11 happy months of the best on-the-job learning under the tutelage of a fantastic crew that included Paul Flowers, Ann-Marie Hillen (now Foster), Chris Capper, Colin Bateman and others too numerous to mention. By the end of it, I knew Bangor pretty well, even for a blow-in.

The life of a junior reporter on a weekly newspaper in those days had a comfortable rhythm that ran something like this (apologies if some days are mixed up in the mists of time):

Monday – Find and write stories, wedding reports and obituaries. Type up handwritten notes from village correspondents. Attend North Down Borough Council meeting in the evening, sometimes till midnight or beyond.

Tuesday – Bangor Magistrate's Court: write up 50 or more cases, some only a few lines, others shorthand-testing contested cases that could run to 30 paragraphs.

Wednesday – Finish off council and mag court reports, and write up late-breaking stories. Stay till 8.30pm to see the paper to 'bed', then relax over a couple of pints in somewhere like Wolsey's or the Ava.

Thursday – Paper published that morning. Mags court again, this time Ards. Or maybe the crown court instead.

Friday – Attend coroner's court and write up reports. Chase up off-diary stories for the following week's paper. The local station desk officer would drop in the police notes. Type up more village notes.

A beat like that lends a fascinating insight into any town – from the Saturday night brawls, to the businessman's wife caught drink-driving in hubby's BMW, and who is – or isn't – paying their TV licences.

Occasionally more serious stuff or the odd juicy story could be flogged to the Belfast dailies or Sundays. All the life of a town and its hinterland, played out in front of your eyes.

The courts were central; the reckoning place of bad boys and shoplifters and a through-the-keyhole peek behind the manicured lawns of the middle classes. Every case was reported – often down to the last line and the finest detail.

No one who appeared at Bangor or Ards Mags was permitted to escape the cold embrace of the *Spectator*. No one. Not even the paper's Managing Director, who was 'done' for speeding one day. His case was promptly reported in the next issue, just the same as all the other speeders: a textbook case of journalistic and proprietorial ethics.

Paul Connolly today

The human flotsam and jetsam that washed across the shores of the courts were a permanently colourful array of characters. Punks and killers, grannies and drunks, clergymen and peelers – the machinery of justice ground on remorselessly if not always efficiently or even fairly. I used to bridle at dads getting serious jail time for fiddling a grand or two from the 'bru', whilst white collar criminals who defrauded tens of thousands were, in comparison, treated more leniently due to a leaden sentencing policy.

The actual magistrates were key. Some were clinically effective, dispensing justice and running the court like clockwork. Too clinical, I thought sometimes. Others were inefficient managers, more focused on the sorry stream of humanity paraded before them. Tom Travers, whose daughter had been murdered a few years earlier, was a frequent visitor: a thoroughly decent man who cared deeply about offenders most of us would gladly consign to long stretches in Magilligan or the 'Crum' without a second's thought.

News being news, tragedies played a large part. My first inquest left me shocked and really quite emotional. It was a poor man who drowned himself in the sea off the North Down coast because of the never-ending agony of severe tinnitus. It taught this in-a-rush 23-year-old a lesson. All those medical terms you read in books or papers? At the end of the day they're not about science or clinical terminology; they're about people. Real people's real lives.

There was a particularly shocking incident when a family in a car were crushed and trapped by a truck that overturned on a roundabout towards Newtownards. I remember the reporter returning visibly upset from the fatal scene and being secretly glad I hadn't been sent on that job. To this day I'm nervous if a 40-footer is beside me on a roundabout.

The Troubles intruded occasionally that year. There were bomb alerts and kneecappings and arms finds and the occasional paramilitary attack that generally missed and hit the barn door instead. Clowns and their amateur little wars, for the most part.

But on 12 September 1988, I found myself standing outside Sir Ken Bloomfield's home in Crawfordsburn. An IRA gang had placed a deadly necklace of four Semtex bombs around the house, blocking exits and obviously hoping to either collapse the structure or catch anyone trying to leave the building. Two exploded and the Bloomfield family had to be carried out past unexploded devices.

It was a major strike at the heart of the establishment and the assassination attempt on the head of the Northern Ireland Civil Service and his family was international news. The viciousness of the attack was shocking, even for the times.

I remember standing there that morning looking around the wealthy homes and gardens and wondering what must have been going through the minds of the bombers, who would have undoubtedly been from the cramped and raw streets of west or north Belfast, as they planted their deadly cargo.

It wasn't all death and disaster, of course. The richness, friendliness and vitality of a special town was deeply apparent, even if I did travel in and out by train daily. That was until I was allowed to borrow the company car. I had arrived!

That first night I pulled up in front of my brother's mates in Belfast's Holyland area – only to be met with hoots of laughter. "It'll be a babe magnet," I shot back, knowing full well I was telling a horrific whopper. The company car was, after all, a rickety red Fiat Panda with *'County Down Spectator – first with the news'* or some other meaningless moniker emblazoned in black, white and yellow on the sides. Their honks of derision reached a crescendo as I tootled off up the street.

There was car colour of a different kind when the Editor, the excellent Paul Flowers who led the team with great skill and dedication, was loaned an awesome Audi Quattro for his motors column. Let's just say we reached a certain speed on the Bangor to Donaghadee road which shall, ahem, go unrecorded in these memoirs lest Inspector Knacker shows a very belated interest.

The *Spectator* staff in general was a talented, committed and hugely entertaining bunch. None more so than Colin Bateman who sat at the back of our section of the ground floor office and kept spirits up with a constant stream of witty dialogue, jokes and word plays.

Colin's wonderfully witty and satirical column was one of the best things in the paper – a foil to the diet of 'firing squad' pictures, planning disputes, council bores, and ultra-local news that is the lifeblood of any successful local paper.

And then there was the famous 'Armalite and Jaffa Cakes' incident where the legal, er, might of the Boys' Brigade was brought down on the paper because of a short Bateman column skit on the BB which included a prediction that the organisation could emerge as the "friendly paramilitaries" with an "Armalite in one hand and a packet of Jaffa Cakes in the other" strategy.

His spoof provoked fury from the BB with members bombarding the paper with complaints and a legal threat. Only too aware of the cost of litigation, even one that might have been fought on the grounds that the comments were obviously satirical, the paper chose to defuse the controversy with an apology, much to the disappointment of Bateman and the rest of the editorial team.

And that was it. After an incredibly short time, I headed off to join the *Sunday News* in big, bad Belfast. The final memory is my leaving 'do'; finishing up in the wee small hours swigging beer and setting the world to rights with Paul Flowers as our legs dangled over the pier in what is now the marina.

Bangor. It was only 11 months, but it was absolutely formative. Great times, on a great local paper, in a lovely town. Thank you.

Colette Maguire
(née Wilson) remembers...

I was at the *Spectator* for seven years but there is one 'marking' I vividly remember covering, and funnily enough so does everyone else!

It was my first proper story – where I would be actually interviewing someone – you know… talking to… wangling information out of and then writing a nice feature about it. That's 'sort of' what Editor Paul

Donny and Marie? No, it's actually Donny and Colette during his visit to Bangor in 1987. 357-9a-34

Flowers told me… but he also 'sort of' missed out initially in telling me who this interviewee would be.

When he did get round to it – to be honest I thought it was a joke. I'd just joined the paper – and when I say 'just joined' I mean it. It was my first day so I thought Paul was having a joke at my expense. But no, it was all true – I was going to be interviewing Donny Osmond!

Even when I think about it today my stomach does a bit of a lurch. Oul Donny, no longer the teenage pop idol of the 1970s, was for a while in the mid-1980s gigging in small theatres and in this case officially opening Top Spin

Colette Maguire joined the *Spectator* in September 1987, having successfully completed the National Council for the Training of Journalists course at the College of Business Studies in Belfast.

During her seven years she was the paper's health correspondent and entertainments correspondent. She left in 1994 to join BBC NI as a traffic and travel presenter. Within months she was reporting for *Good Morning Ulster* and soon

During his visit to Bangor Seventies singing star Donny Osmond also met fan Michelle Conway. Michelle had stayed in Utah with a friend 13 years earlier and ended up meeting the Osmond family at their nearby home. 355-16-34

– a new independent record store at the top of Main Street in Bangor.

Okay so he wasn't as well known, but that didn't mean I wasn't nervous – in fact I was a bit of a wreck. I'm sure photographer Neal Dorman had a good laugh to himself as we pushed our way through the throngs of 30-somethings who'd queued for a peek at Donny.

Did he look as good? Did he still have the fab teeth and smile? I can confirm… yes, yes and eh yes! He was absolutely charming. To be honest I didn't get to ask him much – the shop was mad – people (mostly middle-aged women) screaming, pushing and shoving. I'm sure Donny loved it – I felt a bit stupid about it all.

But after 'the interview' I got a kiss on the cheek and a lovely photo of me and my new best friend Donny who (and this is absolutely true) said I looked like his sister Marie! Okay – he's totally stretching it I know, but it sure made my day!

That picture of Donny and me hung on the wall of the *Spectator* until I left in July 1994, alongside a less flattering picture… one of me hobbling from an aeroplane at Ards Airport. Oh the things I got up to! It was no ordinary plane – it was a Hungarian Zlin… a two-seater with no canopy!

The occasion was a press preview for the forthcoming Ards Air Show, which in the late 1980s and early 1990s was one of the highlights in the Northern Ireland calendar. Being picked to cover the preview was regarded as a 'rite of passage' in the Speccy, so I was thrilled to be picked but oh my God little did I know what I had let myself in for!

As soon as we got to Ards the organisers said reporters had the opportunity to go up in a formation of three in a Hungarian plane – I couldn't believe it… were they for real? I spent around an hour thinking about it – during that 60 minutes I watched colleagues from the BBC and UTV loop-the-loop and fly upside down past Scrabo Tower – all filmed for that night's news bulletins.

I'd like to tell you that I was thinking... is there insurance and am I covered? But no, while I was thinking I could possibly die here, I was more worried about how it would go down in the office if I didn't do it. What would the Editor say – would he understand I was terrified of flying at the best of times and now I had to climb into a tiny plane and do loop-the-loops over Scrabo Tower?

Would I get the sack, or worse – would I be left to cover North Down Borough Council meetings on Tuesday nights for the rest of my *Spectator* career?!

Guess what? Just like the man from Del Monte I said yes – but not before phoning my parents and boyfriend (now husband) to tell them what I was about to do!

Next thing I knew I was strapped into the Zlin by the pilot who hardly spoke a word of English. I was wearing a dress (of course!) so that harness wasn't very dignified! On my right BBC veteran broadcaster Sean Rafferty was also being strapped in, while on my left the chef who'd provided all the food for us reporters (ah those were indeed the days!) was also being put into his harness. Unlike me, he was delighted and excited. I was terrified.

Colette Maguire today

began reporting on *Inside Ulster* and BBC *Newsline*, which she subsequently presented.

Colette also presented the popular consumer programme *On Your Behalf* and went on to report with Stephen Nolan for the TV consumer programme *Fair Play*. More recently Colette worked as Assistant Editor on *Evening Extra* and is currently producing *Talkback* with Wendy Austin.

Colette is married and has two daughters.

All I can really remember is the pilot saying: "We do the loop", with me hanging onto a leather strap above my head and screaming: "Aghhhhhh!"

I'd love to tell you it was exhilarating, I was delighted I'd done it, I was wrong to be afraid... but I can't. I was terrified, it was terrifying and I went into proper shock after we landed. I had

On a somewhat happier occasion, action girl Colette taking part in a training weekend at Stranraer in July 1987 with members of the Territorial Army's Bangor-based Field Squadron 112. *417-23a-37*

to be helped off the plane and I could hardly speak.

Meanwhile, Sean Rafferty and the chef were delighted

with themselves: "Wasn't it brilliant… wasn't that the best thing you've ever done."

Sean could see I didn't share their enthusiasm. "Let me interview you about it – I want to hear your thoughts," he said to me. Well Sean got an interview all right, although an interview is maybe stretching it. Actually he got me saying the word 'petrified' at least 20 times during that two-minute interview!

That was really the only word I could say. But to be fair to him, after that interview Sean said there was only one thing that would sort me out and make me feel better… a brandy – I had to have two!

Helen McDowell
remembers...

The stained beauty board panelling on the walls. The 'cloaking' effect of a thick cloud of cigarette smoke over the editorial department. The thunk, thunk, ping of typewriter keys and returns... aaahhh yes, I remember it well.

My initiation into the industry of journalism all those years ago was a happy one, as a young hack in the Bangor Main Street offices of the *Spectator*.

Helen McDowell back in 1989 in hot pursuit of a big story

A just-turned-19 greenhorn, I entered this heady arena of local newspaper excellence in seamless fashion, when a work experience stint as a student from the Belfast College of Business Studies' respected NCTJ journalism course morphed into a period of probation in the workplace at the end of May 1988, once my studies were complete, and then a full-time job as a reporter.

As a training ground on which to cut my reporter's milk teeth, I could scarcely have asked for better – under the tutelage of such experienced hands in the profession as the then Deputy Editor Colin Bateman, and reporters Chris

Helen McDowell is Deputy Editor of the *Spectator*, having begun her career there as a newly trained reporter in 1988.

Over the years Helen's roles at the newspaper group have included news reporter, court correspondent, elections correspondent, women's editor and council correspondent.

Belfast-born, she lives in Bangor with her husband Stuart. The couple have a grown-up daughter, Naomi.

Capper, Patricia Fox, Colette Wilson and Paul Connolly. Under the editorship of Paul Flowers, we were joined in those late 1980s by Richard Sherriff, Damien Magee and Karen Patterson (forgive me if I've omitted any names).

If variety is indeed the spice of life, my day-to-day work was a veritable vindaloo. One day I could be covering the local magistrate's court or an inquest in Newtownards. The next I was off to one of the many community fairs which spring into life across North Down and Ards, and all the delicious photographic fodder they dish up for a local newspaper, from Bonniest Baby contest to Glamorous Granny, and everything in between.

From reporting on devastating personal tragedy such as a loved one lost in a traffic accident, to covering the intrigue and, more often, banal sameness of local Council business.

And, ah yes, as if I could ever forget them, the dreaded planning appeals which consumed notebooks at voracious speed yet conversely days of my life at a despondently plodding pace, in the spartan surroundings of Bangor's Hamilton House.

One of the first major events I reported on – and still to this day, one of the most significant in terms of its devastating impact on the community of North Down and beyond – was the Kegworth air disaster of 8 January 1989.

The entire *Spectator* editorial department was mobilised to cover this unfolding tragedy.

I recall being instructed to 'doorstep' the local family of some of the 47 victims tragically killed when the British Midland passenger plane crashed near Kegworth village in Leicestershire, en route from London Heathrow to Belfast International Airport. Many more passengers were wounded, some gravely.

Regardless of experience – and in those days I was still a newcomer – it never becomes easier to doorstep or cold call a family in mourning. The whole way to their home, I rehearsed in my mind quite how I was going to begin my enquiry, should a grieving family member respond to my ring of their doorbell.

As I approached the house that Thursday morning, just hours before the paper was due to go to press, my heart quickened as I anticipated the range of possible reactions to my intrusion. I would confess to some guilty relief when several rings of the doorbell failed to yield an answer; the property stood with all curtains closed and no cars in the driveway.

I turned my attention instead to neighbouring houses, only to be met with no response either. It doesn't matter how long you do this job – it never gets easier to intrude on someone's private grief.

On a happier note, I recall interviewing two of the survivors, Bangor couple David and Sonya Seaton, who were among the first to be flown home for treatment after spending almost a week in the Queen's Medical Centre, Nottingham.

Mr Seaton, then aged 35, was undergoing treatment at Musgrave Park Hospital, Belfast, when he and his wife kindly agreed to talk to me about their experiences. I was struck by just how upbeat they were, displaying the light-heartedness of those who realise they were lucky to be alive.

Both had sustained broken bones and extensive bruising but were recovering well, Mr Seaton as an inpatient, and Mrs Seaton having

COUNTY DOWN SPECTATOR
AND ULSTER STANDARD
Est. 1904   THURSDAY, 19th JANUARY, 1989   Price 30p

Mr David Seaton is visited by his wife, Sonya, at Musgrave Park Hospital. Mr Seaton is presently undergoing treatment at the hospital for injuries he sustained in the M1 'plane crash on Sunday evening, January 8. His wife, who was also in the crash, sustained severe bruising, a broken finger and shock. The couple live at Auburn Park with their 20-month-old son. The couple had been returning from a weekend of shopping when they were involved in the tragic BD92 flight.
Specfoto: 15/26-40

BANGOR CRASH SURVIVORS FLY HOME
"Progress so far is excellent"

By HELEN McDOWELL

35-YEAR-OLD Mr David Seaton from Bangor, was among the first of the M1 'plane crash survivors to be flown home for treatment in Belfast's Musgrave Park Hospital after spending almost a week in the Queen's Medical Centre in Nottingham.

Mr Seaton, an aquarium dealer, was flown into Aldergrove from East Midlands Airport last Friday evening on the 8pm flight after he was pronounced ill enough to travel. His 25-year-old wife Sonya, who was also in the 'plane crash, was released from hospital at the weekend but stayed in Nottingham to accompany her husband home along with her mother, father and sister. The couple live at Auburn Park with their 20-month-old son, Christopher.

Sitting up in bed on Monday afternoon in the Orthopaedic ward of the hospital, Mr Seaton displayed the light-heartedness and cheerful joking of someone who acknowledges they are lucky to be alive. "I am feeling absolutely first class, in tip-top condition. I have been treated like a VIP and I wouldn't get any better treatment in a hotel. It's going to be a real come-down when I go home, I won't be getting all this attention," he laughed.

Talking about his injuries, he explained: "I have a fractured shoulder and my eye is badly damaged. I have a compound fracture in my arm and two steel plates in my elbow which were put in in the hospital in Nottingham. My

wife is seeing the same doctor as me, Dr. Calderwood. She has broken bones in her hands and massive bruising near her waist where the seatbelt was. The bruising she has is really incredible, it's very severe."

Mr Seaton and his wife flew into Aldergrove on Friday evening from East Midlands airport: "I was sceptical and nervous; it was very scary," he said, "but as soon as I got on the aircraft I buried my head in the newspaper and never lifted it until I got my coffee."

Since the Flight BD92 disaster some national newspapers have carried stories on how passenger safety on 'planes might be improved, including suggestions that seatbelts should have shoulder straps similar to those worn by the crew. Mr Seaton remarked, "After every accident there is always controversy. They have taken photographs of myself and other survivors to see what our injuries are and how best to stop this in the future. If they decide to change the seating arrangement or the seatbelts then it will be because they think that is best for safety, but as far as my wife and myself are concerned the seatbelts couldn't have been better. We were hanging upside down in the tail piece of the 'plane for a good 45 minutes before we were taken to the ambulance at around 9.30pm. All that time we only had our seatbelts to hold us in."

Mr Seaton will stay in Musgrave Park Hospital until his fractures heal and then he will undergo physiotherapy for his elbow. He said: "I have no idea at all when I will be out of hospital. They won't give me any idea because a lot depends on physiotherapy."

The Consultant Orthopaedic Surgeon who is treating Mr Seaton for his injuries, Dr. James Calderwood, remarked: "I think he could be out in a couple of weeks. His progress so far is excellent."

Mrs Seaton, who is recovering from her bruising with her family, commented: "Flying home on Friday was pretty terrifying but we had to do it because of David's injuries, we couldn't have gone by boat. If we hadn't done it now we would never do it again."

She added: "He isn't in a lot of pain although his knee has been giving him some discomfort. His eye will heal itself in time and he can still see out of it perfectly. He does think he is lucky.

"My finger is broken and I have had bruises mainly where my seatbelt was and on my hands and arms but I am not in any great pain."

Mrs Seaton praised the treatment both she and her husband had received from nursing staff in England and at Musgrave Park, and for the help given to them by British Midland. She added: "BM have been absolutely marvellous with taxis for me to visit David and things like that. We don't personally blame them because things like this happen."

TO GO
By DAMIEN MAGEE

of 7 Ballyholme Road, Bangor, asking him to come and discuss the operation with the council and what alternatives might be open to him. A shocked Mr Marshall said he had received letters asking him to visit the council but this was the first he had heard about a possible closure.

"I've heard nothing about this other than a letter asking me to call and see them, but apart from this paper contacting me

"I have just bought an outboard motor and there will be someone employed to police the operation. The yachts have been in the harbour for the last four years and there have been no complaints. Rowing boats have always been part of Bangor and I can't understand the council's way of thinking because this is a cheap way of entertaining young people and keeping them off the street," added Mr. Marshall.

been discharged from hospital in England before their return home to be reunited with their son, then aged 20 months.

It is humbling that so many people, faced with dreadful and difficult personal events, and in particular the loss of a loved one, can still offer a welcome to the intrusion of a reporter in order to share their story.

Richard Sherriff
remembers...

One of the reasons writing about the 1980s presents something of an onerous task is that, as the old adage of our addled parents goes: "If you can remember the Sixties, then you weren't there."

I was there for most of the former and all of the latter but, I have to say, I don't remember a great deal of detail about either. This is partly because I had just escaped from boarding school and started out on real life. I passed my driving test in '81, celebrated my 18th in '82 and my 21st, predictably enough, in '85.

I went to see Bruce Springsteen at Slane in the same year – got hopelessly lost and hitched a lift back to Bangor, leaving everyone I'd travelled there with wondering where I was. I ended up breaking up with my first serious girlfriend as a result, but the 1980s were just a bit like that.

It was a very sociable period you might say. Although not if you were watching *Nationwide,* mind you, as Barry Cowan, departed presenter of *Scene Around Six,* explained to Michael Barratt sometime in 1980 or '81 that Northern Ireland had the highest percentage of under-age drinkers in the UK and that Bangor was the worst.

Having met people of the same vintage from around the Province since then, I don't believe for a minute that Bangor was the worst – it just caused more middle class

Richard Sherriff in the 1980s

Richard Sherriff was born in Bangor Hospital on 10 April 1964, and was raised next to a hayfield in Beverley Gardens before it became Ardmillan Park.

He was educated at Connor House and Bangor Grammar before he fell out with the school and left after third form. They spelt his name wrongly in the magazine when he left.

Richard finished up at Coleraine where he boarded for five years before training as a journalist in Belfast.

His first job was with the *Ulster Star* in Lisburn before spending eight years at the *Spectator*.

He is currently business correspondent for the *News Letter* and lives in Bangor with his wife Lyn and children Emily and Dan.

Richard Sherriff today

consternation and was therefore (a) more amusing and (b) less hassle to drive to for TV footage.

As a result, with the new decade rolling in, I was in the sixth form common room at Coleraine Inst. calling out the names of friends and acquaintances standing in front of the shelters at Ballyholme Beach, grinning and waving bottles of Olde English and Merrydown cider at the camera.

For the most part, those same people now own houses not too far from the very spot where the end of the world was surely foretold. We are balding and fatter – especially the dads – and we meet at Ballyholme Primary and Bangor Grammar and Glenlola and Cubs and BB and GB and we complain about the fact that our children now appear to favour New Zealand sauvignon blanc, which we can no longer afford given the monstrous rise in house prices. Well, we did.

The other thing is that, for exactly the reasons above, the 1980s were a blur of carefree enjoyment funded by student jobs and ultimately journalism, on which path I was set by the formidable Editor of the *Spectator*, Annie Roycroft.

In fact, it was also my English teacher at Coleraine, Jim Knight, who, as well as persuading the brass to let me sit my English Lit. A-Level even though I'd actually failed the O-Level, also persuaded me that if I got the best marks by writing essays in a free period half an hour before they were handed in, then so be it.

The problem was that at that stage, if not actually anti-Bangor, I just wasn't about to hang around, or so I planned. As the 1970s ended I was intending to go into the Merchant Navy and be off like my dad around the world. Then the British Merchant Navy closed down and my dad, a captain who served his apprenticeship on the Atlantic with Head Line, was laid off and I went back to do A-Levels and have another think about things.

Armed only with an ability to write vaguely intelligent English quite quickly, I decided the only obvious route was journalism and wrote eagerly to about 15 weekly newspapers offering my services. Annie was the only one of all of them to reply, telling me to get myself on the journalism course at the College of Biz in Belfast and to get in touch when and if I managed it – or words to that effect. Unfortunately, her letter arrived several days after applications closed for the year and so I ended up at Bangor Tech for a year.

One of the best years of the 1980s was the summer of '81. I had a driving licence and I got my first car and I spent my time either in The Stables working for Denis Waterworth or on the beach at Portavoe. It was a roasting summer and my friends would come to the pub and then we'd head to the beach. It was magic to pile into the sea after a night working behind beer pumps in a bar which – of course – had no air conditioning.

I completed the journalism course in 1985 and immediately disappeared to England ostensibly to look for a job but I was clueless and it basically turned into a tour of friends and various universities from London to Edinburgh.

When I came home, much in debt, I got a job with Charles Hursts as a finance rep on the road around the garages in a 1.0 litre Mini Metro. It was surprisingly quick – on account of not having a great deal of sturdy metal in it – but it was free which made it absolutely the best car I'd ever had. Then I crashed it a couple of times and the personnel person – that's human resources now – told me I was a danger "to the general public, the company and myself" and 'let me go'.

Not long after that Nigel Tilson, later to become Business Editor at the *Belfast Telegraph,* got me into the *Ulster Star* for some holiday cover, which eventually became a full-time post. I lived in Lisburn during the week but it was Bangor at the weekend and inevitably Jenny Watts.

I had started my drinking career in the Barn above The Ulster Arms (a Saturday afternoon with Ian 'Spud' Magee and Kevin Wykes at 45p a pint) and progressed along with

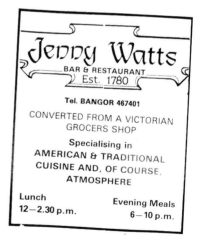

Richard Sherriff in 2012 with children Emily and Dan

the rest of Bangor Grammar to The Tavern on Main Street. How nice it all was then: one night I sent my order in through the front door from the arcade – with money – and actually got the order passed out followed by my change. It really happened.

Anyway, then Bill Wolsey arrived and tarted up The Sportsman's and we all defected from The Tavern. Wolsey's was followed by Jenny's and many a pay cheque was lost between it and Fealty's.

Then Paul Flowers, who had succeeded Annie (via Joy Bannister) in the intervening years, phoned me in 1989 and asked if I was interested in a job and so, after 10 years trying to escape the place, I became the Speccy's latest recruit.

That's only half the story of the 1980s but someone else can probably remember the important bits.

A Final Word
from TERENCE Bowman

Although my wife Averil and I – we had married in August 1979 – were living and both working in Newcastle, County Down, we still spent a considerable amount of time in Bangor during the Eighties. There is a world of difference though between simply being in Bangor and actually participating in at least some of the strands that comprise local life.

Averil and Terence Bowman in America shortly after their 10th wedding anniversary in August 1989

Certainly we ticked quite a few of the same boxes as our Bangor-residing contemporaries – we queued up at the Tonic for blockbuster films and live shows (a tick each for Glen Campbell and David Soul) until its doors finally closed in 1983, we dined out at the Skandia on upper Main Street (they didn't have a licence and the waiter nipped out for the wine of your choice from the nearest off-licence, invariably Blue Nun to accompany the chicken Maryland), we dashed from one expanding shopping centre to another, spoiled for choice, and we strolled along the beach at Ballyholme and round Ballymacormick Point on a summer's day (we even occasionally had good weather back then).

But, in truth, those weekly visits to Bangor throughout the decade had a serious purpose – Averil and I still had immediate family members in the town and we needed to keep in touch. Back then, with the Troubles still capable of producing vile

Jean Bowman (1924-1991)

atrocities that defied description, Newcastle seemed a lot further away that the mere 40 miles marked on the map.

Barely a week would pass without the weekly newspaper I worked for, the *Mourne Observer*, reporting on the terrorist attacks that were destroying innocent lives and devastating property within our extensive circulation area. My mother, Jean, who had somehow managed to conceal any anxieties she had for my safety in the early years of my career, now worried not only for the safety of my brother Geoffrey, in Belfast, but also about a son and daughter-in-law living in an area that many perceived, quite unfairly, as a hotbed of sectarian violence.

The three of us visited my mum regularly, as a way of reassuring her we were safe and always near to hand – all the more so after the cancer that would ultimately claim her life some eight years later was diagnosed in 1983. But between living and working in Newcastle and paying our weekly visits to Bangor, it proved impossible to establish firm roots in either one place or the other. The demands the *Mourne Observer* placed on me, with ever-increasing editorial responsibilities, were such that it was difficult to ever switch off completely.

When first considering my thoughts about Bangor in the 1980s, I'd come to the conclusion it was the decade when I'd finally parted company with the town of my birth in favour of the town where I was now living and working. In reality, my loyalties were caught midway between the two towns and the ultimate winner was always the *Mourne Observer.*

Having read through three decades of the *Spectator* since embarking on *Bangor in the Sixties* back in 2008, it also confirmed my suspicion that the Eighties was the first decade in which I'd had no real involvement in Bangor life. All my important childhood and teenage experiences were reflected in the pages of my local paper – the announcement of my birth at Bangor Hospital in 1957, the 1964 CSSM sports in Ward Park where I was wrongly named Kenneth, Castle Park hosting the BBC's *It's A Knock-Out* in 1969, the highs and lows of Bangor Football Club, and my own tentative first steps into journalism, courtesy of articles accepted for publication by Annie Roycroft while I was still at school. But after I left the town for Newcastle in 1976 there was nothing, bar our wedding photograph three years later.

The story, or rather the lack of one, was the same at the *Mourne Observer* during the 1980s. Apart from the very rare picture where Averil and I were prevailed upon to hand over an award sponsored by the paper (a best-dressed Teddy Bear competition in the mid-1980s springs to mind), my life in Newcastle remained largely anonymous for much of the decade. This also partly reflected the concern we had that one wrongly interpreted word in a story the paper had covered could lead to a late night knock on the door or a threatening telephone call. *Mourne Observer* reporters as a rule didn't look for by-lines, or indeed expect them, which was one of the big differences between the two papers.

> Incidentally, I forgot to mention that the Spectator All Stars football team destroyed the Mourne Observer No Stars a few weeks back in a clash at Bloomfield.

Come to think of it, one of the few times my two lives came together was when the *Spectator* and the *Mourne Observer* met in mortal combat back in the summer of 1988 – actually it was a soccer match at Bloomfield. Thankfully the

> "Dear Colin,
> My coleegs and I were dead offended at the drogatry manor in which you referred to the Morn Obserbor sokker team in last week's colum . . .

Colin Bateman rubs salt in the wound

result has long been lost in the mists of time; let's just say Colin Bateman, by then back on the staff of the *Spectator*, dipped his pen deep into the acid for his next weekly column!

It was around the same time that the seeds were being sown for what would eventually become my first published book – comprising the priceless memories, recorded by my reporting colleagues Amy Dempster and David Telford, of the men who had worked on the railway network that until three decades earlier had spanned all parts of County Down.

After almost 15 years at the *Mourne Observer*, I had found a new literary interest that would take me beyond the South Down boundary that for so long had controlled and indeed dominated my life.

As the Nineties dawned my name began to reappear in the *Spectator*, not only as an occasional contributor – for the first time since the mid-1970s – but also in stories about the factual books that were becoming an important element of my writing career.

The Bangor boy was on his way home, at least spiritually if not physically.

Terence Bowman today

Dear Reader,

I hope you have enjoyed this publication from Ballyhay Books, an imprint of Laurel Cottage Ltd. We publish an eclectic mix of books ranging from personal memoirs to authoritative books on local history, from sport to poultry, from photographs to fiction and from music to marine interests – but all with a distinctly local flavour.

To see details of these books, as well as the beautifully illustrated books of our sister imprint Cottage Publications, why not visit our website **www.cottage-publications.com** or contact us on +44 (0)28 9188 8033.

Timothy S Johnston

BALLYHAY BOOKS